Where They Belong

Where They Belong

Erin Foley

A journey from orphanages to loving families.

atmosphere press

Contents

Introduction...1

THE ORPHANAGE YEARS

We're Here. Now What?.. 9
Nobody Knows What They're Doing 13
Where Did All the Orphans Go? 18
The Corruption Problem 23
The Sponsorship Problem 26
The Volunteer Problem.. 29
Lice 33
MREs and the UN Problem...................................... 36
The Problem of Separating Siblings.........................41
Do the Churches Understand? 45
Too Little Medical Care 49
Sisterhood: Meeting Anny....................................... 52
The Problem of Foreign Adoption 54
The Problem with Double Standards........................57
Cholera and the Problem of Hygiene 60
Vocation Room... 65
The Problem of Separating Mothers and Babies.....70
The Problem of Impossible Choices.........................73
Gatekeeping.. 78
International Adoption Schemes 84
Abandoned Babies..90
Someone Who Needed Rescue................................. 93
The Problem of Low Standards of Care 103
The Problem of Sexual Abuse.................................108
The Return to Cambodia.. 115

THE CHILDREN IN FAMILIES YEARS

Introduction to CIF Years 125

The Heartbeat of Children in Families............................. 130

Anny Joins the Startup 136

The Early Cases...145

Rebecca Nhep and Shifting Perspective............................152

The Government Knows Orphanages Are Bad 165

Creating Best Practices 169

A Foster Care Village..173

The Growth of CIF 181

The Cluster Model.. 184

The Village Who Gave Away Their Kids 188

The Highest Honor... 191

Reintegration with Hannah Won 194

Cultural Abuse 200

The Golden Rule...207

A Westernized Khmer Kid...215

Family of Origin as First Priority...................................226

Foster Care 234

Abortion Baby..242

Flawed Agendas 248

Accepted, Belonging, Loved, Empowered (ABLE).............256

Equipping To Serve People with Disabilities 271

When "Calling" Lacks Wisdom................................... 275

An Advocate for Women and Children............................291

Aging Out 294

Adopting a Boy in a Sea of Girls....................................299

A Childless Couple 306

The Capacity to Love Another Child...............................312

NOW WHAT?

An Introduction to Global Solutions 321
   In Their Own Words—Thailand Orphans 323
   Protecting Families in Thailand...328
   The Tsunami 335
   The African Way 339
   Walking Alongside the Vulnerable 341
   Vulnerable Children Deserve the Highest Care.................346
   Reintegration 353
   Deinstitutionalization.. 358
   Volunteering with Vulnerable Children............................364

AFTERWORD

Our Responsibility.. 367

Author's Note 371
Resources 373

Introduction

The church was in a long, narrow building on a quiet side street in Kathmandu. After jumping out of the back of a beat-up red truck used as a regional bus, I walked the remaining way to this building with an American couple who taught in Nepal. It was exactly one year after the massive 2015 earthquake that claimed the lives of nearly ten thousand people. Yet the city still lay in obvious disrepair, with brick piles next to half-standing homes.

On the way to the house church, the couple I was with shared about different members they had gotten to know. One of those young men had grown up in an orphanage.

Turning to me, the wife said, "It must have been a good orphanage because he's such a nice young man."

She knew I worked in family-based care and was not a fan of orphanages.

I did not argue. I knew all too well that a person could have a lot of internal scars that were not readily apparent from both abandonment and an institutional upbringing.

As the only guest in the tiny church room, I was asked to introduce myself at the beginning of the service. I shared that I lived in Cambodia and briefly explained about my work with Children in Families.

After the service, the members came over to say, "Jai' ma see" (Praise the Lord). A handsome, twenty-something man came up to me as the people left. He shook my hand vigorously and told me how wonderful it was to meet.

"About the work you do in Cambodia," he said in good

English, "it is excellent work. I grew up in an orphanage. I wish someone had done for me what you do for children, giving them a family."

I did not have the heart to explain to him that I was in communications and media and did not directly work with putting children in families, but I was nonetheless proud of the work CIF did. I knew that even if he'd grown up in a "good orphanage," as my hosts called it, institutional care is no substitute for a real family.

Some of my earliest memories are centered around orphanages. When I was five years old, my parents moved to Mexico to work in a children's home. We lived in humble but separate quarters, isolated from the other children.

I remember knowing that most of the kids were not true orphans but I did hear things like, "They were abandoned" or "Their parents did not want them."

My experience on the orphanage playground with the other children was that they were mean. They stole our toys and picked fights. But looking back, I wonder how the kind, tender-hearted among them fared as they had neither parents to run to nor a safe place to hide as I did.

A few years later, we moved to Venezuela so that my parents could start an orphanage. The plans eventually fell through as the government began to create a more stringent legal framework around foreigners taking in local children, thus making it more difficult to build and fill orphanages. But I did grow up believing the world was full of parentless children who were best served in orphanages.

It was not until 2015 when I had been living in Cambodia for a year working for an anti-trafficking organization that I learned differently. I met a staff member of Children in Families at a friend's house, and when he shared about family-based care and that eighty to ninety percent of children in orphanages are there due to poverty, not the loss of parents, I was dumbfounded. I had no idea!

After he gave me his business card, I went home and began reading CIF's website. By that evening, my paradigm of caring for vulnerable children had shifted. One month later, I started working at CIF. Soon I was visiting families, interviewing, researching, and immersing myself in family-based care. My passion has never waned.

If less than an hour of a common-sense discussion about family-based care can convince me that children belong in families and that the institutional model of orphanages does more harm than good, I am hopeful that this book will help either solidify the reader's understanding of family-based care or shift the reader from belief in institutions to more sustainable and loving ways of caring for children globally.

The book is broken into three different sections. The first is following a family's journey of running an orphanage and their conclusion that there is a better way of supporting vulnerable children. The second takes the reader into the founding of CIF, where you will meet many people who helped shift the narrative, change laws, and care for children. Finally, I will address family-based care globally and solutions because this is not only an issue in Cambodia.

I felt compelled to write this book for many reasons, the first being that CIF has been incredibly successful, despite many challenges, and if they can start family-based care in a nation with no foundation for it, others can too. I also felt drawn to write it because, working in Cambodia, I know of several current children's homes where rampant abuse and trauma continues.

The sad reality is that I have not interviewed a single person who worked in or grew up in an orphanage where sexual, cultural, and physical abuse was not taking place. Yet to this day, despite so much data that proves family-based care is significantly better for children than institutions, millions of dollars annually pour into Cambodia for the running of children's homes. I cannot stay silent when I continue to hear stories of Cambodia's most vulnerable children isolated from their families and communities, living in inadequate housing with revolving doors of caretakers, while foreigners plaster their sob stories on newsletters and social media. These same foreigners are applauded as heroes for rescuing the children; meanwhile, they do little to actually care for them. It's a system that is failing these children and delaying their vulnerability rather than solving it.

I write because not one day passes when I don't lament that our soft hearts and ignorance are causing great harm to these kids—kids who will grow up stripped of their cultural identities, in the very cycles of abuse we claim to rescue them from. Yet there are successful models out there to learn from. I write to give you very viable solutions and tools to do better for orphans and vulnerable children.

This book is full of real people. Real lives with stories that deserve our attention and respect. All the people I write about are real and their stories true. I did, however, take some creative liberties around conversations or small details to set a scene or condense timelines for length. I also changed many names, identifying factors, and some locations to protect vulnerable stories. The point of this book is not to name and shame any organization or person, it's to bring you along on a journey to family-based care.

I learned early on while working in the world of Non-Governmental Organizations (NGOs) that none are void of issues and problems. Probably because people are running them. And when people, even those with good intentions, are involved, there is usually a level of brokenness and dysfunction.

Some of the people in this book were victims of their circumstances. Many made poor choices at one point or another. Some repented of their poor decisions, while others never acknowledged their wrongs and continued to hurt and abuse. They deserve our grace but not our approval. I do not tell anyone's story to create heroes, victims, or villains. Instead, I tell their stories so we can all learn and grow in our understanding.

When I met Cathleen, the founder of CIF and a main character in this book, one of the things that drew me to her was her willingness to admit her imperfections. She said to me one day, "I made a lot of mistakes. And I have spent hours, if not days and years, on my knees in tears repenting for the damage I have done on behalf of the children."

I also appreciated her willingness to let go of CIF. Despite the years she spent fighting to protect children and to keep them in Cambodian communities, she handed control of her organization over to others. From the beginning, she wanted CIF to be championed by Cambodians and for CIF to collaborate with other organizations to strengthen families.

My favorite interviews were the ones with her and Ming Anny, CIF's very first staff, sitting side by side, telling stories, laughing, and sometimes arguing over details. Theirs is a friendship forged in the furnaces of struggle and perseverance.

Cathleen and Ming Anny are not heroes. They are two broken people learning, growing, loving, and repenting as they do their best to be obedient to the things of God and the people He placed in their midst. They love children. They love families.

I tell their stories as honestly as possible and as honoring as possible while still protecting identities.

THE ORPHANAGE YEARS

We're Here.
Now What?

The Jones family – Dale, Cathleen, and their children – disembarked their plane in Phnom Penh, Cambodia. The grueling flight was finally over, and five-year-old Loralie and six-year-old Joshua trustingly clasped their parents' hands. Soldiers with weapons directed them to the tiny airport terminal, and as they crossed the tarmac, their weary eyes scanned the war-scarred capital city in the small Southeast Asian nation.

"Jum Reap Suah, Kampuchea. Hello, Cambodia; this is home now," Cathleen thought. It was September 1992.

The Khmer soldiers found the Jones children adorable and their ability to speak Khmer phrases amusing. When Loralie, with her blond pigtails, smiled, the stony faces of the guards softened. The children had grown up in Cambodian refugee housing in America where Dale and Cathleen had worked for several years, so the language and culture were familiar.

Loralie tugged on Cathleen's hand. "Mom," she whispered in English, "I need to go to the bathroom."

After inquiring, they were directed to a corner with a door hanging halfway off its hinges. The little blond, whose bladder was nearly bursting, peeked timidly around the door, then looked at her mother.

"Nope!"

Cathleen glanced in. The single squatty-potty, a toilet at ground level that one squats over, was foul-smelling and overflowing. Green moss poked out from the cracks. At the risk of wetting her pants, Loralie decided she would wait.

Outside in the blinding sun, the only foreigner in sight approached them and reached out his hand to Dale. It was Greg, their country director. After they exchanged pleasantries, he helped lug their bags into the back of an SUV, and the whole family piled in. They'd been anticipating this moment for years.

The dense humidity of rainy season buffeted them as they rode through town. Nearly two decades had elapsed since the Khmer Rouge captured Phnom Penh in the bloody civil war, yet only a few buildings had been repaired. Piles of rubble and bullet-riddled walls mingled with lush tropical plants. The exhausted family passed by *cyclos*, tall tricycles with a seat in the front. Some *cyclo* riders carried paying customers, while others transported loads for the market through the streets. An occasional tank rolled by while jeeps navigated through side streets, heading out to surrounding villages. Very few private cars or motorbikes were in sight; most petrol-powered vehicles belonged to the government or organizations like Dale and Cathleen's.

Later, it struck Dale and Cathleen that most of the people they passed that day were young. Young adult men were strangely missing, but women, children, and a few older people went about their daily lives, all deeply traumatized from nearly twenty years of war. As they traveled through the city, Dale and Cathleen couldn't help but notice the desperate poverty of the people. Worry lines engraved most faces, and many of the children went naked.

At the heart of the city, they passed Tuol Sleng, a memorial to those lost to the brutality of the Khmer Rouge. Tuol Sleng was a prison where countless political prisoners, and anyone else who aroused the ire of a Khmer Rouge sympathizer, were brutally tortured, imprisoned, and murdered. Dale and Cathleen knew about Tuol Sleng but seeing the barbed-wire enclosure was a very different experience. The prison had been converted into a memorial to remind people of the pain and betrayal of Pol Pot's brief but bloody rule. His rise to power and subsequent fall had seemed to happen so quickly, but the consequences continued to echo down the generations.

They arrived at a run-down, mildew-covered guesthouse in the old French section of the city. Greg ushered them into the lobby, where oscillating fans attempted to stave off the heat, and Loralie finally found relief in a clean bathroom.

Most members of Dale and Cathleen's organization had previously settled and were now scattered throughout the city. Many taught English to university students or provided urgently needed medical care. A few were planting churches or running orphanages in other parts of the country.

Sipping instant coffee, they sat down with Greg to deal with the paperwork while the children snacked on a plate of french fries. Greg soon left, and the family found themselves alone in a new country, far from their organization's headquarters. They stared at the peeling paint and the piles of luggage in their room and tried to put together the next steps. No one had given them instructions on finding food and drinkable water, access to cash, or anything else.

The guest house owner was friendly and attempted to be helpful. Thankfully, Dale was fluent in Khmer from spending years living with Cambodian refugees. After the family's initial shock wore off and a second wind set in, they showered with the bucket and dipper, changed into clean clothes, and stepped out into the streets to explore.

Everyone stared. Foreign families were an uncommon sight since the country had only recently reopened to outsiders. They made their way down the street and found some questionable street food to stave off their hunger. Dale chatted with people as they walked along. The Buddhist monks in bright orange robes were enthralled by the white man who spoke their language; if foreigners were rare, even more so were ones fluent in the Khmer language.

During the afternoons, when the heat gave way to torrential rains, the Joneses huddled in their room together, reading and talking about all they were learning. Or they sat downstairs in the lobby conversing with the owners. Several days passed, and they had yet to hear from their mission. Without cell phones or even regular electricity, they had no way to contact headquarters or find it on their own.

Eventually, they made contact with Greg and were informed they would move to the south of the country to take over as directors of an old French orphanage. Six months previously, their organization had acquired it from the government.

Neither Dale nor Cathleen felt called to run an orphanage, and they were certainly not equipped, but at least they were moving forward with plans to serve. They would no longer be stuck in a hotel in the city.

Later they would discover that the organization had no long-term plan for the children or the orphanage. The Joneses would have to figure that out as they went.

Nobody Knows
What They're Doing

Dale and Cathleen surveyed the grounds. Grass grew in unruly patches, and Khmer children ran about the building as the sea breeze wafted through open doors. The full weight of what they signed up for had yet to sink in.

The orphanage had only been with their organization for six months at that point. David, the man running it before them, had come to build the dorms, toilets, and cafeteria. He and his wife were doing their best to care for the forty children who currently lived there, but they had no training in orphan care or trauma care.

In fact, no one in the organization was trained to run an orphanage or deal with trauma. And no one was prepared for the rapid growth they would soon experience. Since Cambodia was just beginning to issue visas to foreigners, the orphanage was mainly a way for their organization to get people into Cambodia and served more as a stepping stone to different work.

After the Khmer Rouge had been driven out by Vietnam, temporary orphanages dotted the landscape out of necessity. Families had been ripped apart. During the Khmer Rouge, soldiers would harm children as punishment for their parents' insubordination, so out of fear parents would pretend not to know their children. Other times murder or starvation caused a parent's death. Separation also happened when fleeing brutality. Some people ran for the Thai border, but others dropped behind in the panic and chaos of gunfire. Those who made it to the border dared not look back. Some fell, while others were hit by crisscrossing bullets; landmines took others. Yet, losing track of a panicked child who darted the wrong way was a reality in all the chaos. Often, they fled in the darkness.

The Russians and French established these temporary institutions after the war, never intending them to be a long-term solution. It was only a way to keep internally displaced children alive until someone could come to care for them. As Cambodia settled and peace loomed, families slowly tracked down their children. Sometimes widows who had lost husbands and children came, taking a few orphans in as their own. However, not all parents or extended family appeared for the children. Some parents survived in refugee camps across the border. Others were decomposing in an unmarked grave; the toll of over three million dead left many true orphans.

"In theory, this is who we came to serve," Cathleen shared. "The structure we stood together staring at was the remnant of a school, now a dilapidated wooden building handed over to our organization."

Dale and Cathleen felt as equipped as headless chickens and were grappling with where to begin. At least they spoke Khmer. How did other foreigners run orphanages without being able to communicate well with staff and kids?

Opening an orphanage was as easy as slapping bricks and a rooftop together while gathering children. However, the real work lies in the long-term well-being of these kids.

"We were naïve. Warm bodies with no training or instruction, not even a calling or vision to run an orphanage. We were not even taught how to manage the finances." The Joneses had essentially been dropped off at the end of Cambodia to fend for themselves and forty children. Overnight, they took on untrained staff, a mountain of corruption, and children whose identities and histories were unknown.

"The first few months were a blur as we found a rhythm.

A growing list of priorities was in constant evaluation. All the while, we learned the names of children and staff."

//

One of the first paradigm shifts at the orphanage came when Cathleen realized the local caregivers also lacked any training. In addition, many were young, unmarried, and childless.

"Most orphanage directors view the dorm parent role as the lowest in the hierarchy," She reflected. "To us, this order of precedence was upside down; dorm parents were vital. Weekly staff meetings and discipleship meetings started immediately. They were expected and seen by Dale and me as the most critical people on the premises since they had direct contact with the kids."

Armed only with her own experience of being a parent, Cathleen already realized children must bond with their primary caregivers. If staff quit, leave, or burn out, it can cause irreparable damage to those attachments. So, in addition to courses on caring for children, they implemented days off and regular breaks. Longevity mattered.

A highly developed system slowly evolved. Dale spent every free moment developing contracts, staff policy, vacation time, wages, and orphanage policy – in both English and Khmer. No template for documenting staff or incoming children existed, so they created and improved it over the years as they realized there were things they needed.

Dale and Cathleen sifted through the file of spotty documentation at David's house and discovered that most of the children had no paper trail. They didn't know where the children had come from nor why they needed to be in the orphanage. There was no system for obtaining or storing records and documents.

Since David did not speak the language, families manipulated and lied to him to get their children into better living conditions at the orphanage where there was access to regular meals and schooling. Many parents were desperate and wanted their children clothed and fed. The little documentation they had was often completely fabricated.

In 1993, an administrative intern arrived at the orphanage. Jessica's role was to document the history of the children. The plan was to give a copy to each child when they aged out. Then they could look at the records and perhaps find family along the way. Copies of sponsor photos were also included in the folders, so the children could trace their growth and have memories of their childhood.

Jessica set up medical records, administrative forms, and incident reports in a practical, organized system. She spent her year of service compiling information.

Years later, Cathleen and Dale were repeatedly sought out by grown children from the orphanage who were requesting their personal information, photographs, and documents. These inquiries left them to wonder what had happened to all those files. The young adults were often told there was nothing for them.

The Joneses are unsure what happened to those files, but they recognized that the children's histories had not been protected. It robbed the children of having the best possible launch into adulthood. It was as though their identities were being erased.

//

Sanitation was horrendous in the early years. Abject poverty, war-torn towns, lack of infrastructure, and lack of education were a recipe for disease. It was a miracle so many survived the bouts of bacterial infections, worms, and viruses that weakened an already undernourished population.

As the weeks passed, more issues became clear. The orphanage and school children used the dense foliage between the school and the orphanage as their mass toilet. The area smelled of urine and human waste. This had to change. Animals foraged in that area, and the heat made the smell unbearable. The children must be taught to use the proper facilities. Diseases were already rampant enough.

Dale sought to understand why the children weren't using the squatty outhouse toilets that were available to them. As it turned out, the facilities were not the issue. The issue was access. Government staff had been left at the orphanage to spy on the foreigners and report back to government agencies. They were incredibly lazy and corrupt, so rather than oversee the cleaning of toilets used by hundreds of children, they wired the doors shut, preferring to spend their time napping in hammocks.

When the toilets were unwired, Dale hesitantly pushed the doors open and was met with absolute squalor. Throwing his shirt over his nose, he forced himself not to throw up.

Dale marched over to the napping government employee with a mop and a bucket. He pointed toward the toilets. The man decided to not show up for his job a few weeks after they threatened to fire him if they found it shut again. It appeared he did not appreciate having to actually work.

"The staff member who wired our bathrooms shut also taught the children to gamble. He used this to steal their minuscule pocket money earned from small tasks around the orphanage," Cathleen sighed.

Even more terrifying than the filthy toilets were the vats of Agent Orange the American military had left in their sleepy beach town. Ignorant of the contents or dangers, locals desperate to scavenge metal to sell or containers to use, emptied these vats, contaminating water and land.

None of their extensive planning had prepared the Jones family to face the early years. Yet somehow, little by little, Cambodia and the orphanage would find a way.

Where Did All the Orphans Go?

Within a few weeks of working at the orphanage, strange themes began to emerge. Dale and Cathleen noticed that a number of the children were often gone. Upon inquiring, they were casually told, "Well, they went home. They miss their mom."

"This confused us because it was an orphanage, and we thought it was full of orphans," Cathleen said. "Their parents were so close they could visit them all the time."

Either the kids needed to be in the orphanage, or they needed to be home full-time. If their parents wanted them, then they needed to stay home. One by one, those kids eventually left.

Other children had been placed in the orphanage because they were related to staff members. With the pressure to fill beds and convince donors their money was going to orphaned children, they had inadvertently created orphans.

One day, an expensive car pulled up to the orphanage, and a clean, well-dressed boy hopped out. This seemed confusing, but they quickly discovered that many families with money paid bribes to get their children into orphanages. Orphanages provided access to education at a time when schools were grossly understaffed or bombed-out husks of buildings.

"He had shoes and socks on, which was astonishing because no children had access to much clothing," Cathleen recalled.

She very kindly sent the family packing. Under no circumstances could this well-fed, cared-for boy with parents live at the orphanage merely for education's sake.

Children's family status became more apparent during Cambodian holidays. The grounds would empty out a few days before Khmer New Year.

"Where did all the children go?" Cathleen and Dale wondered.

"They went home to celebrate with their families," came the staff members' response.

"Their families?"

"Yes. Their uncle picked them up today; don't worry, they'll be back next week."

So it went. As quickly as the children filtered out, they returned. They came back from the holiday excited, chattering about seeing their parents or extended family. After more searching for information, the Joneses realized Cambodia's social norms required them to let the kids return home for holidays.

"When the children went home, they took everything from the orphanage, pillows, clothes, combs, toothbrushes, blankets, etc., to share with their families. When we further questioned the kids, they'd say, 'Yes, we brought these things for our siblings.'"

Desperately poor, the children did not view their actions as theft but sharing of their good fortune with those they loved. They wanted to help amid the glaring poverty. Dale and Cathleen were shocked to find that many of the children had siblings. Why were some in care and not others?

"It was sad that there were whole families in need. Unfortunately, the orphanage only provided for the kids in front of us. Looking back, I see that a better long-term strategy would have been to use the orphanage money for family social services. The kids were happier at home, but they returned hungry because their families could not provide food for them. They missed their families but also really needed to eat."

In their orphanage, only a handful stayed behind during holidays. Less than ten percent were true orphans. There was also a small number of children who were unable to return home because of safety concerns. Cathleen recalled a boy and girl whose parents died from tuberculosis (TB). "They lost both parents but still had older siblings and grandparents. We investigated, and most of our true orphans still had someone who loved and missed them."

That first holiday caused a pivot in the Joneses' thinking. They had gone into their work believing orphanages existed to help children who were truly orphaned, but this turned out not to be the case. Families were still so scattered and displaced by the conditions following the war that the orphanage was full of children who still had families. The Joneses wanted a better system of allowing children into the orphanage. Gatekeeping, they called it. So, they developed an intake form and began conducting interviews and investigations. There would no longer be anyone recruiting children to fill quotas; these beds were now reserved for the highest need, most vulnerable children. This was not a boarding school.

So, they continued to change their approach to documentation. Pictures, identity cards, medical information, and any known history or traceable family went into their new filing system. One day someone might arrive to collect their child. Or the children might have questions about their origins.

The initial documentation oversight was understandable. There was still a lot of chaos when Westerners first gained access to the country. But now they needed to track and document the children in their care. The children deserved to know the truth about their lives and have a shred of history and identity to cling to.

//

Early on, it also became clear that institutional care negatively impacts child development. For example, in a healthy household children hide behind safe adults when strangers approach, or they run back to their homes to announce the arrival of an unknown person. At the orphanage, a stranger stepping onto the premises found themselves engulfed in a sea of children. Each one scrambled to be seen, heard, and touched.

Later they would learn why residential care is toxic for children, especially those of young ages. "Neuroscience tells us," Dr. Delia Pop, an expert with Hope and Homes for Orphans explained[1], "if they [children in orphanages] do not receive proper care, it will always lead to a delay in development." She went on to say there are three main areas of development where these delays take place: cognitive, emotional, and behavioral. These delays are permanent consequences for the children that all stem from institutionalization. Children need at least one healthy and permanent attachment to develop well.

In the Joneses' orphanage, there was no sense of healthy bonding. The children lacked the ability to distinguish a safe adult from one they knew nothing about. Cathleen and Dale recognized their desperation for a consistent parental figure and worked to keep the same house parents caring for their specific small cluster of children.

The children at the orphanage referred to them as "Mom and Dad," which Cathleen did not discourage. Still, the title always bothered her, especially when she sat at her kitchen table teaching her own children in the morning, kissing their scraped knees and holding them in the night when they awoke from bad dreams. She recognized the distinction between how she treated her kids at home versus her care for the orphans. The difference was cavernous. It is not that they did not want to give the children good care; it was that nobody has the capacity to give quality time and attention to forty and more children. She also knew they could pack up and leave at any moment, never to return, which is what eventually happened.

Dale found a solution for the children who were true orphans or whose families were not safe to visit on holidays. In the first two years, he planted two churches in the area. He presented the predicament of the children to the congregation, and local Christian families were thrilled to take the kids in for the breaks. It was a phenomenal success.

Even though many of them, such as local fishermen, were impoverished, they treated the children from the orphanage as their own. If they bought their kids a new outfit for Khmer New Year, the orphanage children also got a set. They sometimes even took the kids on trips with their families to visit other relatives.

Over twenty years later, Taevy, who grew up in the orphanage, shared about the family with whom she had been connected. She still speaks with them on the phone, and if she is in their area, she stops by to catch up.

It started the wheels turning in the Joneses' heads. Each year, they placed the same children back with the same families. Dale and Cathleen hoped that when the children aged out of the institution, they would have a connection to their community and relationships with people they could reach out to. It also planted the first idea that if a biological family did not exist or was unsafe, local families would be willing to commit and take in abandoned and orphaned children in Cambodia.

The Corruption Problem

"Money was scarce. Our mission negotiated with the government for projects like orphanages, clinics, and English schools, but the government hadn't given them any funding for the projects. We hadn't known beforehand that we would be running an orphanage, so we never raised money back home to help with it either," Cathleen explained.

Initially, the orphanage was overseen by government employees. Under communism, constant suspicion reigned, which carried into the years after the Vietnamese left.

The mountain of issues they initially dealt with felt insurmountable. Corruption was also thick. Supplies were siphoned off by all hands touching them, so that even the most basic task of feeding the children became difficult. When the Cambodian Red Cross delivered the donated bags of rice, it was understood that their staff would take a couple of huge loads. Then, the driver would take his cut. By the time the supplies made it to their quiet beach town, many of the rations were lacking. The orphanage directors learned to refrain from questioning this practice if they wanted to maintain relationships and supply lines.

After several months passed, Cathleen began to want an accounting of the food. She felt the rice rations should go farther than they were going. Almost daily, more children were added, and they needed to be able to feed everyone.

Passing by the back of the kitchen one day, Cathleen paused to scratch a mosquito bite. She noticed the cook dumping rice into her bags.

"Bong Reaksmey," she asked, approaching the woman, "what are these bags for?"

Reaksmey's eyes shifted, resting on a tree off to Cathleen's left. She evaded the question beautifully, yet Cathleen was not satisfied with her answer. Walking off, she determined to question some of the other staff later. It turned out it was not a secret. Reaksmey openly took what she considered her fair share of the rice. But, due to the nature of every hand siphoning off the rations, no Cambodian questioned the ethics of this arrangement. Three times a day before serving the staff and children, Reaksmey filled her bags with rice.

After a detailed accounting, they discovered that the cook took one out of every ten bags of rice. Cathleen decided this must be addressed. Reaksmey already received wages for her work, and salaries were challenging to come by.

After a second interrogation, the cook confessed to the theft. "Reaksmey, if you steal anything from here on, we will have to fire you. Do you understand?"

Those shifty eyes lifted to meet Cathleen's. In slight defiance, but mostly resigned to her fate, she shrugged her leathery shoulders and replied flatly, "No rice, no work. I quit." Removing her apron, she handed it to Cathleen and collected her things in silence. It was the last they saw of their communist cook.

That evening, Cathleen laid her head on her pillow, rubbing her temples. She glanced at Dale as he settled under the mosquito net. "What are we going to do about corruption?" she asked. "How do we monitor our staff without smothering them? I cannot be everywhere at once."

Exhausted, Dale promised to think about it in the morning when his mind was clearer. They turned out the lights and gave in to sleep.

Soon Dale had a solution. The staff members were constantly complaining about the poor food. A rotation was quickly drawn up so that no cook would handle the budget alone, and the staff would see what it took to stretch the food for everyone. Soon they were purchasing more to their liking and gaining perspective on what little access they had to meat and vegetable options. Finally, the complaining and theft stopped.

Sometime later, Cathleen was running over the books with a local staff member and discovered that five thousand dollars (an enormous sum in those days) had vanished. How could this be? While small amounts were not unusual to be siphoned off here and there, this was another matter entirely.

She sighed heavily, throwing back her head to stare at the ceiling for a second. She was overwhelmed by the mounting revelation of corruption.

Cathleen traced office staff, interactions, and paperwork until she had one conclusion: the last remaining communist government employee had stolen the money from the office.

Her investigation had taken little time; everyone seemed to know he did it. He nearly advertised it, thinking he was untouchable. Then almost overnight, the man disappeared.

They alerted the local social service branch of the government who tried to excuse and cover up his behavior. He had not miscalculated his ability to get away with it. No one was ever able to catch him.

Because of its extreme embarrassment, the government mainly left them alone after that incident. And after realizing there was nothing they could do about the loss of money, Cathleen thought, "Perhaps it was worth five thousand dollars to be rid of the last of our terrible employees. At least now we can start fresh."

The Sponsorship Problem

In those years, Cambodia was a challenging place to live. Rural Cambodia, even more so. Their only route to and from the city was marked with deep ruts and land mines, not to mention the Khmer Rouge and bandits. Highway 4 was considered the deadliest roadway in the world. Dale regularly drove between the children's home in the south of Cambodia and the school project they managed in Takeo, about four hours north.

Lingering in their minds was the recent kidnapping and execution of three foreigners along the road. They had received bullets to the head from the remaining Khmer Rouge. Cambodia had endured decades of brutality at the hands of the Khmer Rouge and the Vietnamese Communists. It seemed as if no one could win. People languished and suffered. If the guns and explosives did not kill them, starvation and lack of sanitation would.

There was no welfare, assistance, or birth control. The infant mortality rate was so high that children did not receive names at birth. There was no use in bonding if they were going to die.

Disease and active tuberculosis were rampant. Children had whooping cough and chicken pox at such a rate that the orphanage felt as if it were under the plague.

Two years in, when they finally had a nurse visit to examine the children, the ear-cleaning process alone was disturbing. Cathleen gagged at the memory. As if changing diapers and cleaning up the sickness of her biological children were not enough, the fluids and illnesses of over a hundred children proved too much for her senses.

//

In addition to taking over an orphanage without any training, they were given several other significant tasks. In their first year, they helped start two local churches in the area, regularly teaching and training pastors and leaders. They ran a translation office, and Dale was even asked to teach at the Bible school in the capital city, which took nearly a day to travel to. The endless duties made them wonder how they were supposed to raise and care for the orphanage children. The children's long-term best interests didn't seem to have a high enough priority in their mix of duties.

Dale was also put in charge of the school development program. The school project was four hours away from the orphanage, but because of safety issues (they couldn't travel at night) and the indirect route necessitated by the bad roads, it was a multiple-day trip.

It required significantly more work from Dale and took him away from the orphanage about half the time. However, it was the program that seemed to have the most long-lasting positive impact on communities. Here children who lived with their families could attend full-day school and receive regular nutritional soy drinks, daily vitamins, school uniforms, books, and other supplies. It was holistic, and it could be done at a lower cost than running the orphanage.

The majority of funding for both the school project and the orphanage came from a child sponsorship program. The effects of donor loss, however, were different.

If a sponsor dropped a child at the school, it might be sad for the child but not a huge loss. The children did not see their sponsors as the primary source of emotional ties. However,

Dale and Cathleen noticed when a sponsor stopped supporting a child in their orphanage, it was as if the child experienced death. If they no longer heard from a person or received their photos, they felt abandoned again. Many of the children questioned the Joneses. "Wasn't I pretty enough?" "Wasn't I smart enough?" "Why would they drop me?"

Another issue created by sponsorship in the orphanage was jealousy. Some sponsors sent extra money, more letters, or gifts. In contrast, other children received no correspondence at all. The children in the orphanage would compare one another's donors. And the children with a more attentive donor felt superior and more loved. But because the children in the school project were part of a family, all donor letters, cards, and gifts were taken home and shared with everyone.

Over time, Cathleen realized that sponsorship should have been pooled rather than individualized. While the donors felt more involved with an individual child, it created far too many issues on the receiving end.

The school sponsorship program existed in only one community in Cambodia, which begged the question why it was not started in the communities where the orphanages existed. The majority of the Joneses' children could have returned home if their communities had access to full-time school, nutrition, and school uniforms for their children. If families had a little support, the needs the orphanage met, like shelter, food, and education, could have been provided, but the children would not have to miss out on the love and belonging within a family unit.

The Volunteer Problem

Not many months into their work, a man showed up at the orphanage with bags of toys. He told Dale and Cathleen that he wanted to volunteer at the orphanage. They were confused. Who was this man? How did he find them? How did he even get there? Travel was treacherous. Why didn't he just leave the toys at the home office to be picked up later?

Apparently, the man knew someone serving in Phnom Penh. He had come to Cambodia for a month, and without any oversight or accountability, he thought he would spend a few weeks helping orphans.

Cathleen sighed. The schedule was too packed; they did not have time to babysit a well-intentioned foreigner. Dale was better at hiding his annoyance. While the gesture of toys was kind, why did the man's church not bother asking what they actually needed: deworming medication, lice treatment, vitamins, and nutrient-rich meals? However, the man had traveled across the world, and the orphanage had little entertainment to offer the children. A few boxes of toys might be nice, especially for the little ones.

"We had an internal struggle. The gift was a nice gesture, but the guy was young and wanted to do it his way. His condition was that it would be a free-for-all, like Christmas morning. We knew it was a bad idea but had no idea the level of disaster that would come from it."

They decided to let him give the kids the toys, although they made it clear his volunteering was unnecessary.

The children mobbed the man to get to the toys, but he

just reveled in their greed. For a moment, he was a hero, coming in to bring fleeting joy to the fatherless. He grew angry a day later as broken plastic littered the landscape and teenagers fiddled with baby toys. All that time and money from across the globe and the gifts hardly survived twenty-four hours. He would have been even more upset if he'd known that the more entrepreneurial-spirited kids had taken the toys into town and sold them.

A few days later they returned to their sticks and games with broken flip-flops. Cathleen and Dale gathered up the few remaining intact toys and made a playroom with everything in boxes for the kids to share during the supervised time. Unfortunately, the children could not handle the freedoms of property ownership yet.

Cathleen logged the experience into her "never again" memory bank and vowed to devise a better way of distributing things to the children. She and Dale made a pact that people could not just appear on the scene, play the hero, and then disappear into the mist again. It created an unnatural relationship between the attention-starved children and random foreigners. Plus, the kids had no context for these unexpected events.

//

Soon after, a British schoolteacher showed up, wanting to volunteer with the children. Pleased, Cathleen offered to set up English classes for the kids.

"I'm sorry, you misunderstand me; I teach English all school year. I prefer a non-teaching role," he responded.

"Well, what do you have in mind if you don't plan on teaching them?"

"We can play games; I can help around the premises. I'll dig ditches for you. I'll do anything but teach English."

"We don't need ditches dug. Even if we did, we would hire

locals and give them paychecks to stimulate the economy. Those roles are filled. And the children don't need anyone to play games with; there are a hundred kids here. They are not lonely or starved for imagination. English is highly valued and helpful."

He quickly moved on.

//

School breaks were challenging to manage. All the children were on the premises with nothing to do. The boredom gave rise to restless trouble. So, in their first year, Dale and Cathleen brainstormed with the staff and formed a schedule for school breaks. They recruited teachers for physical education, vacation Bible school, crafts, music, and English learning. The kids thrived under the structure, and the staff no longer dreaded these short breaks in their school year.

In their fourth and final year at the orphanage, one volunteer stood out, though for all the wrong reasons. After they arrived from Phnom Penh, the foreign volunteers were briefed. They would run the programs in the mornings and then have the afternoons free. On rare days they might facilitate outings to the beach.

"They worked four hours a day, five days a week," Cathleen stated, "hardly a grueling schedule."

Within a week, a lanky young man lingered behind the rest after breakfast to air his grievances to Dale.

"Mr. Jones, sir," he said, clearing his throat, "I feel like we are too busy. We work all year in Phnom Penh and then come here. There are so many children. Perhaps we could have more time to enjoy it?"

Dale breathed in and calmly responded, "Were you aware you were coming to serve in an orphanage? Did you ask for this opportunity?"

"Yes, sir, I just thought . . ." he paused.

"You thought this would be a vacation to the beach with some feel-good serving thrown in?" It was a rhetorical question spoken gently yet bluntly. It silenced the young man.

He started to respond a few times but could not formulate the words.

"If you wanted a vacation, you should have taken a vacation. We serve over one hundred children here; we lack the capacity to be a vacation boarding house for Phnom Penh teachers. You are welcome to leave if it pleases you. But, if you stay, understand it is not asking too much for four hours daily. This is what you came to do, so please do it."

The young man stood and left. Dale rubbed his temples and prayed for volunteers who came to put the children first rather than fill their emotional tanks with hugs and smiles from cute children merely to disappear again. Although research at the time was lacking, extensive research now[2] shows the lack of long-term healthy attachments for children in orphanages creates lifelong challenges including the inability to develop and maintain relationships, difficulties with trust and affection, and behavioral problems. Dale and Cathleen did not know this, but they were aware the children in their care did not express emotions and behaviors appropriately toward strangers.

Looking back over the years, she and Dale are thankful they ran an orphanage before social media complicated things even more. Otherwise, the volunteers would also be there for photos with hundreds of children, posting for the applause of their online audiences.

Lice

From time to time, the police would arrive at the orphanage with a market kid in tow. Begging and scrounging to survive, these children lived on the streets. They made Charles Dickens's orphans look hearty.

One day, the police brought a boy named Vattan, whose smell greeted the orphanage director even before he laid eyes on the child. Apart from the roving eyes, one could hardly tell the boy—a skeletal being with ratty trousers, scabbed skin, and hair matted in clumps—was alive. It was impossible to discern his age. Severe malnourishment stunted many of the children.

Other than babies and toddlers, most of the kids were at school at the time. This was for the best; Vattan did not need extra sets of eyes boring into him. A large plate heaped with rice and vegetables was set before him. He devoured every grain in a frenzy, fearful he would never eat again. The dorm father gently explained life at the orphanage, reassuring him he was safe and would eat at each mealtime. Then he ushered Vattan into the dorms, where the boy fell asleep even before reaching the mat.

The sun rose and set; the children came and went for a full day. Vattan slept. His dreams were deep and fitful. Other children clamored out of the dank corridors of the market, but his feet were glued in place. Exhaustion from hunger rendered his brain unable to make a quick decision. Strong, heavy hands grasped the front of his ragged shirt and hoisted him off the ground. It was the police. Some were kind, and some brutal. He had learned to turn off his mind to the insults hurled in his face. He had learned to turn off his mind when hunger made him do despicable things for mere crumbs. If he had a family, they were buried in the recesses of his long-term memory and remained unconnected to his current reality.

His brain registered the voices coming and going, yet he did not emerge from the depths of sleep. Something about this environment tampered with his instinct to run.

The boy was near death, with only a few weeks before starvation would have destroyed his body. What had those young eyes seen? What had that mind comprehended? What existence lay before a child whose only objective was survival?

When Vattan finally woke from his slumber, the dorm father took him to Cathleen for a delousing session. All the children battled rounds of head lice, but Vattan also had them in his eyebrows and eyelashes. Cathleen snipped away at the clumps of hair. To her horror, a wave of lice spread across Vattan's head and ran right up her scissors to her arm. She almost dropped the comb and scissors as she watched thousands of lice run away from her cutting. She determined a complete shave was the only option.

The "market kids" like Vattan were challenging to keep in the facility. Wild from being on their own for so long, a structured routine of chores and schooling chafed against their free spirits. Trauma kept them restless. In addition, they lacked the ability to assess risk, so after a while, they would disappear. Sometimes, they would re-emerge and be welcomed back with a meal and a bed; sometimes, they would fade into the tapestry of chaos that ruled rural Cambodia.

There was no social system set up to track them. So, Cathleen and Dale strove to let them know there was always a place for them without forcing any unnatural changes on them. Cathleen eventually developed a system to keep street kids in the orphanage for longer. Several babies had no siblings, so they paired the street children with a baby. The children who got a "sibling" stayed around much longer because they were given a chance for safe bonding and attachment.

The lice, on the other hand, had no attachment disorders. Whether big or small, clean or dirty, Khmer or foreigner, everyone at the orphanage battled lice. Without access to delousing medicine most of the time, a monthly ritual started out of necessity.

Sunday was beach day. Before each child could rush into the ocean, the staff wrapped the children's faces in a towel, sprayed a can of Raid on their hair, and rubbed it in. Once the deed was done, the children would whip off the towel and run madly into the sea, submerging their bodies in the salty waves. With nearly a hundred children to treat, once a month the ocean became a floating morgue for millions of lice.

MREs and the
UN Problem

In 1993, the first elections took place. The United Nations (UN) was temporarily present to oversee the election and ensure it was valid and safe; however, they dug up their stakes and left Cambodia soon after. Government power was now transitioned from the communist Vietnamese back to the Cambodians. The UN also left a trail of illegitimate children throughout the territories.

At this time, the orphanages were still underfunded as the sponsorship program was not fully functioning.

The children were underfed and malnourished because of the extreme devastation of lives, crops, and infrastructure throughout the nation. Although the orphanage was able to offer more food than many households, the children still lacked proper nutrition. Protein undernourishment led to dry, flaky skin and brittle, orange hair. In addition, the never-ending bouts with parasites and worms had depleted their tiny bodies.

So, when Cathleen found out their organization's other orphanage was the recipient of a vast supply of the UN's MREs, prepackaged, dehydrated, calorie-dense meals, she set out to get a portion for her kids. This was more difficult than she had expected. The other orphanage director had not offered to share the MREs.

After Dale pleaded their cause, the partner orphanage relented, and two truckloads were sent south. The empty dorm rooms in their orphanage were stacked floor to ceiling with boxes of MREs.

The staff had the time-consuming task of sorting each pouch and organizing them according to type, so that every breakfast time the children ate the same MRE meal and after school the same MRE snack. The most beloved snack was peanut butter.

"Within three months, all the kids gained weight. Their hair became glossy and black. Their skin glowed. Their cheeks filled in. But as soon as they seemed to be reaching a healthy weight, we ran out of MREs."

Years later, the Joneses learned that many of the MREs at the other orphanage had been destroyed in a flood. They had been stored for later use. Cathleen was thankful that their orphanage had used every last one.

Despite the infusion of MREs, feeding over one hundred children took enormous provisions. By the time the MREs were gone, the Joneses locally had found regular vitamins to maintain each child's nutritional needs. Unfortunately, they had to check each capsule because many of them were filled with flour, a way for vendors to earn a profit without providing the important goods. Corruption was everywhere they turned.

//

"This was a lawless time, a disease-ridden time, and a poverty-stricken time. But family still looked better than institutions in terms of love and attachment."

While families looked better than institutions, the orphanage did do some good. Some children would have died without the immediate care the orphanage could provide, but others died anyway. They'd been too sick to save.

Unsurprisingly, during the UN's presence in Cambodia, many babies born were not fully Khmer. Bulgaria maintained a significant presence with the UN; its contribution was to send communist prisoners in soldiers' uniforms. They were wild and unruly, drinking and gambling and using prostitutes without restraint. As a result, half-Bulgarian babies were born in great numbers in those years, blinking into a world where their fathers were shuffled in and out of the country and their mothers lacked the means to care for them.

A young, severely traumatized woman stumbled into the orphanage one day, clutching a small bundle to her chest. A staff member gently removed the baby from her emaciated arms and drew back from the stench. The woman, eyes wide with madness, pointed at the bundle and spoke through slurred words.

"I'm going back to my home village. My baby is dying. If you do not take her, I will throw her in a ditch."

The smell of death emanated from the mass of filthy rags. Jessica, the office administrator, and Cathleen took her into the baby room where they slowly unwrapped the tatters around her skeletal frame. She was alive, yet in stages of decay. Dehydrated, nearly shriveled, and far too weak to cry, the baby blinked at them through clouded and dry eyes. The women carefully examined her. When they turned her over, they gasped. The baby's entire back was a pressure sore so severe that skin was missing in patches, revealing the muscle underneath.

There were no emergency services. A hospital visit would likely expose her to grave dangers of infection, and she would be left in a corner to die. Tenderly, they worked to clean her.

Then the baby pooped, and what came out of her was like nothing they had seen before. After recovering their senses, Jessica exclaimed, "What is coming out of her!"

Jessica had every reason to be horrified; later a doctor explained that it was the lining of her intestines.

They sterilized an eye dropper, and bit by bit they administered filtered water.

Kalliyan. The name came to Cathleen as the baby finally made a frail sound. The word floated above her, a whisper of hope. An exquisite Khmer actress had this name for a gentle, beautiful woman. The probability of life was dire, yet hope could not be curtailed. Her name was a promise.

"Kalliyan, God is with you," Cathleen spoke to her.

"Kalliyan, *Oum* (a term of respect meaning "older auntie")? Why do you waste such a beautiful name on a baby who will die?" Her staff, having overheard the name, questioned her.

Cathleen explained that she wanted the baby to have a beautiful name that would be a blessing each time a person uttered it.

Jessica and Cathleen began a rotation of constant care for Kalliyan in Cathleen's home. Never to be left alone, she was meticulously cleaned and fed. Her skin was so delicate they could not bandage her sores or exposed muscle for fear the medical tape would peel her flesh off.

The hours stretched into days, which stretched into weeks. Slowly it became evident that Kalliyan was determined to live. Her brown eyes glowed with life. Her cries rose in intensity.

Initially, her pale skin was dry and translucent. However, as she healed and grew, they became suspicious that this baby had a UN father, likely a Bulgarian because she was so fair. Months into her life in the orphanage, Cathleen held her up after a diaper change and took in the baby's transformation. The big eyes met her as a smile revealed her healthy pink gums.

"Kalliyan, you are beautiful! You are so beautiful!" And she was. Soft, light brown curls clung to her forehead. Pale, fleshy skin replaced open wounds. "What a miracle you are."

The mother had refused to give a name or family details. There was no way to track her down.

Kalliyan's father would have returned to his nation, likely unaware of a daughter. Though her parents had given her so little, Kalliyan had a determined spirit. All three of them were victims of the horrors of communism, yet a miracle lingered in the form of this beautiful, strong girl. Cathleen treasured this hope in her heart; after all, hope was difficult to come by.

The Problem of Separating Siblings

Sophea shrieked as she ran through the open field, delighted that she was widening the distance between her and her little brother. With her thick braids slapping her back, she galloped, taunting Vuthy as she ran and hid in the tall grass. Exhausted, Vuthy finally cried out as the distance became too great for him.

"Wait up, Sophea!"

She could barely see his hair that stuck out in every direction, so she paused to allow him to get closer. Everything in her mind was focused, ready to cut and run as soon as he was within reach.

A rustling in the brush caught her attention. Before she had time to look, a searing pain ripped up her leg and spine, sending shock waves into her brain. Her scream rent the peaceful afternoon.

Vuthy darted toward her in time to watch her drop to the ground. A snake slithered away.

Ashen, Sophea fought the rising panic in her chest.

"Vuthy, go get Auntie." Her eyes were pleading as they brimmed with tears of pain and fear.

Vuthy hesitated, torn between comforting his sister and knowing the gravity of her situation. Though he was young and small-bodied, he drew up his chest, brave in the face of dire circumstances.

Mustering his expended strength, he careened toward the

wooden house on stilts, shouting.

Terror set in as the venom coursed through her body. Solid arms lifted her from the ground. The sky grew dim as evening arrived. But it was all a blur.

The witch doctor pressed poultices to her leg. No one knew if she would pull through.

A while later, her foot, completely black, fell off. She learned to hobble around on the exposed bone stump. Life was forever changed.

There had been very few days of joy and even fewer days of innocence for Vuthy, Sophea, and their two sisters. Their parents were shadowy memories. Their father disappeared one day, never to return; it was believed he was dead. Mother was frail and heartsick. Sophea mostly remembers her with a vacant stare and gaunt arms wrapped tightly around her chest. Then, in a vague memory, Mother faded into those shadows, never to return.

Dear Auntie, the strength and bright spot of their world, worked her hands to the bone to provide for them, but eventually, tuberculosis consumed her weather-aged body. There were no options left for the children's care. So, she packed a small parcel of rice each, washed their ragged clothes, did her best to tame their unruly hair, and pointed them down the dusty path toward the beach town.

"You will find a big home there. One full of children. A wonderful place where you can learn and play. Where a foreign couple can feed you." Pausing to cough blood into her stained rag with one hand, she embraced the children with her free one.

Once she recovered enough to speak, she gave them further instructions. A single tear slid down Vuthy's face as she spoke. Auntie scolded him in her most loving tone.

"Vuthy, you are the man. A handsome and strong man. I know you can do this for me. No more tears. This is our fate. We must meet Fate as it comes."

Auntie slunk back as another fit of coughing took hold. Finally, a firm pinch on each cheek sent them on their way. Sorrow crossed Auntie's face for only an instant. Sophea thought perhaps she imagined it. The sternness quickly returned. Hand in hand, Vuthy, Sophea, and their sisters turned toward the path. They would never see their Auntie again.

Several months passed, and the children were now settled at the orphanage. Each one had been placed in a separate room due to age, creating a deeper separation. It took a while to adjust to the boisterous activities of being surrounded by so many others. Cathleen tended to Sophea's old wounds.

Cathleen took Sophea to the nearby hospital for more assessments, and she was slated for surgery. Despite her anxiety about the unknown, her fetid wound was surgically removed higher up on her calf. She was then fitted for a prosthetic.

One day, she bubbled with joy as she chased a pack of children around the grounds. Laughing until her sides hurt, she tumbled into the grass with a few of the girls. While her gait would never be normal again, she realized she hardly noticed her differences. Nostalgia caught her off guard at that moment. Was it possible to feel this way after so much hardship?

She and Vuthy's cheeks filled in a bit more, and they were beginning to understand the sounds that matched the shapes called letters taught at school. Her dorm parent was a delightful, moon-faced young woman who took her job seriously and cared well for the girls.

Yet at night, when the trees rustled and the frogs raised their song in chorus, Sophea would allow her mind to wander back to that crooked, wooden house. To the days when Auntie smiled at her as she stirred the rice over the fire. To a time when, although hungrier and more shabbily dressed, she knew she was loved.

Would the feeling of love fade, like her memories of Mother and Father? Would the outline of Auntie's high cheekbones and full lips also become blurred and unrecognizable as

Mother's had become? Curling on her side, Sophea prayed to whoever would listen that she could hold that feeling forever. That Auntie's face would stay sharp in her mind, that the loving pinch would linger on her skin, and that Vuthy would not become just another boy at the orphanage.

They interacted with over one hundred children daily, and Vuthy had a different dorm parent in the boys' section. Before life in the orphanage, the two had been inseparable. Vuthy still sat with her during their few free hours of homework or playtime. She wondered how long it would be before the boys he spent his afternoons with would usurp her company. She and her sisters had already drifted apart.

Their favorite day was Sunday, with no school and many times a trek to the beach. In the water, Vuthy still clung to her sides as the waves lapped higher and higher up their legs. Looking at her, he smiled, revealing a recent missing front tooth. Looking down at his bright eyes, she smiled back, her soul longing to stamp that memory into her mind forever. His hair was wet and stuck up in several directions. She compulsively pulled him into her arms and held tight.

Their bond never completely frayed, yet over the years their memories of family faded into the backdrop of life. They tried to talk of home, to keep it alive. But Vuthy, so young, began to remember out loud only for her sake. Remembering may have felt worse than forgetting for her two sisters. Yet Sophea never forgot her first home.

Do the Churches Understand?

Despite the drama that can occur with a hundred traumatized children, a rhythm of school, meals, and bedtime developed. The staff members were beginning to thrive in their roles now that they had proper training and job descriptions. And the bigger children gently guided the new kids into their way of life.

A few years in, Cathleen felt she could breathe a bit deeper. Stopping to take in her surroundings, she smiled as the palm trees swayed gently. There could be worse places to live.

"*Oum* Cathleen," Leak called. "Dale returned from Phnom Penh. He wants to discuss some news with you."

The calm shattered. Cathleen turned to walk back to their house. Her heart was grateful that Dale had returned safely across the treacherous highways, yet she knew that news from the home office usually meant more work and stress. "What did they want now?"

As if their time and resources were not stretched taut already.

Sitting at the dining table, Dale looked spent.

"What did the home office want?" she asked, deliberately calming her internal turmoil.

"They want us to take a new volunteer. She is barely nineteen. But she comes from a church that donates a lot, so we don't really have a say."

"We don't have the time or resources to watch someone's teenager from America, Dale! We need nurses, counselors, and people trained to work with children. Why can't we get volunteers with skills?"

Dale was well aware of these facts. He sat silent, allowing Cathleen to release the pent-up pressure of keeping so many children alive.

At times, it felt like the orphanage was less like a home for the children and more like a zoo where wealthy foreigners could gawk, take pictures, shed a few tears, and feel good about themselves. Later, Dale and Cathleen were told by her parents that they sent their defiant teen abroad, hoping she would see those less fortunate than herself and have a change of heart. Their intentions were good; however, it was a risk for staff and children alike, not to mention for the girl. They did not seem to think through the amount of extra work it would put on the Joneses to care for a problematic young woman in a potentially unsafe foreign country.

After the silence lengthened between them, their eyes met. "We don't have a choice, do we?"

Dale shook his head. "No."

"When does she arrive?"

"She flies to Cambodia next week. I'll pick her up when I head to Phnom Penh to check on our school project."

For the safety of the children and volunteers, the young woman was slated to live with the Jones family. In addition to homeschooling their children, running an orphanage, overseeing several local church plants, and overseeing a school project in another province, the Joneses now took on a challenging teenager sent to Cambodia for a summer to "build her character."

The haughty girl arrived the following week; her attitude soon put the family on edge. The orphanage did not meet with her approval: the food was too little and too "same-same," as the Cambodians might say. At times the Joneses felt like they were living with Goldilocks, that difficult-to-please children's book character. The girl was hardly settled before regular tantrums started. She disregarded safety procedures and demanded unreasonable privileges.

She chafed under the restrictions and the smothering Southeast Asian heat. However, from time to time, some promise in her character would shine through. Some days she gladly ran office errands or played with the children after school. Starved for attention, they would hurl themselves at her in delight. Yet her demands and door slamming raised the household tension. Which version of the intern would they get today? The helpful, cheery version, or the passive-aggressive, brooding version?

Having a steady personality and sense of humor under all her practicalities, Jessica, their office administrator, built rapport with Ashley and managed her mood swings well. One day she invited her on errands to town. Balking under her constraints, the girl agreed and trotted after Jessica.

The two were not far down the road when inspiration struck Ashley. "I want to pedal a *cyclo*! Here, Jessica, you sit in one, and I'll take you to where we are headed."

Jessica did not dare tell her not to ride the cyclo. She hesitated at Ashley's request but then saw the eagerness in her face. A *phu*, "uncle," in his floppy hat consented as they handed over a few hundred riels to take his *cyclo*, which was less than one American dollar, and the promise of returning it shortly. Jessica sat demurely in the front basket while Ashley perched herself atop the driver's seat. Getting the *cyclo* to move took more effort initially than Ashley anticipated. Standing up to put weight on the pedals, she strained as the men guffawed at the sight.

"Careful not to hit that pothole," Jessica called out too late; as her sentence finished, the *cyclo* nearly tipped.

The process took longer than walking, but both women wore grins until the pedals snagged Ashley's sundress. Before she could react, a loud ripping noise and the pulling force of the fabric almost caused her to fall. She attempted to stop, but it was too late. A generous portion of her sundress was violently wrenched from her body, tangling in the chain and pedals, halting the bike. Screaming and attempting to pull the fabric back out drew attention from all and sundry headed to the markets or selling food on the roadsides.

Starved for entertainment and with rare *barrang* (French or white foreigners) sightings, a crowd formed. The *cyclo* drivers could not staunch the explosive laughter. Women muttered, embarrassed for the girl yet unable to keep a few chuckles from escaping. None could look away.

Jessica scrambled once she realized what happened and attempted to gather the fabric of the dress up and cover Ashley's rear end as she tried to shield her from further embarrassment. She also did a marvelous job of restraining her own merriment.

The two *barrangs* did their best to make a straight line back to the house to get Ashley new clothing. She hid in the room for the remainder of the day, unsure how she could show her face in town again.

Dale and Cathleen tried their hardest not to laugh when Jessica recounted the incident. Thankfully, she seemed to take it in stride. At the end of their rope, Cathleen and Dale begged the home office to find her some work in Phnom Penh to finish out her time. Looking back, the amount of extra work and tension she caused during her stay was significantly greater than her contribution. The risk to Ashley and the children in the orphanage was far too great.

Did the churches back in America not understand the incredible amount of work and strain taking on a teenager required, let alone the cultural implications and all the other responsibilities they had to deal with? Rural Cambodia in the '90s was not a camp for character-building. It was a nation rebuilding after war and tragedy and was still extremely dangerous.

Too Little Medical Care

The orphanage continued to fill beyond bursting, yet they always found room for another in need. While it never felt like they could stretch their resources any further, stretch they did.

One day the orphanage heard of a baby with major physical issues. His parents had abandoned him due to congenital disabilities, but his grandmother still wanted him. Nisay had been born without an anus. His grandmother had taken him in for colostomy surgery within days of birth. But with several other siblings and cousins, Nisay was left in a hammock for much of the day because his grandmother was overwhelmed. Over time, it became evident that he would not thrive in his grandmother's care.

She knew he needed extra care if he were ever to have a chance at life. So, with a heavy heart, she brought the baby to the orphanage.

Cathleen and the staff did not know enough about his congenital disability at the time. Many years later, Cathleen learned that Nisay had been born with a severe midline defect. Developmental problems occur along the vertical axis of the body and, depending on severity, can affect the brain, spine, heart, genitals, and midline of the head and face.

Every six months, the staff would deworm all the children at the orphanage. Worms would start working their way out of Nisay's stoma, where his waste exited his abdomen into a bag. Keeping the stoma clean and preventing Nisay from playing with the bag was a constant challenge. At six months old, his hands were always in his mouth or pulling at everything within reach. His bag was prone to infection. Little Nisay was worth all the battles, but he kept the staff at constant attention.

His grandmother faithfully appeared at the orphanage to visit him. When she could find time away from the tending of his siblings and cousins, she would make the trek from the countryside and run her hands gently across his cheeks. Gazing into his big round eyes, she delighted in his improving health.

Everyone thoroughly enjoyed the babies, from the toddlers to the teenagers to the staff. Babies made life feel more like family. Because of his condition, Nisay could not be entrusted to the older kids like the healthy babies could be, but they still loved to pinch his cheeks and tickle his feet, hearing the gurgles of joy rise from his tiny throat.

As his one-year birthday approached, the staff began to note several health concerns. Cathleen and Dale decided to take him to Phnom Penh for oversight by a specialist. Braving the highway of bandits, they made their way to the city. His diagnosis was heart failure, but at that time no one in Cambodia performed heart surgery, and the hospital refused to keep him in their care. They did not want another death recorded in their books. Because of his congenital disability, his heart was damaged, unable to cope as he grew and plumped up.

The drive back was silent. A deep sadness settled over Dale and Cathleen. A few days later, Vanny entered the office, eyes wide with concern.

"Cathleen, you must come. It's Nisay. He is blue!"

Cathleen sprinted to the baby. She knew he was dying the minute she looked at him. He was blue and gasping for breath. Frantic, they rushed him to the local hospital. The emergency room was just an open-air corridor with people milling about. But Cathleen did not even notice them. The doctor grabbed the baby, threw him on a table, and began to perform CPR. But it was CPR for adults and not for children. Cathleen watched in horror as the doctor crushed Nisay's ribs, terribly hastening his death.

Coldly, the doctor placed the dying Nisay in Cathleen's arms and walked away as if this baby's life meant nothing. Regret surged through Cathleen as she struggled to catch her breath. Why had she not just let him die in peace in her arms?

She cradled Nisay's crushed body. He turned cold in her arms. In her grief, she leaned against the wall for strength. How could she have failed another one? A year. He'd had one painful year of life.

Cathleen returned to the orphanage and requested that the staff inform his grandmother of his death. But she never followed up with them, and a few weeks later, Nisay's grandmother arrived as she always did, faithful to visit him. The old woman staggered as they told her of his fate. Her precious boy was gone.

Sisterhood: Meeting Anny

"Cathleen," Dale said as he lifted his head from his Bible study, "next time we go to Phnom Penh, we should connect with Heng and see how he and his organization are doing."

After settling in Cambodia, Dale remembered a Khmer man he had met at a conference in California years earlier. The man had an organization in Phnom Penh that sounded like a good connection. They were all serving in Cambodia, so why not support each other?

So, the next time they navigated the mine-blasted highway up to Phnom Penh, they paid a visit to Heng at his mission office.

After a tour of the facilities, Dale and Cathleen enjoyed an encouraging conversation with Heng. He insisted on introducing them to a Khmer pastor and his wife and two young children.

In walked a man and his petite wife, Anny. Little did the Joneses know that this would be a lifetime connection. A friendship where trial, heartache, triumph, and victory would knit Cathleen and Anny together in an inseparable bond. This frail woman who had battled health problems her entire life had an internal fire the world could not quench. Her strength would be tested and come out true time and time again.

Originally from a village in the south of Cambodia near the Vietnamese border, Anny survived the Khmer Rouge. After nearly starving to death several times, she finally found herself in a Thai refugee camp. In the camp, she met Christian missionaries serving the displaced Cambodians. There in Thailand, in some of the worst conditions on earth, she surrendered her life to a God who promised to guide her. She was desperate for the hope He could give, and her total reliance on Him would change her life.

After returning to Cambodia alongside her pastor husband, she dedicated her life to loving her people who were broken from decades of war.

Anny smiled at Cathleen. Finally, she could put a face to the *barrang* woman she had prayed so fiercely for.

"I have heard of you, your family, and your orphanage," Anny told Cathleen. She poured out her heart for them and the hundreds of children in their care. Every day, Anny said she petitioned God on their behalf. Now, as their eyes met, Anny knew God would answer her prayers for the children of Cambodia.

"My heart swelled as Anny shared her prayers for the orphans. So many people said they cared, but I knew she meant it. She lived it. Living so far from the capital, we felt cut off from people, and I longed for deep relationships with other adults. People who shared my heart. I found that in Anny," Cathleen shared.

The Problem of Foreign Adoption

"We cannot possibly take one more child!" Cathleen vented to Dale. The orphanage was bursting at the seams. All the staff were overworked and overwhelmed. But what option did they have? They could not turn away dying and abandoned children. Their baby room was filled with sickly little ones whose lives hung in a delicate balance.

Then came Nhean. Critically malnourished, the baby teetered on the brink of death. Cathleen feared he would be lost forever if she put him in the baby room with all the other needs. Memories of holding dying babies haunted her. Yet all the exhaustion in the world could not keep her from finding the energy to pour into him. So, Nhean moved into their home and received round-the-clock care.

His malnourished stomach and bowels could not process any food, so everything came straight out of him after he ate. If cuddles and prayer were a form of nourishment, that was how Nhean survived each hour.

About a month into caring for Nhean, a family came from Phnom Penh for a holiday. Cynthia, Tom, and their children had come for a much-needed rest. The extreme living conditions in Cambodia were taking a toll on them, body, soul, and mind. A common theme among foreign workers.

One day while visiting the Jones home, Cynthia stepped over to Nhean, who began to wail and kick at his thin blankets. "May I hold him?" she asked Cathleen. She gently lifted him into her arms, cradling his frail form near her heart. She melted as those saucer eyes met hers.

Cathleen glanced at Cynthia with the baby asleep in her arms. A small smile crept across her weary face as she noted the tenderness in Cynthia toward Nhean. She seemed perfectly at peace with him, and it was nice to have an extra set of hands to care for him.

As their vacation was nearing an end, it was no surprise when she sat down next to Cathleen to talk. Twisting the cotton of her skirt nervously, she looked at her hands. Trepidation in her voice, she said, "I was thinking. You are busy here, and I am falling for Nhean." At this point, she glanced up to meet Cathleen's eyes. The longing was clear. She had spoken with her husband, and he was supportive. "We can love and care for this baby so well. I promise to do everything I can for him to have a healthy and happy life. My husband and I will take care of all of the adoption papers and process ourselves."

Cathleen knew she meant it, and they seemed to have a plan, having friends who went through the same process.

Later, Cathleen would realize that adoption with a foreign family was much more complicated than with a local family and that there was no follow-up to ensure that the child and family were bonding well. At the time, however, all Cathleen could see was a best-case solution for Nhean in an overwhelming situation. Instead of being one in a few hundred children, he would have the chance to have a family. And he would get the specialized care he needed to survive. He was so severely malnourished that he needed more physical care than any orphanage could provide.

After verbally processing with Dale, the orphanage staff, and Cynthia's family, Cathleen sent Nhean to Phnom Penh.

//

Despite her long rest, Cynthia had continued to struggle with her health. Her heart was pure, and her intentions were good, but some days putting one foot in front of the next was about all she could manage. She hated to admit it, but all the love in the world could not give her the energy necessary for the medically needy infant.

She loved him, yet somewhere inside she knew he would be better off in another family. She and her husband realized they couldn't give Nhean the attention he needed.

One day a solution walked through the doors of their church. A sweet local married couple stepped out of the sunshine into the gathering. Ten years into their marriage, they still had no baby. Nhean was soon placed with this childless couple. They would be his permanent family.

Although sadness enveloped Cynthia for the baby she could not keep, she and her husband made a selfless decision. And they remained faithful to loving him by financially supporting Nhean through school, as well as any health costs his family could not pay.

Cathleen took away valuable lessons from their experience. No more children would be put in foreign homes. The other lesson was that local solutions needed to be found.

The Problem with Double Standards

"Awwww, Mom, do we have to?" Josh and Loralie whined at the mention of going to Phnom Penh again. The thought of spending most of a day in a car traveling to the city, then sitting in the back of a meeting room for a weekend while their parents gathered with other adults, was not a fun prospect for the two kids. They would rather stay home.

The Jones children usually handled life in rural Cambodia very well. They rolled with the constant changes and their parents' hectic schedules and rarely complained about anything. When it came to these meetings, however, they made their wishes known. Not that Cathleen and Dale disagreed. They hated the long drive and sitting through meetings too.

Unfortunately, their kids were offered no form of entertainment or even learning experiences during these meetings. It would have been nice if a missionary from the city had offered to entertain the kids, but no one did.

Dale and Cathleen sat down and discussed the options. The kids were friends with many of the children at the orphanage and knew all the adults. So, after running it past their local orphanage administrator and house parents, they agreed to try leaving their children for two nights at the orphanage while they went to Phnom Penh.

Loralie and Josh responded joyfully at the prospect. A sleepover! The following day, when the Joneses arrived at their gathering childless, they were surprised by their team's shocked responses.

"How could you leave your children there?" was the standard response. The feedback was discouraging.

Cathleen began to doubt their decision. Was she a bad mother like everyone seemed to think? However, a worse doubt crept in.

Why was the orphanage considered unsafe for the missionary kids, yet it was championed as a way to care for the local kids? She and Dale had not abandoned their children; they would be gone for only a few nights. They trusted the staff to care for over one hundred children, so why wasn't it OK to trust them with their own children?

The double standard stared Dale and Cathleen in the face. They realized that none of their organization's families would ever consider placing their children in an orphanage, even if they were to die suddenly or be faced with financial hardship. All mission workers had provided for their children in their wills; they had family members or close friends who would raise them if necessary.

This revelation disturbed Dale and Cathleen. What exactly were they doing to Cambodian families?

//

When they first moved to Cambodia, Cathleen discovered there was a transitional orphanage nearby.

"Dale!" She burst into the office on the day of this discovery. "The French are building little houses where a small number of children would live with a house mom, more family style. They would cook and clean together. I want to go check it out. I think we can learn from them."

When she finally found a break in the chaos of responsibilities, she made the trip and was astonished as the director showed her around. This was a much better model of care.

She imagined how so many children got lost in the shuffle of their big orphanage. Here they would have some semblance of a family structure. Yet as she marveled, jealousy tightened in her stomach. Their top-down leadership in Phnom Penh and big orphanage model boxed in creativity.

While she put the concept in the back of her mind, there was no opportunity to implement this structure.

Cholera and the Problem of Hygiene

Access to adequate medical care was almost unheard of. This was a nation whose doctors now occupied shallow graves on the outskirts of Phnom Penh. They had been executed for the crimes of having been trained in modern medicine and of rejecting the ancient practices of the East and witchcraft.

After decades of the murder of the educated, few doctors remained. There were even fewer supplies and sterile environments. In remote areas, like where Dale and Cathleen were serving, this was a harsh reality.

The scene outside hardly matched the interior of the hospital's mildewing plaster. Outside it was a near paradise. Frangipanis exploded with flowers, perfuming the bright blue skies. Birds sang from the tops of the mango trees. All the while, a hell on earth existed within those walls.

Cathleen mopped the sweat from her face. The breeze off the sea hardly gave relief in the oppressive heat of the hot season. The humidity built for months as the days grew warmer and warmer. Eventually, the clouds would burst, soaking the land in sheets of rain and giving temporary relief. As quickly as it came, however, the sun scorches the land, and it was as if the water never touched it. The pressure would build again, creating a torturous cycle, only broken when the wet season arrived. Hot season was a terrible time to be ill, let alone dying.

As she pulled up to the hospital, Cathleen could smell

the effects of cholera long before she breached the breeze-way connecting the wards. Her muscles tensed at the sight of children writhing in pain, pooled in vomit and excrement. Wobbly folding chairs cradled emaciated beings who glanced up through hollow, fevered eyes.

She could not peel her eyes off one boy whose bodily fluids drained so quickly that the two IVs piercing his frail arms emptied noticeably. Stomach lurching, she turned away as the raw stench hit her in waves. Then, steeling her mind from the harrowing scene, she pressed on to check on the children and staff from her orphanage. Running was not an option. People were dying.

No one had prepared her for this; it wouldn't have mattered if they had. How many times in the past few years had she felt like there was no measurement for the level of suffering and injustice she witnessed?

There was no manual that could teach a person how to cope with watching a village die off from lack of sanitation and clean water. The local medical staff were overwhelmed. Their resources were draining as quickly as their patients' fluids. Was a brutal war and a country dotted with land mines not enough for Cambodians? Did they also have to die from a lack of basic hygiene?

After returning home from the hospital, she peeled her sweaty shirt away from her skin in a futile effort to cool off. Wishing she could erase the tortured images of that place, she turned to Dale. Their pleading eyes met: how much longer could they endure?

She and Dale sent a desperate message to their directors in Phnom Penh. They had five minutes daily over a HAM Radio. Then their communications were cut. Phone lines did not exist, and the office in Phnom Penh did not like the static of the HAM radio, so they turned it off for the rest of the day. People outside the city were incredibly isolated.

In their five minutes, they tried hard to convey this was

an emergency. Many people were sick and dying, and some orphanage children and staff were among those rendered ill by the disease.

"Please send medical help, one of the nurses. Please! People are dying. Some of our children are sick and in the hospital." The words caught in Cathleen's throat. The hollow eyes of the frail and dying bodies clung to her memory.

Static. Then a clipped response: "We'll look into it and let you know tomorrow." That was all. No prayer or word of encouragement. No offer of support. They anxiously awaited the next day's communication.

But relief never came. The following day, she repeated her plea for medical support. This time it was met with a resounding "No." The director had called the World Health Organization (WHO), which said there wasn't a confirmed cholera outbreak in the province. So, headquarters refused to send help.

Cathleen clung to the desk, willing herself not to be overcome by the crashing waves of despair. Would the suffering never end? Why didn't they believe how desperate the situation was? Hundreds of children's lives were at stake, and not one nurse or truck of IV supplies would be sent.

Dale's strong presence stood nearby; she lifted her head, their eyes locking. The "No" was echoing in his mind as well. There was nothing they could do but cry out to God. They sank to their knees on the kitchen floor.

"God, show us," they implored. "Show us how to stop this."

They joined with the groaning of creation, and after a time of pleading passed, there were no words left to pray. They picked themselves up, determined to face the day.

Dale walked to the orphanage to settle into a day's work. His circumstances were unchanged since their time of prayer, yet faith rose within him. Somehow, today, help would come. After stopping by the office and chatting with the staff, he made rounds throughout the dorms. As he entered a far building, his eyes glimpsed a boy at the opposite end of the room.

He watched curiously as the child bent over the mop bucket. Dale's breath caught in his throat as the boy scooped the water into his mouth for a drink. Rather than go to the water filters installed in every dorm, the children were using the mop water to quickly quench their thirst.

He had found the source of the cholera.

Those same buckets were used to collect kitchen scraps to feed the pigs' swill. Then, because all resources were precious and few, this bucket would be rinsed and filled to mop the floors. Children and staff would help themselves to a quick drink.

Soon after, staff and children alike were educated about the dangers of unclean water sources. The cholera abated.

//

From the beginning, getting the children to appreciate hygiene was challenging. Most had little concept of cleanliness. They knew only war and poverty; soap was either a luxury or a foreign substance.

The older boys were the most recalcitrant, and they were the ones who needed showers the most. They refused to take off their clothes when bathing, but a volunteer nurse cured them all with one conversation.

Working in men's urology back in her home country, she knew about the need for male hygiene. So, one day, she gathered together all of the boys for a class about personal cleanliness. Dale stood nearby, ready to translate.

It was not a captive audience. Many let out a heavy sigh, rolling their eyes. They were slapping each other, laughing, talking, and doing anything but listening.

Undaunted, she began to tell the story of a patient who was old and unkempt. He was so dirty and infected that his penis fell off. Fell off. They had to perform emergency surgery to save his life, but his private parts were never recovered. Dale almost couldn't hold himself together long enough to translate, yet he somehow managed to keep a straight face. The health of the children depended on it.

Her audience was now captive, eyes glued to her solemn face.

She continued her hygiene session, but this time her voice and Dale's were the only sounds in the room. At the end of the class, even before Dale finished dismissing them, there was a stampede to the bathhouse.

No male teenage orphans were cleaner.

Vocation Room

Bright blue shutters were flung open. The staff surveyed the room as the morning light poured through, reflecting off the orange and white tiles. Rows of looms lined one wall, while sewing machines occupied the other side. They anticipated the thrilled looks on the faces of the teenagers when the room would be revealed that afternoon as everyone flocked back from school.

In the mid-'90s the public schools were terrible, especially outside the city. Pupil numbers in each classroom were unmanageable; teachers were barely trained, equipped, or compensated. Most children had trauma histories and no access to good early childhood development. They struggled in the traditional rote-learning setting.

Established on memorization and regurgitation of information, the Cambodian school system was neither adequate nor appropriate for many of the orphans. In addition, the house parents needed more capacity and knowledge if they were to help hundreds of children with their homework.

The Joneses pondered how best to meet educational needs. One day the children would grow and age out. They supplemented the meager local schooling by hiring a full-time teacher for the orphanage. Skill sets and education were vital. In a traditional home, children would grow up with their parents' trades displayed to them regularly. Daily life involved helping to cook, clean, farm, patch roofs, fiddle with engines, sew, and weave, among other domestic tasks. In an institutionalized setting, there was none of this exposure. Thus the need for the vocational room.

//

As soon as school let out, the kids rushed to the door of the new vocation room. They were packed so tightly in the doorframe that a house father had to dislodge tangled bodies and craned necks before he could push through and explain the care and rules of the tools. Then, squealing with delight, the teens gathered around the machines, marveling at the potential of each facet. Petite Mony ran her hand gently across the black surface of a sewing machine, her smile so large it almost covered her entire face.

The next day, a dorm mother who was talented in weaving and sewing swept into the room. A young seamstress from the local church stepped in behind her, and silence fell on the children. They were delighted that these two women would be coming regularly to teach them sewing and weaving skills.

It was not long before students who could barely stitch a sentence together were happily sewing simple items. Older girls, who found starting school late difficult, were now weaving. Their nimble fingers flew as shutters click-clacked and spools of cotton unfurled. A few showed incredible skill and talent, while some less patient ones spent half their lesson untangling knotted threads.

Mony had walked with her head down before, but now she beamed each time she entered the room. She had found her passion and something at which she could excel. Several others budded in confidence and looked forward to their time with the aunties. Patterns emerged as the proud weavers held up the *kromahs* (traditional Khmer scarves) they had made. In time, several kids were making school uniforms, scarves, table covers, and even curtains.

Those with aptitude were allowed to create more technical fabrics after starting with basic cotton scarves. All the boys and girls were required to learn basic sewing as a life skill.

Cathleen would walk past the room only to hear giggles as the whir of sewing machines filled the air. Stepping in one day, she noticed a group of young boys at a machine. She pulled out her camera and snapped a photo. Dimples and toothy grins appeared as the little faces looked up from their concentrated work. Almost three decades later, this photo still graces her album. Teaching the children to weave and sew was one of the things she felt they got right in their years at the orphanage.

It was never Dale and Cathleen's goal to turn out professional sewers and weavers. However, they wanted the children to not only have a grasp of their local culture and to learn skills their parents would have taught them in the home but also to give them new things to learn and keep the teenagers productive with positive activities as well as earn pocket money for the work they did.

The children upgraded the look of the school and orphanage. They were now at least minimally equipped with a few skills for life out in the world. Cathleen often lost sleep over this very issue. The orphanage was not a natural setting; the children were shielded and unattached. Would the orphans be able to make it on their own?

"Mother! Mother!" Cathleen heard. She looked up to see Mony beaming. Mony gave a respectful bow, then shyly showed Cathleen a brand-new pair of sandals. "I saved for these with my pocket money. Aren't they lovely?"

While made of poor-quality material, they were the first things Mony owned that were not a donation. Cathleen looked into her eyes, the pride evident, and she grinned at the girl. "Yes, those are perfect."

Unfortunately, the next orphanage director dismantled the whole program a few years later. He threw away the looms, stating it was "poor people's work." He predicted silk fabrics and *kromahs* would soon be a thing of the past in Cambodia. He didn't know the Cambodian economy or that a whole revival of this trade would emerge in years to come.

Instead, his focus became sending all the children to college. American supporters loved the idea of sending orphans to college; this helped the director raise a lot of money. At the time, Americans had little value in teaching trades and craftsmanship. Skilled work was deemed less necessary than a university degree or not ambitious enough. Why shouldn't they impose their cultural lens on a nation they did not understand halfway across the globe?

//

The orphanage had begged for helpful volunteers for two years. Finally, Emily, a volunteer nurse, was sent to them. She worked full-time caring for the children as viruses, dysentery, lice, cuts, scrapes, and normal kid illnesses were rife. Everything was multiplied by having so many children in one place. In her free time, she taught the staff English and played the piano.

"Emily was a God-send!" Cathleen remembered. "She improved the children's health, got them on a vaccination schedule, and organized the medical records. In addition, she advised them on extreme cases that came in."

In their free time, the children gathered around Emily's piano. They loved to sing, and they invented actions for many of the songs. Inspired by the African children's choirs that were hugely popular in American churches then, Emily and Cathleen formed a small choir. Wanting to expose the children to the arts and bring joy to other people because the children were on the receiving end of so much generosity, they decided that an upcoming Bible college dedication was the perfect event to showcase their hard work. They had been sent a formal invitation to the event after the Bible school leader had heard the children sing at a church in Phnom Penh.

Voices rang out across the grounds as they prepared for the event. Whether they were doing chores or playing in the field, the children were always singing. They learned how to follow the director and raise or soften their voices as instructed. Happiness was etched upon their little faces when they were told they would perform in Phnom Penh.

Similar to the vocational training, the choir became a catalyst for the children to find delight in a skill set. They were no longer a single face amongst hundreds. In the choir, they felt both collectively special and individually unique. A few of the more shy and quiet kids even found an outlet in music. Singing wove a deeper thread of identity, belonging, and talent into everyone's hearts.

During practice one night, Cathleen caught sight of a little boy who had had a particularly traumatic early childhood. He missed his mother terribly. She was deaf, and at that time, there was no help for the deaf. It was hard for her to find work and care for multiple children.

But there he stood, shoulders back and head high, singing with his entire being. Cathleen could not pull her eyes away from him and his newfound boldness. It was as if she were watching an entirely different child stand with pride alongside his peers. For a few minutes, all her griefs and regrets were forgotten as she watched each precious face declare hope through song.

After their performance, the van full of children headed back to their sleepy beach town, the children chattering non-stop in excitement over their performance and the chance to see the capital city. This small event was enormous in the hearts of the tiny people whose lives rose and set in a tiled dorm full of paid staff.

The Problem
of Separating
Mothers and Babies

One morning, a woman appeared at the Joneses' home. She was so impoverished that she borrowed a neighbor's dress to visit. With bone-thin arms and legs and with heavy breasts and a sagging midsection, she claimed to be the mother of newborn triplets. She implored the orphanage for help. With four older children, her oldest being only five years old, she lacked the means to keep her tiny premature infants alive.

Cathleen and a staff member went to investigate the situation. Despite all they had experienced over the years, nothing had prepared them to enter the abandoned, crumbling building with squatters dwelling in dark crevices. Stepping over rubble, Cathleen glanced at the sky shining through missing ceiling tiles. Rubbish was strewn about; the stench of human waste assaulted the senses.

Eyes adjusting to the dark, they followed the mother as she led them to a low, wooden platform in one corner with a premature baby girl lying on a pillow. Filthy toddlers peeped from behind a hammock and fallen beams. In the hammock slept two even smaller boys, who appeared identical.

Dumbfounded, Cathleen hardly heard the mother's pleas to keep them together. She stared at the triplets, taking it all in. This woman had given birth in the hospital, then returned home to squalor a few days later with no support. Nevertheless, she had managed to keep four other children alive and had the strength to trek to Cathleen's home within days of delivering the triplets. Not only would the emaciated mother need to breastfeed three premature babies and keep them sanitary, but she would also have to do it with barely weaned toddlers. She stood there, wringing her hands in desperation, begging Cathleen and her staff member to help her babies stay together. Even in the worst of conditions, family mattered to her.

She had been offered money for the baby girl but refused because she wanted to keep her babies together.

"The mother needed money badly, but she cared more about the bond between her babies," Cathleen remembered.

The weight of responsibility for their survival clung to the damp air. At just over a kilogram each, the babies hardly uttered a noise. They were completely exposed as the mother had no blankets, clothing, or hats. Death was imminent unless they intervened.

Cathleen and her staff took the babies to her home and then called the doctor. A few hours later, he examined the babies grimly, not expecting a good outcome. As Cathleen suspected, their survival was unlikely. Apart from keeping the babies warm, he had no other advice.

They put the three infants in the baby-care home in the Joneses' downstairs and set up a baby assembly line with Jessica, Cathleen, and another staff member. Each baby was bathed and put into clean clothes, their diapers fashioned from cotton towels and disposable zipper bags. The three women fed the premature infants every two hours with formula, and the babies slept together in their crib just as they had for seven months in their mother's womb.

When Dr. Samnat returned a few weeks later, he let out a loud victorious cry, jumping up and down and clapping his hands. He celebrated the babies not only being alive but gaining weight. He marveled as he took the vitals of each. The grin on his face appeared permanent. It was incredibly undignified behavior for a local doctor, but he didn't care. His joy bubbled over because he had never seen triplets survive.

Cathleen still has a photo from the orphanage days. In it, three healthy toddlers stare at the camera, the boys in matching plaid shorts and white polos, the little girl with black hair in a bob cut and plaid dress. Two are grasping hands. They look like they were interrupted from playing with a nearby wagon.

Grateful that they lived and grew up healthy, Cathleen still mourned the situation. "Their mother wanted to keep her family intact; she understood how they needed one another, but they were just incredibly impoverished. Had she kept them, they would have died because it was too unsanitary. Yet what if our mission had considered caring for the wholeness of an entire family and not just the babies?"

Recently, another member of the organization passionately defended their orphanage model: "I know those triplets. Sure, they have issues from growing up institutionalized, but their mother is crazy. They are better off growing up in an orphanage."

But what difficulties had that woman faced that caused her emotional instability? Decades of starvation, abuse, neglect, and war can wear down a person's heart and soul as much as they wear down a person physically. What did losing her babies do to her? Did that unimaginable loss lead to behavior that others considered "crazy"? Despite her imperfections as a mother, she cared enough to fight for her children to stay together. There must have been deep love inside of her that knew it was right to keep them together. What would have happened if the church had seen her and valued her as much as it valued her babies? Perhaps all their stories would have a happier ending.

The Problem of Impossible Choices

Phally carefully worked out the kinks in her curly black hair with her wooden comb. Her heart sank in her chest as she felt the baby kick. Belly bulging from the advanced pregnancy, she could not quiet the flutter in her chest. It was so much stronger than her hunger pangs. How did it come to this?

She looked around at the cracked plaster; she had memorized every line in the walls. Water stains from the wet season made darkened patterns. She remembered the wet seasons when he was still there. They were poor but content. Together, they could always make it. They could raise their daughter together and feel the joy of parenthood. Yet she didn't know where he was. Was it the Khmer Rouge or bandits on the highway? Did a land mine or accident take his life? Or was it something as simple as another pretty face, one not swollen with pregnancy? One not focused on a toddler?

After his disappearance, her whole life spiraled. She had no money for medical care, and the taut skin across her belly reminded her there would be another mouth to feed soon. And she had no support. All her family was missing or dead from the civil war, which continued even after Pol Pot had been removed from leadership.

Phally set her comb down and pressed her hand against her aching heart as Davi lifted her beautiful bright eyes, awakening from her sleep on the mat in the corner. She seemed to sense the sorrow in the room and remained quiet, unblinking, as her mother looked back at her.

Phally steeled herself. What if she lost this perfect little girl? The child she and Ratha yearned for years to have. Davi was not flesh and blood, but she might as well have been. Ratha and Phally had scratched together savings to buy Davi from the market. There was no adoption available in Cambodia at the time; however, women rendered childless through disease, war, or starvation could find a child if they knew where to look. Infertility brought shame on a family, so couples who could not conceive sometimes bought children. There was a high price to pay, considering the poverty of the place, yet it was worth it.

More than a year ago, Phally first held the tiny, red-faced baby in her arms, and her heart had been knitted to the child. Her little girl, whose kisses were sweet and whose smile was even more endearing. The communists had robbed Phally of so much, but she felt Davi was a balm, a redemption from sorrow. Yet here she was about to inflict even more profound sorrow than she thought possible.

Her precious little girl was now penniless and fatherless; how life had changed. "Fate, how cruel you are. Meting out suffering upon suffering, while others live in lavish comfort."

Phally had seen the large white man and his family before. She heard they were kind. Their orphanage brimmed with children, and she hoped there was a place to keep Davi safe. What other option did she have?

The toddler pulled herself near her mother and gently placed her hand on Phally's belly. She looked up at her mother with a question in her eyes. Did Davi know? How could she?

Phally ran her fingers lovingly through the tendrils of dark silk on Davi's head, messy from a night of deep sleep. "My sweet love."

Rising slowly, Phally went to the corner where the cooking pot was. She spooned out the rice that she had cooked the night before. Having not eaten herself because this was all that remained, she carried the rice to Davi and slowly spooned the white fluff into the child's mouth. She cherished every detail: Davi's curling and uncurling fingers, her tiny perfect teeth, and her smooth brown skin with a faint flush of pink on each cheek. Phally and her husband had named her Davi because it means angel, and this child embodied her name.

When the meager meal was finished, Phally cleaned Davi and combed her hair, tying up the soft waves into pigtails. She rose again, her ankles swollen, and hefted Davi to her hip. She was about to embark upon the longest journey of her life. She hoped they would agree to take her child; she had no other choice. There was nowhere else for her to go, nowhere to turn but up the hill to the orphanage.

Cathleen had finished homeschooling and was checking on the staff at the orphanage. She went to the baby room first. Several new babies were very frail and sick from malnutrition and disease. Most had been abandoned at a few days old. Their baby room was filling up faster than they could find the staff to care for them, yet somehow these babies were determined to survive.

She brushed the cheek of the smallest as she talked to the caretaker about his feeding schedule. The little one was hungry, no doubt about that. The formula was worth its weight in gold, but these babies were worth infinitely more.

One of the teenage girls knocked on the door. Looking at Cathleen shyly, she asked in a barely audible voice if she could hold Srey Oun, the plump baby with the long eyelashes that framed her almond eyes. Srey Oun's emerging personality was spunky and had a bit too much power behind her cries.

The staff allowed some of the older children to take the babies for a period. It taught them responsibility and child-rearing even as it bonded the babies in a sibling style. The girl squealed with delight when the staff member plunked the freshly changed Srey Oun into her arms. The gummy baby grin was a reward in itself.

Cathleen watched them go, then snapped back to the reality that she currently had over a hundred children. How could their budget keep stretching? Yet, having overseen the finances, she knew that every week was a miracle. Somehow, they kept feeding and caring for everyone.

After a few more rounds, she wiped her brow and made her way to the office. In the distance, she saw a petite woman, clearly near her due date, hefting a toddler toward them. Taking in the scene, Cathleen could tell they were poor, yet clean and well cared for.

The woman's dusty and swollen feet revealed a long journey. Cathleen invited her to sit. Sorrow and hesitation filled the woman's eyes. Cathleen had seen this look far too many times.

Phally explained her situation, pouring out her life story. The death of her family. The abandonment by her husband. "I have no one. No money."

Then the conversation shifted. Phally begged to be paid for Davi. "Please, I need the money to have this baby," she said.

Her voice cracked. She broke eye contact as she toyed with the hem of her skirt. She was desperate, and Cathleen's heart twisted. "We can take Davi. We will give her good care but cannot pay for her. This is our policy; we absolutely do not pay for children."

Filled with compassion, she watched the young woman's last shred of hope flicker. Now two hearts were breaking.

"Oh God," Cathleen's heart cried in a silent plea. "How would you respond? I know I cannot save everyone, but she's right in front of me. How do I turn her away?"

She looked at Phally, examining her closely. Then, softening her speech, she leaned in. "Please, we will care for Davi. We cannot pay you, but she will be safe and fed. Please let us take her." Cathleen stopped short of saying the word love. They would do their absolute best, yet she knew that no love from the staff or the hundred parentless children could match a mother's love.

Phally gently brushed her fingers across the toddler's soft arms. Torn between her critical need and her affection for this little one, she hardened herself. Then, knowing what must be done, she rose to leave. She needed money; they would die if she did not get money.

Cathleen gave one final plea for Davi, who clung to her mother. Then she rose with Phally and walked her out. She watched the slow shuffle, swollen belly, and straining arms until they disappeared in the distance. Cathleen never found out what became of them, and their faces are permanently seared into her memory. This moment was her tipping point.

"Something is wrong here, Lord. That woman needs help. I feel so trapped in a system of orphan care. I cannot help her, and it's the mother who needs me the most. What if we're helping in the wrong way? Are good intentions enough? What if we could keep them together? What if mothers did not have to sell their children to survive? Even in desperate poverty, could families make it if they were given a chance, hope, and support?"

Phally, Davi, and her unborn baby will never know, but they were the impetus that would carry Cambodia into family preservation, a concept above and beyond orphanages. Their suffering came at a high cost, but it would lead to a different outcome for thousands, if not tens of thousands, of children.

Gatekeeping

After realizing that most of their children were not orphans, Dale and Cathleen began setting boundaries for whom they could take into residential care. Most people in Cambodia had needs, and they could not help everyone. The budget and food were already scarce, and wages for the staff needed to be higher. In the first six months, the orphanage capacity doubled, placing enormous stress on already-tight resources.

Overwhelmed by the volume of children, they knew if they took in more or did not place some back into their families, the level of care they could provide would be poor. They wanted the space for those desperately in need. In the pre-Internet days, Cathleen used her limited free time to search for literature about "gatekeeping." There was almost nothing available on the topic. Dale and Cathleen didn't have any access to other long-term orphanage directors who could offer wisdom, so they had to figure it out for themselves.

They developed a stringent vetting process. Did the child have parents? If not, did the child have an extended family? What were the living conditions? Were they safe? Did the child have medical needs their families could not meet? Were there alternatives to residential care?

Over time, the list of protocols and requirements grew and began to stem the flow of children into their care. The task was difficult because it meant turning away vulnerable children. On top of that, there seemed to be some competition among the organization's orphanages. Who had the most children? Who was taking in the most babies? How many programs were they running? Leadership seemed to think that the more challenging the situation, the more donors would give. And they weren't wrong.

In hindsight, Cathleen realized that her internal compass told her they needed to become more family focused. Still, at the time, she cared too much about what others thought, so she did not rock the boat or question her leaders.

//

Not long after the triplets arrived at the orphanage, Sokhum appeared at their gates with twins, a boy and a girl. Her husband had disappeared a few weeks after their babies were born, a sad reality for many families. So many men had died in the genocide that there was one man for every five women in the country. A lot of men absconded from their wives and children to chase another woman.

How could women both work and care for their children? They had no support or family to help them because oftentimes their parents, siblings, aunts, uncles, and cousins were dead or separated.

Although disadvantaged, Sokhum appeared intelligent and capable as she held the squalling infants. A house mom took one baby from her to relieve her as the three women talked in the gazebo. It was a beautiful day and the wind was off the sea, which made being outdoors a relief from the oppressively hot buildings.

"Please take my babies and care for them," she implored after pouring out her story. "I do not have enough to eat, and my home is small. I don't know what to do anymore."

Her anguish was palpable. Cathleen touched the soft tuft of black hair on the little girl. A twinge of pride gripped her heart; these babies would be healthy here. The staff loved the tiny ones, and the orphanage up north had recently boasted of a young sibling group they had taken in, complete with a beautiful infant. Twins would make for an exciting newsletter.

Cathleen quickly squelched these thoughts, brushing aside the selfishness in her heart. She looked into the face of this woman, brokenhearted at the thought of losing her babies. Sokhum had made a great effort to care for them during their first weeks, but it had not been enough. It wasn't for lack of love or desire. The man she loved was gone, pursuing younger women. And when he left, he took her only source of income to clothe and feed his children. Any new mother, no matter where in the world she lived, would be devastated.

Sokhum could not envision a future. But after having turned away Phally and her adopted daughter, Cathleen knew there had to be another way. This woman needed hope and help, but the solution could not be for her to relinquish her children. After a long conversation, Cathleen made it clear they would not take the babies. She shared with Sokhum how important it is for babies to bond with their mothers; the orphanage staff could never replace her.

"However, we will help support you in caring for your babies. Since you are nursing and do not have enough food or time for yourself and the babies, we will give you infant formula each month." Sokhum perked up a little, but she was also a bit angry. Cathleen's response had been unexpected. She twisted her kromah in her hands, unsure of how to respond.

They invited Sokhum to dinner. As they shared their meal, Cathleen and Sokhum agreed on a plan. Sokhum would return each month with one baby each visit, swapping them out every second month so the orphanage staff could do a checkup. In this way, she could keep her children, and they would remain healthy. They promised to assess her situation each time, measuring the babies' progress and providing her with another month's worth of food and formula.

After dinner, they sent Sokhum off with two gigantic containers of formula in a bag. It came from Thailand in a canister big enough to last a month. A house mom gave her a rundown on bottle sterilization and how to mix up the powder, so she had what she needed.

One month later, Sokhum appeared at the gate, the baby girl in her arms. The following month, it was her son. The babies grew plump and rosy under this arrangement.

"They were the cutest babies," Cathleen remembered. They had a healthy and cheery disposition.

Then a miracle took place. A few months into this unusual arrangement, Cathleen and her staff began to see a shift in Sokhum. Her strength was growing; she walked with her head slightly more erect and no longer appeared despondent.

Around the eighth month, as Cathleen reached out to take the chunky infant in her arms, Sokhum looked at Cathleen and said in an earnest voice, "Thank you for making me keep my babies. I was so angry with you for not helping me enough. I was so desperate. These two are the light of my life. I cannot imagine my world without them."

After a year, Sokhum took both babies and never returned. They never knew what happened to the family. However, Cathleen is reasonably sure it was because Sokhum was finally able to care for both babies herself.

"Looking back, I wish we had done a house check. We did not monitor her situation. I had no idea who she lived with or what their home life was like. There was no follow-up after that first year. I know better now, but I also know we did the right thing in helping her keep her children. We were unable to give her transportation; she walked a long distance with an infant and formula every month, which showed her commitment to loving her children. The babies were in good condition every time she came, so she must have been doing a reasonably good job of caring for them at home, which is reassuring."

Sokhum was a poor, single mother, but she was still worthy of keeping her children. Her love for them sustained her through difficult times. Sokhum needed help, not having her children ripped away from her, even by choice.

The Joneses began to wonder if more parents just needed a little assistance. What if parents could keep their children?

//

After Sokhum's success, a man arrived with his six children. His wife had died in childbirth, and he wanted to remarry. Unfortunately, it was and still is common in Cambodia for remarriage to come with the assumption that spouses will dispose of their children from a previous marriage.

Because of their new policies, the orphanage refused to take the man's children. He was capable of providing for them. His only reason for wanting to dump them at the orphanage was his and his future bride's selfishness. After their refusal to take the kids, he stormed away, leaving his children on the doorstep. The toddler wailed in her older sibling's arms.

Undaunted by his behavior, Cathleen stood her ground. Staring at six unwanted children was not easy. The staff sat the children on a bench in the shade outside the gate and occasionally peeked out at them to ensure they were fine. It did not take long before the kids' auntie arrived. She gathered them to herself like a mother hen and marched off with them. Cathleen watched this scene, satisfied that she had done the right thing but hoping they would be loved and cared for by their family, yet wishing she could do more.

//

"Ruth, what are they going to do?" Cathleen questioned, looking her in the face.

"I don't know!" Ruth snapped back. "Make up something for them to do. Paint a mural, sew some curtains . . ." she trailed off.

"But the kids already make all of our things in the sewing room."

While down on a short beach holiday, Ruth, another orphanage director, had stopped by in a whirlwind, leaving Cathleen on edge. Ruth wanted to put together a team of women from her home country. She needed to find things for them to do and thought showing them around the orphanages and creating menial tasks would make them happy.

Cathleen understood the desire to share what they did with others across the globe, but this approach felt unhelpful and disruptive.

Cathleen took a breath and explained, "You want us to create a need unnecessarily when we already have so many real needs for these children. I understand that we want people to partner with what we are doing, but this is not the way."

Cathleen thought of all the relationships that had been broken in the children's lives, leaving them feeling abandoned over and over. She did not need to add a team of doting foreign women to the list of people who would walk away after a week of non-stop attention.

"You will lose your funding if you don't find a way to accommodate these women," Ruth retorted.

Later, Cathleen processed with Dale. He stood firm in her initial assessment. It was not suitable for the children, and it was not helpful for the orphanage. The children's best interests were more important than donors' feelings and the creation of fake opportunities for short-term teams.

A pared-down version of the team did eventually visit Cambodia and later made their way to the beach for a holiday. They were very nice ladies who seemed content to spend a few minutes chatting with Cathleen, who popped by their guesthouse. This quick meeting prevented the children from being further harmed, however it put them at risk of losing funding. This was a key moment to think through what short-term mission teams were actually there for.

International Adoption Schemes

While international adoptions existed in Cambodia in 1994, most organizations were against it because of the rampant corruption. Unsavory characters recognized that international adoptions were lucrative. Selling children as true orphans brought in a lot of money. While in reality, most were separated from their families due to poverty.

A few years after the Joneses had taken on management of the orphanage, a beat-up 4-Runner rattled into view. Out stepped Ruth. Cathleen came out of the office into the glaring sun to greet her. With hardly a glance in her direction, Ruth indicated she wanted to check on their baby room.

Cathleen sighed and followed her.

"Why is she here again?" Cathleen wondered. "Last time she scrutinized, judged, and nitpicked every detail."

Ruth was a fellow team member who had just one more year of experience in the field than the Joneses. But her strong personality could be intimidating.

As they quietly stepped into the baby room, Ruth's eyes settled on Pisey, an abandoned baby girl whose rosy cheeks and sweet chuckles made her a magnet for adoration.

"What's this baby's story?" she inquired, plucking the sleeping girl out of her cot.

"We believe her father was a UN soldier and her mother was a local single woman. Another woman tried to raise her when she was abandoned. However, she didn't have enough money and brought her here for care."

"So, no one will return to ask for her?" Ruth asked.

Cathleen hesitated; what was Ruth getting at?

"Well, as far as we know, no relative has ever come searching for her. We are unsure if her family is alive or not. If the story we were told is true, we do not think anyone will come. Pisey is so beautiful." Cathleen continued to share the baby's difficult beginning, how malnourished she had been, and how she was flourishing now.

Cathleen paused for a second, then asked, "Why are you asking?"

"My cousin wants a child," Ruth continued.

Flushed with confusion and a sense that something was wrong, Cathleen did not know what to do about the uneasy feeling in her heart.

"You know we are not supposed to be involved in adoptions," Cathleen responded. She noticed the frustration rising in Ruth and stumbled over her next words. "Our leadership made it clear that we are not allowed to be involved in adopting our children internationally," she continued.

Even though it was not strictly illegal to adopt children out of Cambodia at the time, their organization had made it clear from the beginning that international adoption was not an option. The message had been relentlessly hammered into them: "You will not get involved in international adoptions; that's not what we are here to do."

Yet rumors abounded. Under-the-table adoptions were taking place, and people seemed to be turning a blind eye. With no monitoring from the government and little oversight from their leadership, children could unfortunately be taken out of the country for a price.

Ruth looked at her, tight-lipped. The sweet little one did not appreciate being awakened from her nap and then dumped back in her cot. Cathleen didn't know what to say next. She wanted to scream like Pisey was now doing. How could someone just walk in and peruse the children? Did the boundaries of their organization mean nothing? What impact would an international adoption have on the children's lives?

Conflicted, Cathleen wrestled with what was right and wrong. She knew these kids needed families but felt this was the wrong way of going about it. The international adoptions she had heard about were full of corruption and bribes, which was precisely why her organization did not permit them, but here was a woman promising a loving home for one of the abandoned children in their care.

Although confused and conflicted, Cathleen let Ruth know she could not take Pisey. At the time, there wasn't a label for it, but now these kinds of actions would be considered "trafficking." At the very least, this behavior set a precedent for bypassing systems designed to protect children from being taken away from their families, communities, and country. While some kids were placed with good families through bribery and false documents, this practice opened the door for more nefarious enterprises to traffic children. So little monitoring took place in those days that unethical people could always find work-arounds if the right bribes were paid.

At one point, after Dale and Cathleen had watched several babies pass through the hands of foreigners and out of the orphanages, the facilitator remarked, "It's just easier to change the documents and make the kids true orphans."

Cathleen knew that this had to stop.

//

During the four years Dale and Cathleen spent at their orphanage, many couples rotated in and out of the other orphanage their organization ran. When one couple went home on leave (also called "furlough"), another couple would take their place. This resulted in a constant turnover of caregivers for the children. The couples who worked at the orphanages desperately needed the time off, but the effect on the children in their care was to add more trauma to the pain they had already endured.

One year when Ruth and Michael went on furlough, Bryce and Emily filled in for them. The workload wore them down. Their marriage and faith in shambles, they were too exhausted to continue, and they made a sudden return to America.

In their absence, an unexpected issue was discovered. Bryce and Emily had chosen a child from the orphanage to live in their home and become part of their family. They treated her like their own child, changing her name to Samantha. She wasn't growing up in the orphanage with the other children, but Bryce and Emily had no legal claim on her. So, when they left, Samantha was confused. She thought she was their child, but the law dictated otherwise.

Dale and Cathleen went to Phnom Penh for a meeting with their director about the situation. Looking at them across his desk, he asked, "Can you please take Samantha into your care until legal documentation can be arranged for her to be with Emily and Bryce?"

"At the time, we lived upstairs in a house near the orphanage, and the orphanage babies were kept downstairs for more constant monitoring, but the baby center was full. Several staff and I cared for all the babies, and I also homeschooled my children, so it was not feasible to care for Samantha in my home. She was used to more time and attention than I could give," Cathleen said.

One of the dorm mothers had a small group of children to look after, and she was fantastic with the babies and toddlers. With their leadership's permission, Dale and Cathleen arranged for her to take responsibility for Samantha, giving the love and attention the toddler needed.

"The dorm mom loved her," Cathleen said. "She and the children in her care doted on Samantha. She was the princess of the room. They dressed her up, and she was so cute. Her standard of care was exceptional."

A few months into this arrangement, Samantha was settled into life at the orphanage when Cathleen got a call on the HAM radio.

Ruth's voice cracked across the expanse, "I'm coming today. I'm coming to get Samantha."

"What are you talking about?" Cathleen asked. "Samantha's fine."

Ruth signed off, not responding. Half a day later, she blew into the orphanage and wrenched Samantha from her new room, hastily packing up her things.

"Ruth drove down to 'rescue' Samantha from her life in the 'evil orphanage,'" Cathleen reflected. "She came without any input or consent from our leadership and took Samantha to keep in a room she had arranged for children who had been set apart for American adoptions. There was no thought to the trauma inflicted on the child by yet another change of caregivers."

Bryce and Emily trusted Cathleen with Samantha's care. Their organization entrusted hundreds of children to Cathleen's care. Yet it was not good for Samantha, and she was now being isolated and treated differently than the others. Cathleen further processed the circumstances: "If we believed orphanages were good for children, then why were people so set on adopting them to foreign families? Why adopt in the first place if orphanages are fine to raise children? Deep down, Ruth and the rest of us knew this wasn't the best place for kids to grow up."

Over twenty years later, while Cathleen was speaking with a friend from their organization, the friend questioned, "Should someone tell these adopted kids their real ages and family information?"

Cathleen gaped at her, "Yes, a resounding yes! They deserve to know they have family in Cambodia!"

As a result of the black market of international adoption, an entire generation of adopted children are now adults in America and Europe with no idea what their real names are and that they are not orphans.

Cathleen addressed the overarching issue in their orphanage and institutions across Southeast Asia and globally: "There is this incredible pride of ethnicity that we have. It's discrimination. We think they are better off if they get to live like an American or raised by foreigners. As if we need to rescue children from their culture and families. It's a 'Cambodia is less than' attitude. It is so prejudiced."

Abandoned Babies

Toward the end of the Joneses' time with the orphanage, two more sick babies were brought to them. The first baby was brought by the woman who had found her, but nothing could be done. Malnourishment and dehydration had already taken hold, and her frail body was consumed by death within a few days.

Not long after, a radio call came from Phnom Penh. Someone had found another abandoned baby girl. A local pastor and his wife had been alerted and were caring for her as best they could. They were feeding her sweetened condensed milk with added sugar to keep her alive until the mission organization could get her. Suffering from dehydration and unabating diarrhea, the baby was in desperate need of medical care.

The Joneses took her to their orphanage. She was in a sad state but not without hope.

The worst shock, however, came when Cathleen removed her clothing and saw evidence of severe sexual abuse.

Even though she had experienced wave after wave of human suffering and demonstrations of brutality in their four years in Cambodia, Cathleen could not control the emotions surging through her. She was consumed with both rage and pity. How could anyone rape a baby?

Shaking, she stepped back from the baby, dropping the clothes in the process. What level of seared consciousness must one possess to inflict this perversion and abuse on an infant?

Taking a deep breath, she calmed her shaking and faced

the task set before her: a sick baby girl. At a certain level, as with all their difficulties, they had no choice but to bury their need to process these burdens. A baby was dying. A living baby, right in front of them. Despite all the heavy questions life in Cambodia brought to the surface, Cathleen and Dale repeatedly had to set them aside. Over a hundred children needed them. There was no time to wrestle through the theology of suffering and sin fully.

Given the utmost care, the girl became another valued member of their orphanage. They slowly weaned her off her sugar addiction as she initially refused pure formula, and they kept her in their home until her health improved.

As Cathleen finished telling me the story of this little girl, she said, "She lived. She is a beautiful young woman now."

Not only was the orphanage model difficult on the children, the reality was that it was hard on the adults running it. No one is equipped to deeply care for and meet the needs of so many children, especially not the trauma so many entered the institution with. And because of their workloads, they did not have the time to process the constant difficult situations with which they were faced.

//

One of the girls in the orphanage contracted encephalitis. She was in the hospital for months. She survived, but her brain was slow to recover.

Dale and Cathleen worried about how the other kids would treat her, since many believed in the cultural idea of karma that said those who suffered deserved their suffering. Additionally, the children who were experiencing their own trauma tended to make very hurtful remarks to one another.

Christmas came, and Dale drew names from a hat to determine who could go pick a gift from the pile of donated gifts. This girl got the first pick. She rose from her seat at the back of the room and, with the assistance of a staff member, walked to the front. Suddenly, clapping started. Then, feet-stomping spread. The children were making a cheerful clamor as the girl approached the table spread with presents!

Spontaneously and in unison, they erupted into a cheer on her behalf. More than one hundred kids celebrated that she was walking, smiling, and alive. They cheered more for her success than they ever did for a personal toy.

"There were some days when it all seemed worthwhile, and that was one of them," Cathleen said as she relived the memory.

Someone Who Needed Rescue

Taevy had been abandoned by her Khmer mother and Vietnamese father. Her father's parents had taken her in but hated her because they hated her mother. So, they forced her to work with their cattle all day, leaving her starved and neglected, only giving her attention when they hurled insults at her or beat her.

One day, as she tended the cattle, ankle-deep in mud from the hard rains, a stranger approached her. This woman appeared wealthier than any of the neighbors and not from their area. Taevy paused as the woman navigated the field to draw near.

"I know your mother!" she shouted as she approached. "I know your mother in Cambodia, and she sent for you."

Taevy could hardly believe her ears; after all this time, her mother wanted her. Soft-spoken, the woman acted genuinely distressed about her poor treatment. Concern etched her voice.

The woman shared details that seemed true, pouring out promises of giving her a better life. How else would she know her mother had been gone a long while and was in Cambodia?

After sharing more information about their journey, the woman indicated they should leave quickly. "Your grandparents will not approve since they hate your mother. It is best if we leave without them knowing."

With a lifetime of misery, Taevy had nothing to lose.

The woman led her to a waiting rammork (a large trailer

pulled by a motorbike) piled high with supplies. Taevy had never seen her reflection in any surface to know just how pathetic she appeared, but she recoiled at the spiritless and emaciated human staring back at her from the rammork.

Broken in body and spirit, she pulled herself up into the trailer, already packed with weary-looking travelers, and they set off for Cambodia. It was arduous.

The day grew impossibly long. It slowly dawned on Taevy that this woman was bad. They were not going to see her mother; the rammork was approaching a port town. They would be taken by boat to an island where Thai slave traders were waiting to purchase them. She and the others were to be sold by their captor as slave labor, or worse. Yet with nothing left in her to fight or run away, she surrendered to her fate. Shifting to relieve her aching legs, she tucked one leg under herself and let the other hang freely from the back of the cart.

Fear squeezed her heart, and she began to pray to God, Fate, or anyone who would hear. "Please let me die and give me a new life with joy and love!"

A terrible noise broke her prayer. Snapping her mind back, she looked up and saw a van careening toward her.

"This is it! This is the moment I die." Peace flooded her as she breathed out. In the next instant, the van ran directly into her.

Time slowed. Glancing down, she saw her right foot and lower calf hanging by a thin strip of skin. Before she could register pain, she found that she could no longer hear, a cold sweat beaded her brow, and then her world faded away.

//

Just before dusk set in, Rithy drove home, trying to make it before dark. Despite being a local police officer, he feared the dark and the empty streets where men were murdered for their motorbikes or even a few *riels* padding their wallets. He rounded a treacherous curve in the road where many crashes happened, slowing down to be sure not to strike any oncoming vehicles. The hair on his neck stood on end. Surely, he saw wrongly; that could not be a body in the ditch. Downshifting, he felt it was his duty to take a second look.

Yes, it was a body, a little girl. Bile rose into his throat for fear of the condition he would find her in. Her limbs lay unnaturally positioned as though a person had dumped her. He put down his kickstand, cautiously looking in all directions for danger before sliding down the small embankment when he saw her bloodied leg, bone crushed, foot blue. Before he could stop himself, he vomited.

Her eye twitched. He leaned in, and sure enough, there was shallow breath in her lungs. She's alive!

Panic quickly replaced his joy. He had to keep her alive. This poor starved child, almost dead! He'd seen his share of death and atrocities over the years, yet it never robbed him of his compassion and humanity. A voice within him urged him to hurry. Told him that she must live.

Cradling her light frame in his arms, he lifted her out of the dust. He positioned her on his motorbike as he raced back to the nearest city where a UN hospital was located. Dark or not, resolve pushed away any self-concern.

After what seemed like the longest ride of his life, his headlight lit up the entrance to the UN hospital. Calling out, he roused the guards, who rushed at him. They gently removed the bloodied child from his embrace. Staff rushed a stretcher out as an older French doctor sprinted to the yard. Rithy poured out what happened, keeping pace with the racing feet of the medical staff.

As she entered surgery, they held him back. Hours later, a nurse approached his slouched figure, napping in the corridor with his head slumped against the wall. It was late at night. Generator-powered lights dimly flickered. The nurse offered a hot, watery tea.

"The girl's leg had to be removed, but she will live. All

thanks to you, *Phu*," the nurse told him, placing a firm hand on his shoulder. "Now drink this, and we have a mat for you in the yard."

//

Taevy roused. Confused, she felt scratchy sheets beneath her. Her mind was still clouded as she glanced about the hospital ward. Morning light filtered through smudged windows; birds sang in the palms outside. An IV ran into her arm. As she grew more alert, she remembered Vietnam. The woman. The long ride. The van. As her memory recalled her foot dangling by skin, dull pain registered in her body.

Frantically reaching down, she felt bandages and a stump on her right side. Slowly her heart rate decreased as she attempted to make sense of her situation. A nurse approached her.

Soon, a litany of confusing questions were flung at her. Who was she? Where was she from?

Although she knew Vietnamese and Khmer languages, she could not mask her Kampuchea Krom accent, marking her as a despised Vietnamese. Due to the generations of fighting, Vietnam and Cambodia hated each other. She was no better than a dog to the Cambodians.

The French soldiers filtered in to check on her throughout the day. The French doctor had such a tender manner, speaking gently to her, explaining what he knew from Rithy. But the Cambodian doctors looked at her as if she were dung, a blight on their hospital.

Learning the little they could from her, the UN doctors conferred and decided to look after her, feeding her from their own rations until they could connect her with long-term care. Her road to recovery would take a while.

Despite her circumstances, Taevy smiled after a while. A nearby woman who was nursing her son glanced at her. "Why are you so pleased? The doctors just said you lost your leg.

You don't care?" The woman was blunt but kind.

"It's OK, in a few months my leg will grow back!" Taevy responded perkily. Her mind was completely empty of concern.

"What do you mean?" The woman appeared puzzled.

"Like the crabs in the fields, when you remove their pincers, they grow back." Genuinely believing this reasoning, she smiled at the woman. Surely, that explained everything.

The woman looked stunned. Sitting in silence, staring at the half-starved child, she spoke, "Girl, are you insane? Do you know nothing? Your leg will not grow back. We are people, not crabs!"

Undeterred by the woman's comments, Taevy remained hopeful with only a hint of niggling doubt. Later when the nurse came to check on her fluids, she inquired. After she repeated her crab explanation, the nurse gave her a similar confused look. A lengthy, unbelievable explanation followed.

The foot is gone, and it will never return. Not in a month. Not in a year. Not ever.

Instantly, more of her innocence and hope was erased. A completely blank future stared back at her. Again, she found herself crying out to God, if there was a God.

//

Dale and Cathleen felt as if it was almost ritualistic to bring children to the hospital. Worms, dengue, typhoid, and a slew of jungle diseases, waterborne illnesses, and general childhood viruses kept their tab at the hospital long.

On their recent visit, a head UN doctor told them about an abandoned girl found with a terrible leg wound. She had no family to speak of. He felt they were a potential solution to her plight.

The next morning, the doctor took them to meet her. While the Joneses had seen so many children in shocking health conditions, this girl had an even more forlorn look about her. Not only starved in body, her spirit seemed to be screaming for human connection.

Cathleen sat gently at the edge of Taevy's cot and leaned toward her without intruding on her personal space.

"We hear you've had a difficult time and you have no family to care for you. We want to help. May we ask a few questions?"

Her Khmer language skills were decent, although a strong foreign accent prevailed. Her husband, on the other hand, spoke Khmer flawlessly. If she closed her eyes, Taevy was sure she was not speaking to a gigantic, blue-eyed man. Despite his size, however, Dale was so kind she felt safe in his presence. She wanted badly to answer their questions, but her life had no timeline, and she really had no idea where she was from.

After that, each afternoon, people from the orphanage would visit. So many years of no one caring about her, and now there were kids, adults, and foreigners alike, all coming just for her. They brought hand-picked bouquets, hand-drawn cards, and food. They asked her questions and shared about life in the orphanage.

//

One day, an orphanage girl who had a prosthetic leg came. Taevy and Sophea were close in age, and the girl shared her journey of losing her leg to a festering snake bite. While she enjoyed the company of everyone, Sophea was her favorite. Well, next to Dale, whose fatherly, calm presence brought her a peace she'd never felt before.

After a month, the hospital released Taevy into the care of the orphanage. The French doctor had assessed every corner of the orphanage to be sure he was comfortable giving her into the Joneses' care.

The orphanage was not the best option for many of the children, but for Taevy it was heaven on earth. "I was profoundly grateful to be there. I had no one, and life had been so hard," she said. "I had to break the habit of waking up in a panic, however. For a split second, I thought I had slept through the hard labor. Each time it was a relief to realize that wasn't my life anymore."

For the first time, she could attend school as well as learn trades. Hungry for knowledge, new worlds unfolded for her in the books and school lectures. She drank in information. The kids would tease her because she became close with their staff tutor, who helped them study at the orphanage. While some of the children found excuses to miss school, Taevy wanted to learn day and night.

Her absolute favorite subject was Bible and prayer. Starved for love, she learned about God. A God who heard her prayers, saw her, loved her, and created her with a purpose. She, a simple, skinny, half-Vietnamese child who had been abandoned and was missing a leg, was known and pursued by the God of the Universe!

One day, as the beauty of the Gospel washed over her heart, she saw God in her past. In the food brought by neighbors. Even in the way he pulled her out of being trafficked to Thailand. Not knowing God at the time, she had prayed to him, and he had answered.

"I lost my leg in that accident, but I gained my life," Taevy said.

She also found forgiveness for her family. It did not come immediately, but as time went on and she grew to know this God in the Bible, she found she harbored no resentment against those who had wronged her.

Having not been institutionalized until her teenage years, she saw each opportunity as a gift, sought out information, and asked questions. Accustomed to neglect, she did not require constant entertainment. So, the adults naturally liked her. She was more at ease in their midst than many of the children, whose maturity and development lagged from lack of family.

The favor she garnered from the adults did not go unnoticed by her peers. Most of the conflict with other girls was over her relationships with the teachers.

The institution created deep-seated issues in the children. Not only was healthy attachment impossible, but the children were spoiled. They expected material possessions without learning the value of caring for their things or earning them. Several of the children looked upon their privileges as if they were owed it.

Sophea, her best friend, would come over to finish her homework, slouching on a nearby bench. The silence was comfortable. Taevy had never had a friend before. It was nice to have someone who understood so much. An incredibly humble and gentle soul, Sophea made a wonderful best friend. As Taevy read the words in her Bible next to Sophea, she prayed a silent prayer of thanksgiving, "Thank you, God, for your love. Thank you that I am safe, and I have Sophea, teachers, and so many people who care for me. Thank you that I can play, grow, and learn."

"Taevy," Cathleen said, "was the kind of kid we wanted and needed to help. While I do not agree with the orphanage model anymore, it was the best place for her at that time. She was not safe in her family and she thrived in the orphanage. But I do wonder how much better she could have done in a good family?"

//

The orphans were exposed to life outside the high walls when they went to stay with local Christian families over holidays. As extended families gathered, they played games and shared stories late into the night. The kids slept together on mats under mosquito nets. The families had little to give, yet whatever they did have, they shared with the orphans. Taevy bonded with her holiday family and is still in a relationship with them more than twenty years later.

However, as she grew older, she realized the orphanage model was insufficient. She said, "I feel it [the orphanage] was too big. I was not cared for on the same level I would have been in a family. If one of the dorm moms got close with you, the other girls would be super jealous. So, then you were put out from being close to the other kids."

Not only were they lost in a sea of faces, but their primary caregivers changed frequently. Dorm parents got married, had their own children, and left. Or they found other jobs. The kids called Dale and Cathleen "Dad and Mom," despite the Joneses not insisting on it and not living on the premises. They, too, would leave after about four years, and a new couple would take their place.

When the new directors arrived, they changed the procedures and schedule. With their own methods and ideas, the staff and kids had two new personalities to adapt to.

Taevy was about to age out when they came. She described the orphans when they learned the Joneses were leaving.

"I had so many tears. It was terrible. Well, at first it was terrible, but, eventually, we all adjusted. A bond was broken, however, and a new system and way of doing things started."

In that moment, however, all she could think about was that she was abandoned. Again.

Former children at the orphanage reflected in adulthood that the biggest difference between the directors was that the Joneses tried to love each of the kids equally. They would listen to both sides of a story before making decisions.

The older kids would say Cathleen was strict but that she loved them equally. And they did not favor the staff over the kids or not believe the kids. They said, "Mom's [Cathleen] so strict" but when she left, they complained that the new director was much worse.

One particular orphan found the transition as a chance to come out ahead of the others. She was opportunistic and manipulative; the girl flashed a pretty smile and ran to the new couple, engulfing them in hugs. She kissed their faces, sweetly calling them Mommy and Daddy from the start. The other children held back, reluctant to give their hearts away, while she battled for position.

Taevy said, "It gave her power over others and caused jealousy. The new orphanage parents gave her authority, clearly preferring her. She began to tell them lies and get those she did not like kicked out."

The girl made herself unpleasant to the others. Yet in hindsight, this was the atmosphere created by institutionalizing children. Without consistent caretakers, the system groomed children to become conniving to get ahead.

The Problem of Low Standards of Care

It is common for institutionalized children to find their way back to orphanages as adults. Those high gates and the constant ring of tiny voices echoing the halls are comforting. Rarely are they properly prepared to face life outside of an institution. With no family to teach them practical life skills, such as how to run a household or interact within a community, they return to the known.

Soon after aging out of the orphanage, Taevy found herself working in one in Phnom Penh. It's there she met her husband, Nak, who ran a computer shop across the street.

Four years into their marriage, the extremely poor Taevy and Nak were approached by James, a foreign worker and Nak's mentor, to run the orphanage he had started in Phnom Penh. Dale and Cathleen had returned at this time, working in another capacity across the city, yet they maintained a relationship with Nak and Taevy.

Feeling a pull toward helping the children and loyalty to James, Nak worked tirelessly for a very meager wage. He and Taevy chose to live off the premises, but from sunup to sundown Nak was there as director, carrying most of the responsibility. The orphanage was much smaller and more basic than the Joneses' orphanage where Taevy had grown up. James did not want to spend money on anything, so Nak opened his thin wallet to cover additional expenses for the children.

James failed to keep up with the laws and underpaid his

staff. Soon after they established the orphanage, James and his family returned to his home country, only returning once a year to check in. He still held all the purse strings and made ridiculous demands of the caregivers, but was rarely there.

In the meantime, the couple had a daughter. Tragically, a live-wire electrocuted Taevy when she was pregnant with their second child. It killed the baby, and she never conceived again. She busied herself working and mourning her loss. Then one day an abandoned baby boy was brought to the orphanage. James had decided not to accept any more babies, but once Taevy picked up the tiny boy, she fell immediately in love. Baby Noah became their son.

James initially offered to provide for Noah's care, though he quickly reneged on his word. Nak and Taevy never regretted their decision, and they loved their son deeply. However, more work and expenses were added to their already stretched lives.

As Noah grew, kids teased him for being adopted. Taevy looked him firmly in his big, beautiful eyes and told him, "You may not be from my womb, but you are from my heart. You are mine."

//

Over the thirteen years that they served there, Nak remained faithful to James and the children, despite so many reservations about his work. For one, all the children had families. Their care was minimal since James rarely gave money for anything beyond basic survival. Staff did not stay long, leaving the children without consistent bonds.

It reached a point that local Khmer would support the orphanage to give the children fun parties at holiday times and extra food. The very community handing their children over to institutions for care, convinced they would have better lives raised by foreigners, was stepping up to care for the children because the founder lapsed in his responsibility.

After a while, Nak began to research the lives of the children more deeply and set up his own gatekeeping policies, only taking in those who had no other options. This cut down on the intake. Nak had keen instincts and was good at finding the underlying cause of many false stories, enabling him to place children back in their communities.

Being very intuitive, Nak also decided to teach the children local skills. He trained them in motorbike maintenance and housecleaning, and he found apprenticeships for the older children. That way they would have skills when they left the orphanage.

Cathleen described Nak: "He was not your typical director and has a compassionate heart. He genuinely did his job because he wanted these children to have a better future. When he took over, he thought, 'They need to know how to do daily things in the home as if they had a family.' He was a natural teacher who wanted them to learn how to sell things and run a small business because that's the Khmer life."

James, however, was furious when he found out about the vocational training. Feeling the work was beneath "his orphanage," he tried to discourage Nak. American success was university, good salaries. James didn't care whether the children wanted further study or how they would adapt to life outside his tiny kingdom.

The salary was so low, it forced Nak to hire people too young to legally work at an orphanage. No one else wanted the responsibility and terrible wages. It imploded when a young woman working for them threw herself at Nak, flirting and making advances. Dale pulled Nak aside and told him to fire the underage staff before anything bad could happen. Dale and Cathleen also reminded him that the law forbade people that young to be caretakers.

After a while, Nak became discontent. James grilled him over buying higher quality clothes for the children, despite the assurances it lasted longer. Every little detail was scrutinized from a distance.

Nak was so frustrated as the kids grew older and showed signs of institutionalization. He did not realize at the time that it was related to their upbringing. The kids were unable to break out of the institutional mindset, always wanting a handout.

Taevy and Nak poured hundreds of their own dollars into the kids who aged out, helping them get motorbikes or work, only to have the motorbikes crashed or stolen and the young adults not show up for their jobs. The children quit halfway through their studies. Nak realized the children were not launching well into life. James never stepped in. Some of their kids eventually figured life out after failing a lot, but most ended up in cycles of addiction, poor choices, and broken relationships.

Finally, James gave up the pretenses of care. He notified Nak that they would not take in any more kids. It seemed like a good transition, so Nak took the opportunity to look for other jobs. He knew he needed a new career once it ended.

Another blow came when James found out about his job search and fired Nak on the spot. James felt it was a betrayal, even knowing the end was near. Nak and Taevy were not even allowed to say goodbye to the remaining children.

Cast out after years of loyalty and pouring their lives and finances into James' children's home was incredibly traumatic.

Then, James immediately closed the orphanage. The kids who were old enough were set out on their own with no preparation. The teenagers were placed with a former disgruntled staff member who abused them, and the younger children were cared for by his single twenty-one-year-old son in a remote corner of Cambodia, which was illegal for a number of reasons.

The older children all ran away and tracked down Nak for help, furthering the sudden rift in the relationship with his mentor. One of the teenagers was a disabled girl, incredibly vulnerable to abuse and exploitation.

Taevy and Nak have both moved on to completely different careers. The Joneses remain their family. Loving Dale and Cathleen so much, she and Nak purchased the lot next door to the Joneses and built their home with a gap in the fence. Rarely a day passes when they do not see one another. They also still visit Nak's "orphans" from time to time.

Sadly, James's lack of care toward the children is more of the standard than the exception. He poured little of his own time and resources into their lives, giving out the absolute basics for their physical survival while completely neglecting their emotional and spiritual well-being. And, when his bottom line was threatened, he put out his staff and the children overnight. Nak, the local staff, alone is the only reason any of these children stood a chance against the world they were brutally kicked into.

The Problem of Sexual Abuse

Cathleen's world came to a grinding halt as Josh, her son, innocently poured out details of abuse that he had been subjected to for the past few years. Her vision tunneled, and she looked into those big eyes. Her boy, her baby boy had been sexually abused in the very place that was built to help children!

Her mind reeled. How had she missed the signs? How could they have had a predator in their midst this whole time? For her son's disclosure included other victims at the orphanage.

All the boys, including her son, had trusted her and Dale for protection. How could they have failed these kids? These boys lived full-time with a person hired and trained to nurture them, yet he became an abuser.

Her son's disclosure rocked her world and her faith. His innocence had been stolen from him at a mere eight years of age. She grasped for a chair to sit in, pulled him close to her, and stroked his hair.

Reassuring him, she whispered into his ear, "You did the right thing to tell me. This is not your fault. This is not your fault."

He clung to her as she tried not to reveal her inner storm. Her mind ran through every interaction, every scenario. Like a yo-yo, her emotions bounced from rage to deep sorrow and right back again. Were they neglectful parents for doing so much work and letting their children run and play with the children at the orphanage? What about the other victims? Again she asked herself, "How did we miss it? We were there. All of this happened under our nose."

Fortunately, they were scheduled for a furlough soon and they needed it desperately. The years of relentless work were taking their toll.

The man in question had been moved to another branch of their organization a few months earlier because he had enraged too many coworkers. Although he was charming and intelligent, he had a way of infuriating those around him with his superior attitude. After he left, Josh realized that the man would not return, and he felt safe enough to reveal the abuse.

After Dale and Cathleen related the abuse to their mission, the organization hurried them out of the country to get Joshua help. As they reflected on the incident, they saw more clearly the inequality of justice between their children and those in the orphanage. No thought or attention was ever given to the Khmer victims of molestation.

From the beginning of their time in Cambodia, Dale and Cathleen realized that the kids in the orphanage needed emotional healing. So, when they begged for counseling for the children displaying signs of previous abuse, the response was always, "Love these kids. They just need love and Jesus, and they will be healed."

Cathleen's frustration threatened to burst. "Love these kids! We can hardly clothe and feed all of them, much less give each one of them the personal attention they deserve."

Previous abuse and neglect were constantly surfacing in the children. Symptoms of attachment disorders were also bubbling up. One cannot adequately love hundreds of children. What they could give was not enough to bring healing from the trauma of a war-torn nation and poverty, let alone abandonment. Or worse.

"Waiting outside Josh's counselor's office in America," Cathleen reflected, "I wondered why my son mattered, and the children in the orphanage did not. Who would right the wrongs done to them? Who would comfort them and teach them that the abuse they had experienced was not their fault? Who would reassure them that abuse was unacceptable?"

It seemed to Dale and Cathleen that their organization looked at the Khmer children as expendable, and it wasn't just their own NGO that treated the children this way. Kids were mere props that brought in millions of dollars of funding through harrowing stories of poverty and loss. Instead of being cared for as human beings, they were used as tools. These tiny people were an expedient salve to the souls of people who wanted to feel good about giving but who did not want to invest sacrificially in long-term ways, in the lives on the other end of their money. The charitable organizations filled beds and congratulated one another on a job well done while keeping the children at arm's length.

Cathleen said, "To my knowledge, not one of those boys in the orphanage ever received any kind of counseling or care for their molestation. Later, I was told that most of these abused children were kicked out of the orphanage because they were exhibiting inappropriate behavior. They were acting out their trauma through child-on-child sexual abuse, which is typical behavior for abused children."

Instead of receiving tender, loving care, they were pushed into a broader community to fend for themselves. They were punished for being victims. Some, in turn, would become perpetrators within their community.

Looking me dead in the face through tears, Cathleen said, "You tell me if my mission agency cared one bit for those children. If they did, my son would not have been the only child to get help."

The Joneses spent a year in America, sharing at churches, visiting family and friends, and healing. The kids in the orphanage got a new set of temporary caregivers. The abuse, and their pain and confusion, were never spoken of again.

"It was hugely devastating on so many levels," Cathleen reflected. "We felt let down by God, our mission, and ourselves for not seeing it."

However, rising inside Cathleen was a deep sense that something was wrong with the system and that she needed to do something about it. Four years of watching children suffer and families be separated had impacted her profoundly. The revelation of abuse was the spark that caught hold and ignited all her misgivings into a flame.

She and Dale had seen firsthand that packing traumatized children into buildings to be cared for by paid staff does not work. It is haphazard and negligent of the basic, fundamental needs of humans. Children might have daily food and access to an education, but people need so much more; we need to be known, loved, and cared for.

//

The abuser was one of the many staff members inherited from the previous couple who oversaw the orphanage, so it was assumed that he was trustworthy. At that time, child molestation was not a topic for discussion, and no one did background checks or thought about child protection. Even if their organization had seen the need for background checks, proper documentation would have been unavailable.

Cathleen said, "Early on, as we trained staff, we did take a common-sense approach. Unmarried men and women were not allowed to be alone, and male staff could not be alone with girls. I had noticed that the older teen girls developed a quick affection for Dale because he was a kind father figure, but some tried to get his attention by engaging in sensual behavior. Therefore, Dale was cautious in his interactions with the girls, still kind and loving but never rewarding inappropriate behavior."

At first, there was little question about Vin and his behavior. When they arrived, he was eager to please. He had been significantly better educated than most of the Khmer staff members, helping immensely with translation work.

In hindsight, they realized that he spent an unusual amount of time with the teenage boys; however, his job was as a house parent, so they naturally assumed that he was like a big brother to them. Quick to learn new skills, he was gradually moved into the role of assistant director, as his English and managerial skills were unrivaled. He lived in a private room on the grounds after moving from his houseparent role because suitable off-site housing was difficult to find.

Dale and Cathleen allowed their kids to play with the children in the orphanage once their morning homeschooling was finished. Their son and daughter found it difficult to relate to children their own age, so they naturally gravitated to the older ones.

"Our family was isolated because of our skin color and culture, and we did not realize that our son was so vulnerable. Vin showed him favoritism, and we were busy. Too busy."

Eventually, the staff almost mutinied because Vin's superiority complex became unbearable to most of them, so he was transferred out.

Soon after Vin was reassigned to work in Phnom Penh, Josh told his parents about the abuse. The Joneses told their organizational leaders in the city, who called Vin into a meeting to address the molestations. He confessed to abusing Josh, and he admitted to doing even more.

After deliberation, the organization's leadership forced him to sign a "gag order," a document swearing that he would never work with them again. He had to sign off that he would never take work involving children.

Nothing was stopping him from victimizing more children because Cambodia, at the time, was focusing on survival and there were no laws or procedures to take action against predators. Instead, he merely moved to another part of Cambodia and offered his language services to other organizations, which had no idea of the risk they were taking.

At that time, there was no justice or recourse. If they chose to prosecute Vin, they would be the wealthy foreigners picking on the poor Khmer guy, and their organization had no precedent to deal with that.

A few weeks later, the family was packed up and on their way to America.

"It took Josh a while to grasp that what he went through was abuse. It's haunted me that the Khmer kids never got the counseling they needed. I wish we had been given a chance to transition out better. I wish we had been able to help the others. Over the years, we had to do some follow-up for him. However, he now is able to share his story in the hope that it might help someone else. The injustice of the treatment of the local kids compared to our own is the worst part of what we all went through."

Sadly, this was not to be the only incident of sexual abuse to occur in the orphanage.

Report[3] after report from the last fifty years indicates that the rate of sexual abuse in institutional care is significantly higher than for children who grow up in a family structure. While all children have a certain level of vulnerability, those in residential care tend to be desperate for love and attention from adults, making them easy prey.

There also tends to be a revolving door of caretakers, causing attachment disorders and giving abusers much easier access to children. The rate of child-on-child sexual abuse is incredibly high with so many traumatized and abused children packed into one location. With children also being unrelated and much of their actions going unmonitored, abuse can go unnoticed and unseen for a long time. As in the Joneses' orphanage, these children do not receive the help they need after being abused, so many of them (knowingly or unknowingly) act out their abuse on others, thus perpetuating the cycle.

Cathleen finished, "We [all of us who worked at the orphanage and our mission agency] did not treat these kids like our own. Dale and I really struggled with this."

The Return to Cambodia

During their furlough, Dale and Cathleen spoke at church services and missions conferences, about 130 total. At one conference, a man took the stage and promoted a child sponsorship program. He shared about the children in his program with an air of intimate knowledge. Cathleen's ears perked up as he mentioned Cambodia. Suddenly, she realized he was telling stories from the lives of their orphanage children.

Afterward, she entered the lobby and approached one of the display tables. As she inched closer, listening to the conversations, she saw that the table was scattered with photos of the children from their orphanage. Pictures and biographical data stared at her. They had taken those photos to put in the children's folders, along with a copy that went to the home office in Phnom Penh. The information they had gathered for documentation of the children's histories now stood on display in America.

"Look at this one; he's so skinny," a woman tutted, sifting through the pictures of kids. "Oh, now, isn't she adorable? What kind of mother would leave a child who looked like her?"

One of their girls, her front teeth missing, stared back from the photo paper, hair in plaits. Cathleen smiled at the thought of her and her silly laugh.

Others scooted in closer.

"Poor orphans."

"Is he cross-eyed? I hope they can fix that in Cambodia."

"Look at this little peanut. I would sponsor a child like

this. Who could say 'no' to those eyes? If I went over there, I'd snatch them all up."

On and on, people sorted through the photos of their kids, commenting and picking apart their looks. Cathleen felt like they were judging the children's worth.

Indignation rose within her. She and Dale had no idea that their kids were being marketed like this. How dare people treat them like items of pity to sift through! They had lives, thoughts, and dreams. They were people with dignity, not objects.

Cathleen felt sick standing there as she realized that she, too, had been guilty of these thoughts and behaviors. How disconnected they were from the truth of the whole situation. She did not begrudge sponsors. Their gifts helped the school programs and funded the orphanages. The way the children were being marketed, however, felt terribly wrong.

As she heard one more lament about "poor orphans," she almost burst out, "They're not orphans! None of them are orphans! Their parents live down the road."

She no longer saw in the photos what everyone else around her saw: unsmiling children in their school uniforms. She knew their names, she cleaned their scraped knees, sat near their hospital beds as IVs refilled their fluids, and held the half-starved infants, waking them hourly to feed them.

As the crowds waned, she spoke directly to the man who had given the presentation. He appeared genuinely interested and appreciated hearing her input. She understood how necessary raising funds was; however, the way people spoke about the children made her realize that the model was inappropriate. These children were much more than a stack of photos to elicit emotions and open wallets. And, so many times before, she had failed them. They deserved better than this. The whole model of care, including how they shared about the children, was deeply flawed. As she mulled over this, she knew she needed to explore other types of care for vulnerable children and learn more.

//

In 1997, after a year of home leave, the Jones family returned to Cambodia humbled. They had changed markedly in the five years since their arrival in the bombed-out city of Phnom Penh. Cambodia was changing too. The scenery looked about the same, but UN troops no longer patrolled the country. Hun Sen was now the head of the government, and the remaining Khmer Rouge and rebels were hiding out in pockets near the Vietnam border's forest and hills.

While they were on furlough, Dale and Cathleen had asked to be reinstated at the orphanage, but were told they were reassigned to use Dale's language and administrative gifts. Other workers were taking care of their orphanage, and they were not allowed to have contact with local churches they had planted. They were required to ask permission to connect with the orphanage. They felt saddened and bewildered that they could not return to the kids whom they cared for for so many years. Instead, their family was to stay in Phnom Penh where Dale would work at the main headquarters.

Cathleen had spent time during their furlough thinking up better ways of caring for the children and creating more of a home-like atmosphere for them. She had done research, including small group-home models, and wanted to set up the orphanage in small group homes with different-aged children like in a typical family. The houseparents would teach them how to do chores, and they could eat together. She was disappointed not to be able to implement this new model.

Once again, Dale and Cathleen faced the reality that these kids would go through three sets of directors in only a few years. It was not just about bonding with the caretakers; each couple ran the place in completely different ways. The children would get used to one routine, only to have it changed, creating more stress for the already traumatized children.

Later, when they met the man who had replaced them at the orphanage, they realized the real reason for their replacement. Ray had a big personality and could raise lots of money. He could get things done, but he did not seem interested in children's histories or the programs that had been put into place before he came. He had his own way.

After obtaining permission, the Joneses were finally able to visit the orphanage. They could barely contain their excitement. When they arrived, shouts and screams erupted. The children stampeded Dale, Cathleen, and their kids, shouting, hugging, and vying for position. Ray stood by snapping photos.

However, on their second visit, none of the children or staff spoke with them. It was strange as everyone kept their distance and eyes were averted until Ray left the premises. As soon as his motorbike was out of sight, the Joneses were crushed by joyful children.

A few weeks after that visit, Cathleen ran into a trusted house mother who was in Phnom Penh for a medical visit. Cathleen asked her about the puzzling behavior. The woman looked at her. "Our loyalty is to Ray. We cannot show that we like you, or he will be angry."

Dale responded, "We would never expect you to choose between us. So, why do you feel that way?"

It turned out that Ray had threatened to fire them if they spoke with the Joneses. Later, some of the older children, who attended university in Phnom Penh, told them that Ray had lined all of the children up and said, "You have only one Poppa. I am your Poppa. You can leave if you think you have any other Poppa than me."

So, the children were terrified. They knew they would be kicked out if they showed love to Dale and Cathleen.

//

While Dale was busy in his new administrative and leadership roles at the head office, Cathleen took on a kids' club in their neighborhood. Their new home was in the north part of Phnom Penh near a notorious red-light district. Hundreds of children throughout the community gathered in front of their house for the club and tutoring time. It included teaching, games, snacks, songs, and dances, and it would not have been complete without a puppet show in Khmer.

Most '80s and '90s ministries involved puppet shows. The children thoroughly loved them. Cathleen got a kick out of watching hundreds of kids hooting and laughing over these characters made of felt.

Dale and Cathleen missed the orphanage kids, but they realized they did not miss the massive amount of work it took to keep it running. Working with kids who were in their community and in their families was like a breath of fresh air. They found a new routine in the city, but kept wondering where they could serve best. Over the past six years they had been shoved into jobs with unreasonable hours and been asked to fill countless holes in different ministries.

People popped in on their work, took photos, and sent out shining newsletters but never engaged with the children or acknowledged Dale and Cathleen's hard work. No one asked how they were doing, and eventually, their bodies, mental health, and marriage began to break down. They loved Cambodia, but they knew their ministry needed to change.

After four years of working at the orphanage and less than four years of working in Phnom Penh, Dale and Cathleen reached a burnout stage. The trauma from the orphanage years, the abuse of their son and other children, and being overworked and undercared-for all compounded into personal and marital issues.

They returned to America on the brink of divorce and were

in danger of becoming bitter. Unfortunately, this is a common story among people serving in orphanages. The husband of another couple who ran an orphanage entered a hospital after having a complete emotional and mental breakdown. Decades later, he shared his story with me. He had healed and returned to a neighboring Southeast Asian country more humble and robust, but it took years of pain and working through severe issues.

In a hurry, the Joneses exited the country and ministry for a second time, not knowing if they would ever return. Their time in the States was focused on healing and counseling. It became a season for them to reflect, truly and deeply, on the previous years of ministry.

Their reflection became holistic. Slowly, all the pieces of the orphanage puzzle began to fall into place: desperate parents who need support, children with trauma and attachment disorders, extreme poverty, unhealthy leadership, and money taking priority over people. There had to be a better way to support the families and children of Cambodia.

When they ran the orphanage, Cathleen and Dale tried to visit a well-established orphanage in a neighboring country with their denomination to learn more. To be more equipped. But their leadership denied the trip. Then, they attempted to create a group with the other orphanage directors to collaborate. It became more judgmental and competitive than helpful. The other leaders lacked interest in changing or finding better solutions for care. Finally, Cathleen sought literature and research on how to run a good orphanage. But without mail or the Internet, there was little for her to access. Internally, she knew this model of care was not right and that there must be a better way, but it felt like doors kept closing.

Now back in America, doors began to open.

As Cathleen shared more of her story, she said, "Sometimes people who come to help are lazy; they don't want to work with communities and adults. Kids are easy to control. You can make decisions for them, but they are too little to have a voice. My repentance has been mainly over making huge life decisions for the children in our orphanage so quickly and flippantly without considering the big picture or the long-term effects."

A lump caught in her throat as the fire in her eyes was quenched with tears of remembrance. The years of humbling and sleepless nights washed over her. She had taken their lives into her hands.

An immediate benefit for one may cause irreparable harm to many others in the wake of that decision. "You must look at the many the same way you look, feel, and act for the one. You cannot jump over legalities to save the one because it ends up excluding others who also need help.

"Do we think God is so weak and powerless he cannot reach families and communities? If I look at a poor woman placing her child in an orphanage, I need to look beyond the pitiful child. The woman deserves our love and attention. Her community and nation deserve as much as that child. The decisions we make in programs need to be at the root level and should impact the greatest number for the greatest good possible."

Despite the many people claiming to have a calling and heart for children, Cathleen saw limited expressions of it. Family-based care did not exist in Cambodia. Yet.

THE CHILDREN IN FAMILIES YEARS

Introduction to CIF Years

When we take a look back at history, we see that the establishment of institutions often entailed people in power (whether government or religious) to single out classes of people or particular races, deeming them unworthy of raising their own children. Whether it be the single Irish mother, poor mothers in the UK, or the aboriginal children of Australia ripped from their culture and family, the intentional fracturing of families is not a new issue. It has been castigated and publicly apologized for again and again, yet it continues.

In any given economy, the poor receive the harshest judgment. Their ability to care for and love their children is questioned significantly more than those with material wealth.

In my journey of learning about family-based care, I have had to sift through my preconceived ideas about what caring for people truly entails. For example, I had to ask why institutions began to transition to foster care in the early 1900s and ended in America and Western Europe around the 1960s, yet even today, we send people to developing nations to establish and run orphanages. If institutional care is not good for children in the cultures that send us, why would we assume it's good for children in other cultures?

And I had to examine my prejudices about the culture in which I serve. When the heat and the noise of Phnom Penh became too much for me, I complained about Cambodia, finding very little to endear it to me. I began resenting Cambodians, lumping everyone in with the few who had lied and ripped me off. Finally, a friend of mine, Pheap, sat me down and gently reprimanded me.

She shared about a family in the private school where she worked. A single Khmer woman, older and widowed, took in a baby thrust upon her in desperation. The father violently abused the mother, who feared for her boy's life. So, she dropped him on this older woman's doorstep and went into hiding. With little more than a piece of tin to pull across the opening in her shack, this stooped auntie rose before the sun each morning, pushing a bulky metal cart and selling cooked eggs along the roads.

Every day of her life, for fifteen years, she rose and sold eggs to care for this boy. They did not share DNA, yet she loved him deeply. Her purpose became focused on more than her own personal survival. The boy joined her in the evenings, selling eggs.

It was a joyful day at fifteen when he received a scholarship from the school, no longer relying on Auntie for all his needs. Tears slid down her wrinkled face as she looked pridefully at her beaming boy. This woman could have had a nicer home, taken a day off, or eaten more food. Yet her labor spoke of immeasurable love for an abandoned baby.

As Pheap finished her story, I reluctantly admitted my wrong attitude toward Cambodia. What if, in our drive to fill orphanages, we're robbing people of homes filled with love and opportunities to use their God-given abilities to care for children without parents? I cannot believe for a second that boy would have been better off in an institution. Nor would his auntie.

International data estimates that family-based care is eighty-five percent cheaper than funding orphanages. Just fifteen percent of the money needed to raise a child in an institution is enough to support a child growing up in a healthy family. In 2015, fifty million dollars poured into institutions in Cambodia.[4]

Rebecca Neap, Australian Christian Churches International (ACCI) Kinnected Program founder, researched and analyzed the numbers for money flowing into orphanages in Cambodia. She then assessed what we could do nationwide for that amount. It was astonishing. With that amount of money flowing into Cambodia to care for vulnerable children, there should be little excuse for poverty to still exist, let alone poverty at the level of families losing their children. Millions of dollars are poured annually into orphanages in Cambodia alone. Yet that same amount of money could provide better education, nutrition, clean water, and other opportunities, to all the communities in need throughout Cambodia.

There is absolutely no reason for a healthy child in Cambodia not to be in a family. The amount of vetted, good families waiting for children, especially babies and toddlers, is much longer than children without safe families. CIF has a waiting list of Cambodian couples who want to adopt or foster.

"To this day, over a decade later, the same orphanage we ran in the 1990s has healthy young children. We could place every single one of those into a family tomorrow. Yet we still find them in orphanages, and orphanages are still claiming to be their only hope," Cathleen told me.

Rebecca, who was involved with CIF in the early years, also observed, "Donors of orphanages might see happy children, but when those children are ready to leave care, they are ill-prepared to go out into life."

She asks rhetorically, "Who is driving this?"

Many residential homes exist because they are fundable. There are people who *want* to fund orphanages. Orphanages then become attractive projects for people looking to raise funds.

The other hurdle, possibly the most significant, was also educating well-intentioned but shortsighted people who fueled the orphanage industry.

Rebecca breaks down the issues through several lenses. First, the theology behind orphanages is flawed. What does the Bible say? Both New and Old Testaments talk about supporting vulnerable family units. "Religion that is pure and undefiled before God the Father is this: to visit orphans and widows in their affliction, and to keep oneself unstained from the world." (James 1:27 ESV). The orphan and the widow are a family in and of themselves, not separate charity projects.

Orphanages also involve discrimination and bias as children are often placed on an economic basis. Poverty is a driving force. But is it right to remove a child due to poverty?

"There are different classifications of poverty," Rebecca shared. "We can discriminate against the poor by removing their children because we are not considering the same value systems for others. There is also cultural discrimination, looking at how different people live and how families are structured based on cultural dynamics. Finally, there are concerns about the child's spirituality in the Christian orphanages. The driving force is 'better discipled in an orphanage than a community,' which is wrong and not a long-term way to think about discipleship."

CIF has seen entire communities shift their view on Christianity because we include everyone. Rather than removing children from their families and cultures to mold their pliable minds in an institutional setting, we care for the whole family structure.

The children's home strategy creates significant trauma for the children in them. Yet orphanage directors and volunteers failed to question the impact these separations have on those in their care.

Once as Cathleen Jones and I discussed this issue, she told me, "God's heart is for the world; it includes all the people of the world. If God loves all the children of Cambodia, then our actions need to be loving toward all the children of Cambodia. It has to be a solution that is best for everyone, not only those in your specific program. Many 'rescuers' can only see what is right before them. Loving children requires you to get beyond yourself and your agenda."

This is not a new phenomenon. The orphanage issue today does not stand alone. It originates from a greater context of how people feel about other races, poverty, and socio-economic classes. It comes from a mindset in which children are things to manipulate and control. They do not have a voice in their futures.

There is good news, however. Solutions in the form of family preservation and family-based care exist across the globe and are gaining ground. This is why I am so passionate about sharing the story of CIF. It is one of many organizations in the world working to shift how we care for vulnerable and orphaned children.

I believe "God sets the lonely in families." And CIF was founded to do just that while honoring Cambodian communities and culture.

The Heartbeat of Children in Families

"By setting up programs only for children, we are not respecting birth families. Instead, we should look into how we can support them as well. Communities and parents matter as much as children. This problem required me to shift my mindset and heart."
–Cathleen Jones.

Returning to Cambodia for the third time with a new organization, Cathleen looked over at her sleeping toddler curled next to her. She and Dale had fostered and adopted their third child while back in the States. All that Cathleen learned over the years at the orphanage had culminated in becoming foster parents during their time of healing. She knew the ins and outs of American foster care, the brokenness of the systems as well as the really positive aspects. The issues were with the system but not with family-based care.

She and Dale had discussed at length what it would look like to keep Cambodian families together. And when there were not safe biological options for children, finding loving alternative families. This time, it would not merely be theory. The Joneses cared deeply for strengthening the communities around them, and Cathleen was determined to use the difficult lessons she learned to shift the narrative. She brushed the soft blond curls out of her toddler's face, then turned back to her notepad where she was brainstorming all they needed to start.

The early church was known for taking in orphans and abandoned children. Not on a large scale, but individuals would take children into their families. The church provided for widows so that they could care for their children. This model became a guiding force for Cathleen in decision-making. It propelled her to stem the flow of children into orphanages across Cambodia; it caused her to research family preservation.

Across the country, kids were flowing out of their homes and into institutions at such a high rate she knew she had to start somewhere. First, she needed to identify just one way to keep children in their homes. Cathleen referred to this process as "throwing up a dam." She knew she wouldn't start out with a perfect system. Then, as things developed in the laws and communities, she could work up the river and put more dams in place like more preventative steps.

She jotted down, "God gave these families their kids. Our role at Children in Families (CIF) is to help Cambodian parents fulfill their God-given responsibility to their kids. Not to take their kids away."

//

When Cathleen had attended a gathering for people establishing family-based care programs globally, she met Ruslan Maliuta, the founder of Ukraine Without Orphans, she asked, "What is your biggest challenge in getting children out of orphanages?"

He answered, "The Western churches are coming over and building orphanages and putting kids into them."

Before family-based care existed in Ukraine, he believed that children in institutions needed to be in a family. He challenged the Ukrainian church to care for children who had no family or whose families were not safe. Working hard, he made the local church aware of the plight of children growing up in institutions. After just two years, domestic adoption jumped by 30 percent. This pattern caught on in Belarus, Russia, and surrounding nations. His organization grew into World Without Orphans.

Cathleen's research later led her to data from Korea. After the Korean conflict that divided the nation, mothers abandoned children at an alarming rate. This trend continued so much that orphanages became packed. Then they sent the kids off to America for foreign adoption. Yet Korea found that when they began to support the mothers rather than only focusing on rescuing children, the rate of abandoned babies dropped significantly. Once there was care and structure in place, women could keep their children.

Cambodians needed to heed the call to care for vulnerable and orphaned children, and Cambodian families needed to be supported holistically. This is where her organization would start. But it also needed the support of local laws and government officials who believed in the cause.

"The outside perception said, 'Cambodians won't take care of children who are not their flesh and blood.' However, I saw a very different narrative living in refugee housing in Minnesota. Widows took in and cared for orphans."

Many Khmer refugee families claimed children who were orphaned or separated from their parents in fleeing Cambodia. These caring adults took them in, even falsifying documents to enter America as a family.

Taking what she had learned from this experience, she sought to understand why Khmer families hesitated to foster children. The answer was almost unanimous: "We do not want the child taken away from us."

Their hesitation to foster children was not a lack of care; they were guarding their hearts against possible separation. Many foster families eventually took in a second or third child because the DNA of Khmer culture involves siblings. Parents felt bad about raising a single child. Or they had concerns about the age gap between their biological children and the foster child.

This cultural DNA is why orphanages are so countercultural in Southeast Asia. There is a tribal and family-centered perspective versus the Western individualistic one; however, the arrival of orphanages chipped away at the social structures.

Another hesitation that was prevalent among Cambodians came up as Dale and Cathleen spoke with their church-plant communities. "Orphanages are better for children, aren't they?"

Families who placed their children in orphanages were rewarded with better food, education, and sometimes medical care.

Cathleen jotted down on her growing list, "How do we convince families that what they offer their children is better than an orphanage? Love, attachment, identity. What if we help these families with food and education, so they can be rewarded for keeping their kids?"

//

Although Dale's name rarely features at the forefront, he was crucial to CIF. He was part of Cathleen's processing and decision-making. CIF would not have started without his immense support. She said, "He's my best friend, and I've always talked to him and asked for his input in everything."

His passion and experience in fostering and running an orphanage were the backbone, calm, and reason that kept Cathleen pushing through all the trials and uncertainties they faced.

However, Cathleen knew she and Dale could not do this alone. They needed local staff, people who could navigate the legal systems, and like-minded NGOs as partners.

//

Cathleen settled into the hard, wooden seat at the roadside café. Sipping her Cambodian iced coffee, heavily laced with sweet, condensed milk, her friend arrived. Quickly, they caught up on their families.

As Cathleen mentioned how Children in Families was getting started, her friend interjected, "I must tell you about the funeral I just attended."

She then launched into the horrifying story of the orphanage recruiter. The widow and her children were in the midst of their grief as the funeral pyre consumed the body of her beloved husband. Both mother and children were utterly distraught, dealing with the immense anguish of their loss. When the man, sent by a local orphanage, began to gather her children to himself. He assured her that they would be well cared for and get plenty of food. The widow was not emotionally in a place to make any life decisions about her family's care.

Recruiters earn income by going into villages to gather children for orphanages, most of whom already have a home. Cathleen's friend stood in shock as she watched the recruiter shamelessly round up the widow's children before the guests could even pay their proper respects.

Devastated but unsure of how to respond, she watched the children scream and thrash, being led away from their remaining parent.

The proper response in any community would be to find a way to support this mother and her children, especially while bereaved. Institutions claim to have the children's best interests at heart, yet ripping them away from their mother mid-funeral is unloving and cruel to the remaining family members.

Both women paused, silently soaking in the mental image while thinking of their own families.

Orphanage recruiters will even go to village chiefs and

request their "poor list." Then, they go to the homes of the most vulnerable families, convincing them to give up their children. Sometimes, just one or two of the children. Not even bothering to keep kids together, they may take only one to alleviate the burden of the others. The level of abandonment pain is immense for the child placed in residential care.

Sadly, this theme arose when I spoke with former orphanage directors in multiple nations, including Cambodia and Thailand. It was incredibly common.

Anny Joins the Startup

Fear clutched at the little boy's heart. He had heard some of the adults saying that he and his sister should go to an orphanage. He wailed and clung to his mother while silent tears streamed down his sister's face. Their mother, Anny, trembled, steeling herself to be strong and courageous for her children. "They were my life. I had already lost so much; I could not lose them."

Anny was Dale and Cathleen's friend from the orphanage years, who prayed for them and the children in their care daily. Her pastor husband of a decade had left and disappeared with another woman almost overnight. Rather than care for the widow and orphan as commanded by the Bible, the church rejected Anny and her children. She found herself alone and penniless as her place of honor in long-term ministry was stripped away. When he abandoned his responsibilities, judgment for his sins fell on his family.

She needed to find a place to live and work because she knew her friends wanted to place her children in an institution but she could not bear to lose them. Leaving her children with their grandparents in the village, she scoured the city for a decent wage and a home.

Their father's sudden absence was traumatic enough, so the idea of their mother placing them in residential care struck panic in their hearts.

"No matter what, my kids wanted to be with me because I was their mother. They missed me and were frightened."

She first learned about God in a refugee camp, and her

faith had sustained her over the years. Now that faith cut through all the negative voices fighting to be heard. She knew God would give her a job, and she would not lose her children. Not now, not ever. Her children's bloodshot eyes were reason enough to fight to keep her family together.

"When I left the church, and it was just my children and me, it had been so traumatic to lose my husband. Giving up my children would have emotionally finished me off. While I hunted for work, a friend tried to take my children to an orphanage, convincing my parents it was the best for everyone. But wailing and screaming, the kids made the drop-off impossible."

That moment solidified to Anny that children do not want to be in orphanages.

"I knew that kids do not want to leave their families. So, I would do whatever it took to keep mine. Later, I always asked children in orphanages where they wanted to live. Maybe only one in one hundred prefers the institution. I always find out those children came from abusive families. The others respond that they want to be with their families but have no choice. They want to attend school and know their parents cannot afford it."

Finally, Anny found a job teaching cross-stitch to vulnerable women and former sex workers. The income was small but enough for her to take her children back and care for them.

Around the time Anny found the job teaching cross-stitch, she ran into Cathleen. Their paths had crossed occasionally over the years, but they hadn't seen each other in a while. Dale and Cathleen were back in Cambodia after their long stint in the States, fostering and adopting a daughter out of the system. In 2002, they were looking for a place to live when they ran into Anny, who set to work helping them find a home in Phnom Penh.

Dale and Cathleen had a vision for a house that was both countryside and city. Praying, Anny had no idea how to find what they wanted, but she also did not give up easily. Taking a jarring ride down a small dirt track beyond the dyke road into the swampy southern part of Phnom Penh, she saw a sign on a gate. With a massive garden, it sat back from the road. After negotiating the price down, she brought Dale and Cathleen to it. It met every expectation.

After helping find the Joneses a home, Anny returned to her monotonous job. Sighing, she surveyed the room of women bent over their work, realizing that she did not enjoy teaching cross-stitch. Moreover, she felt caged because the women in the organization's care had to stay locked inside their safe homes all day. Even their tuk-tuks had guards for their safety when they went out. As the walls seemed to close in on her, she reminded herself that the income allowed her to keep her children. But she longed for more intellectual stimulation.

She kept in touch with the Joneses as the years passed. So, in 2005 when Cathleen was trying to figure out how to start CIF, Anny came to mind.

"Anny is amazing," Cathleen later said. "Her son and daughter knew their mom was always there for them, no matter what happened. Anny understood firsthand how important family is."

Anny's phone rang one day. Seeing that it was Cathleen, she answered immediately. Cathleen had previously shared her heart with Anny regarding family-based care, so she was not caught off guard as Cathleen poured out her vision for Children in Families and asked Anny to join her. Anny's experience with nearly losing her children was raw and honest, making her the perfect Cambodian counterpart for the role.

A partnership sparked that day. Finally, Cathleen had found a Cambodian who would invest in this vision and fight to keep families whole. She could not have picked a better person to start CIF alongside. Anny is a fighter, survivor, a teachable woman of God who relentlessly pursues what is right. So, Anny started work part-time and oversaw kinship care while getting trained.

When she became discouraged, Anny would think of her kind mother and grandmother, who adopted two kids and loved them well. Her family's legacy of loving and taking in others was part of her spiritual DNA. They were Cambodian and it was their instinct to care for children in their family unit. Anny's loss experience spurred her on, and the bond with her children inspired her.

Initially, Children in Families was entirely grassroots and a small, two-person operation working out of Cathleen's house in Phnom Penh. People thought they were crazy. Many people, especially in the NGO world, indicated that family-based care would never work in Cambodia.

But they persevered and abided by this principle: decisions would be discussed and made together. If they disagreed, they would have to seek middle ground. When others joined the team, the inclusion increased. CIF would not succeed with one strong leader taking charge.

"I knew I did not know everything. I knew I needed other people with experience and knowledge to give input, to learn from. We welcomed constructive criticism and questions from the beginning," Cathleen said.

Internal collaboration was one of many core values. Cathleen and Anny knew they also needed to partner closely with other organizations. Not an international NGO, they had to learn within the culture. Cathleen shared, "We believed in Cambodians doing the work and that God created families to care for children."

Soon after inception, they applied for NGO status. Cathleen found Anny with her head in her hands one day. "The dilemma," Anny said, looking up, "is that the government wants to see a track record of our work. But that would mean our activities would not be entirely legal or recognized initially. We want to start but we also need NGO status to start legally."

She quietly lamented that she felt like she was chasing her tail.

They copied another NGO's by-laws and created a board of directors with a CV of who they were. They also needed an office address but operated out of a downstairs room in Cathleen's home. After running in circles, the government continued to insist on an office address, so a friend let them use her NGO's office address. The government continued to scratch their heads that this work would involve Cambodians caring for Cambodian children in their family homes, not a group home. So, they cast their vision to the government, helping them understand.

During that time, NGOs were cropping up all over the city. They were easy to set up in the country in the early 2000s. All these organizations came in with big budgets, renting huge buildings and slapping up fancy signs. Sometimes others looked down on them because they did not fit the "official NGO" stereotype. Yet they focused on their work, not their office. Khmer like it fancy and official. CIF was neither.

The government struggled to understand that CIF did not have a center. Cathleen actually feared having outward signs of status because people might think they were an institution and start leaving their kids at the door.

//

Anny pulled her scarf tighter around her neck, shivering against the cold of Seoul. She stood outside Incheon International Airport with a delegation of Cambodian government officials as they waited for their bus. A few years earlier, Anny was a single mother, fighting desperately to keep her children. Now she traveled internationally with leading officials to a conference about implementing foster care.

Cathleen and Anny had devoted their time to learning as much as possible. When they presented the concept of family-based care to the Ministry of Social Affairs, Veterans and Youth (MoSAVY), the ministry invited Anny to travel to

Korea with them to study child development and to learn from Korea's experience of implementing a foster care system. Most of the delegates had to pay for the trip, but the Cambodian government paid for Anny to go because they believed so strongly in the vision of CIF. She returned full of inspiration.

"The training taught us what worked and did not work in the Korean foster care system. Then we took that information and compared it to knowledge of the Australian system and Cathleen's work in the American foster care system," Anny reflected.

There was no foundation of laws or procedures in Cambodia. The policies regarding care for vulnerable children were so new that most government employees were unaware of them. In her first years, Anny met with ministries, learned laws, and visited countless officials and offices. She knew the government offices so well that she could have made the journey blind.

Meanwhile, Cathleen laid out the purpose of CIF and the programs they would develop. The scope of what they wanted to do seemed insurmountable.

As the two invested in relationships with government officials and like-minded organizations, more people and agencies began to catch their vision of family-based care.

Anny reflected on all the initial work, saying, "Yesterday, I went to visit a child. When we found him, he was almost dead. Now he has a family and is healthy. He gets to go to school. Our vision was that every child would have a family and grow up in their community. We're beginning to see it fulfilled."

//

Children In Families' very first baby was a premature boy who survived. A Khmer Christian pastor and his wife had a daughter, but his wife's first pregnancy had been difficult and incredibly traumatic. She sobbed at the thought of giving birth again. They longed for more children; however, her fear kept her from trying for another.

Cathleen was caring for the baby when she heard this couple's story. CIF was not doing adoptions then, so it was not directly involved, but they introduced the birth mother to the family. The village leaders and local police then oversaw the whole process and were there to sign the adoption papers. The meeting needed to be a local affair, and CIF was not in attendance.

The birth mother was elated to meet this kind family who immediately loved the infant. Everything went well. Within weeks, the boy was thriving in the care of his new family.

A few months later, however, the leader of an anti-trafficking organization found out about the adoption and was furious. The biological mother had once passed through the woman's NGO, so the NGO leader felt she had the ultimate authority over the young woman and her baby. She preferred the baby to go to an orphanage, the usual choice of anti-trafficking organizations with unwanted pregnancies, than live with a loving, local family. The NGO leader raised trouble in the expat community, implying Cathleen and Anny had coerced the mother into handing over her child. Furious, the woman tried to block the adoption from going through and attempted to take the baby back.

However, the wise village chief had the papers in order. CIF had not been present at the adoption, and everything was legal. She could breathe threats but was powerless to take the child.

Although slight in stature, Anny is not one to be intimidated by anyone. This incident, however, rattled her. She knew they had to tread lightly where certain NGO leaders were concerned.

Meanwhile, the young boy thrived. Loved and pampered by his parents, sister, and extended family, he is now a young adult. And his adoptive mother, wounded and terrified from a difficult pregnancy, felt God had answered her prayers. She had a baby to love without another birth.

//

Before they had other staff, Cathleen and Anny had to implement strong accountability between the two of them. Since they were the first emergency care providers, they had to keep each other from growing too attached to the children in their care, knowing they would soon go into their forever family. They helped each other with emergency care to avoid getting overwhelmed. As difficult as it was, their experience helped them develop a system for emergency care families. Their steps to guard each other from getting too attached also kept them from burning out as they had sick children in their care and were working hard to get CIF off the ground.

Initially, they had hoped to use small orphanages for emergency care. After all, that's what an orphanage model should be, a short-term, temporary safe place to put children until a suitable family can be arranged for them.

They met with the orphanage director and agreed to the terms of emergency care. Children would only be there long enough to get healthy if they were ill and a suitable permanent caregiver was found.

Within twenty-four hours of placing the first sick toddler, Cathleen returned to transfer the child to a Khmer foster family, but the orphanage refused to give her back, stating, "God sent her to us. We just love her too much; she is ours now."

The small Christian orphanage had already given her a new, Western name and entered her into their long-term care. Cathleen's jaw dropped. "We agreed on the terms just a few days ago. We have a good family for her."

The director was unrelenting, barring Cathleen from seeing the child.

Thankfully, the paperwork and witnesses all documented

the little girl being under the authority of CIF and the Cambodian government. The orphanage put up a fight but had no legal ground to stand on and had to return the toddler to CIF, who placed her in her new family.

Cathleen and Anny decided they could not trust orphanages to hold up their end of the arrangement and had to care for the children until local families could be trained for the role.

At one point, they had a colicky baby in emergency care. He screamed his head off. After working all day and being up all night with the little one, Cathleen was exhausted.

One night, she fumbled about the dark, preparing a bottle. She put three heaping spoonfuls of formula into his bottle, then took it to him for feeding. He kept pushing the bottle away, crying even louder.

"I flipped on the overhead light to see what was wrong with him. I looked and saw a heaping pile of formula on the kitchen counter. The bottle was just full of hot water. I was so tired that I completely missed the bottle with the powder."

Prayer is what fueled them in those early days. "We had weird things happen," Cathleen said.

The Early Cases

Ratha had a difficult start to life. He was born without an anus, so his birth mother took him to the hospital for surgery and abandoned him there. His auntie felt sorry for him and picked him up, but she knew she could not care for him.

A missionary couple living nearby heard of his plight and took him in. A few months into his care, it became clear to Barb and James that Ratha should be in a Cambodian family. They began to plan for surgery overseas while seeking a local placement. However, they doubted the possibility of finding a Cambodian family who would know how to properly care for a baby with multiple congenital disabilities and health issues.

When she heard about CIF's work, Barb contacted Cathleen to line up a family for him. During the initial meeting, Cathleen and Anny found the baby incredibly weak and pale, yet clean and dressed nicely. Unfortunately, though Barb was sterilizing bottles and carefully measuring out his formula, she had not been feeding Ratha enough. She was used to American formula measurement, which at the time had larger scoops, twice the size of those in Cambodia. Thus, Ratha was receiving only half his needed daily nutrition.

After Anny took him to her home for temporary emergency care, he plumped considerably and gained strength. A later visit to the doctor confirmed that he was malnourished and also that one of his kidneys was in his abdomen. Suffering from a massive urinary tract infection due to his kidney not draining correctly, poor little Ratha was miserable. The heat and humidity wreaked havoc on his stoma bag. Infections were unavoidable, so they had to find a better solution.

Barb was sorrowful about the formula mix-up, but she remained committed to providing support for Ratha. She began to search for a way to send Ratha to America for surgery; meanwhile, Anny and Cathleen found him a family.

Both Cathleen and Anny were skeptical of her plans. There were world-class hospitals in Southeast Asia, so why not look for something closer to home? Somewhere that would allow his new foster mother to accompany him? They also reflected on the cost of sending him overseas. Those same funds used in Cambodia would cover multiple children's medical care. Cathleen explained to Barb that the baby did not need a big expensive trip; local care would be just as beneficial.

He desperately needed medical care, but he also required love and bonding as much as surgery.

Placed in a loving local foster family, Ratha received meticulous care. Soon, they set him up to get surgery with a Singaporean doctor who specialized in surgeries of this nature.

Members of the foster family traveled to the north of Cambodia with Ratha for the surgery. He was their child, and they loved him fiercely.

The specialist surgeon explained that Ratha was an extremely complex case, but he came out of it a success. Additionally, he did not have to leave his Cambodian culture and family to travel to America.

He's a healthy teenager now, still in a relationship with Anny due to his foster parents' bond with CIF. He calls Anny regularly. She played me his voice message, where he left jokes for her. He also left a message asking her to pray for his legs as he still has minor congenital disabilities. She said Ratha's voice messages come constantly, he loves her so much. Every time she goes to his village, he mauls her with loving embraces. She said he's a brilliant and hilarious child.

Many years later, another baby with similar issues came through CIF. She ended up being placed with the same family.

They had room in their hearts and home for another child, so she grew up with a big brother and parents who understood her condition well. Had he been sent away, his little sister may never have found such an advocate and support in him.

//

Above collaboration and holding one another accountable, Cathleen and Anny were devoted to prayer.

Prayer and devotions play a considerable role at CIF. Together they prayed over each new kid who came into their care. They prayed to find suitable families, to get money, and to steward it well. So many children who passed through CIF had survived trauma, illness, and difficult circumstances. Yet through nights of prayer, babies lived, and they found solutions to complicated problems. Prayer seasoned all these two women did.

Over a decade later, a visiting Australian high school student asked Anny, "What do you do when you come up against a problem that you've never seen before and don't know how to solve?"

"I start with prayer," she responded in a firm, humble confidence.

In a meeting with UNICEF, someone asked a similar question. She answered the same. In a room full of hundreds of people with considerable influence and deep pockets, Anny told them she turned to God for answers.

"I get on my knees and ask God to show me the path for this child. Then, I ask God to provide a family for this child."

"All the training I had to do with CIF was a lot to take on," she said. "No one was doing what CIF did in Cambodia. We needed God's guidance."

//

In the early days of CIF, Cathleen and Anny placed several children in doctors' families in Phnom Penh. Educated people with means and experience of the world knew that the old way of getting children by buying babies from poor women was not the best way to continue if the nation were to develop and improve, yet they still desired to adopt a child.

So, they came to CIF.

In the years after the war, people sold children to families. Many went to people who genuinely wanted a baby and were good to their children. But, unfortunately, this was only a cultural practice, and legal adoption had no clear avenue.

"Some of the kids who were sold ended up in good situations," Cathleen and Anny explained, "but with no monitoring and screening, you just could not know. So, CIF placed the kids to ensure they would go to good families."

The doctors who fostered through CIF showed forethought, desired accountability, and wanted to do things the right way. Many people understood the importance of regulation. They were dispelling the myth of fostering to exploit or for monetary gain.

//

A firm, concerned voice addressed Anny over the phone. The head of a Christian NGO in a dilapidated area of Phnom Penh called. Although he was calm, Anny noted the worry and tension. There was a baby for sale; would CIF intervene?

Anny gathered her things and flagged a tuk-tuk. She did not know the neighborhood well but knew it was unsafe. The hair stood on her neck as they approached the described location. Anny found the woman selling the baby. Aged well beyond her years, the woman was missing about half her teeth, and deep lines implied a difficult and tragic life.

The baby was not hers but belonged to a relative, a young bar girl who wanted the baby in an orphanage. The relatives, being hard up for cash, decided to sell the baby instead. Crudely, the auntie demanded payment for Anny to take the baby.

As resolute as ever and determined to leave with the baby before dark, Anny stood her ground, "We never pay for children. Please, give her to me. I will take her to be well cared for."

Anny got nowhere with the woman and eventually gave up. The day was fading, and this neighborhood was unsafe. Her driver insisted they leave.

She left, praying daily for the little one.

A few months later, Anny was back in this out-of-the-way location, summoned by the same man. This time, the auntie had no desire to keep the baby. One look and Anny was horrified; the infant was near death. Starved and diseased, she only stared at Anny with saucer eyes, silently pleading for rescue.

Anny fought the guilt rising in her. Why had she left the baby?

The entire ride, she feared the six-month-old would not make it. Finally, at Cathleen's house, she set the baby on the couch for her and Cathleen to examine. Opening the blankets, signs of severe neglect became more evident. Panicked, they immediately rushed her to their trusted clinic and neither stopped praying during the short journey.

The doctor said, "Take a look into her mouth. I've never seen thrush this bad!" The baby's mouth looked like thick, white fur was covering the inside.

After being given medication, the baby gagged and then vomited huge gobs of thrush. She was skeletal, bald, and extremely dehydrated. The doctors at this local clinic were skilled and had saved many of CIF's emergency cases. The doctor expertly put IVs in the tiny body as they pumped fluids and more medicine into her.

A day later, the scene was repeated as her body rejected more thrush. This process went on for days. Unsanitary bottles led to the thrush growing and filling her mouth, throat, and stomach.

Without a miracle, she would not survive.

In the meantime, Anny tracked down her mother, a young

woman who was HIV positive and whose outlook for life was grim. Hardly capable of caring for herself, there was no way she could take back her baby. No longer trusting her relatives to care for her baby, the mother signed her over to CIF.

Meanwhile, a childless couple yearned for a baby. After being married for ten years and struggling with infertility, they put their name on CIF's list. As teachers, they could hardly pass their days surrounded by children and not long for one of their own.

Meanwhile, the baby fought for her life and won. Despite thrush, severe malnourishment, and absolute neglect, little Sovy pulled through. Soon, plumper and healthy, she was placed in the arms of the two educators. The course of her story was altered as her new parents' hearts expanded in ways they could not believe. She was their miracle. She grew into a stunning little girl.

Over a decade later, only one of her biological relatives is still alive. They all succumbed to their unhealthy lifestyles and abused bodies. Sadly, her birth mother passed away at a young age.

But Sovy is incredibly loved and grows more beautiful each day. Well-educated and an accomplished pianist, she was the teachers' only child for a long time. Much later, CIF placed a little brother in her family. "Both kids became part of an incredible family under the worst of circumstances."

//

Despite having to start from nothing and fumble their way forward, when Chab Dai (an organization that monitors and strengthens NGOs to collaborate and maintain training and standards) did their first evaluation of all their members, Helen Sworn, the founder of Chab Dai, met with them.

Sitting across from Anny and Cathleen, she marveled that CIF was further ahead and more developed than many other organizations.

Helen listed their merits, "You have job descriptions, contracts, health insurance, set working hours, paid time off, child protection policies, staff development plans, and a constitution. Not to mention, CIF has a board of directors who actually meet and are registered with the government with a memorandum of understanding (MOU)."

Anny's heart swelled as the reports came back; it was so encouraging to know they were starting well.

Rebecca Nhep and Shifting Perspective

"Sixty years of global scientific research shows that living in residential care can harm a child's social, physical, intellectual, and emotional development and has long-term impacts in their adult life."
–ACCI's Kinnected Program

When I met Rebecca, she swept into a small cafe with a large, stylish sun hat on her head, carrying herself with a natural confidence that commanded respect. She looked more like an Australian woman headed to a fancy afternoon tea on some lawn rather than an advocate warrior. She smiled brightly.

As soon as she started speaking, I knew I was out of my league intelligence-wise. Her brilliance would be intimidating if she weren't so incredibly kind.

Throughout our interview, she only spoke of herself as a way to point to others, to help and advocate for them. The conversation was never about her, only about what she had learned through trials to teach others a better way.

In her early twenties, she moved to Cambodia. At the same time that Cathleen was beginning to conceptualize family-based care in Cambodia, Rebecca began her own unexpected journey that would play a vital role in CIF's formation as well as protecting vulnerable children and families.

It was 2000, and Cambodia had only been open to foreigners for about eight years. Amid language studies, teaching

English at a local school, and doing research for her project on oral communication systems and their development, she lived atop a school run by the mission in Phnom Penh.

There were no cell phones at the time, but a call came through the school office from a man with her organization who ran an orphanage in rural Cambodia.

His voice crackled across the line, "Hi, we've hardly met, but I need you to pray about a girl here. She's in my orphanage and has been staying with our family in our home, but she is just not doing well. We've secured a job for her teaching English at the school, but can you consider having her live with you?"

As the story pieces fell together, Rebecca realized she'd be living with this sixteen-year-old who grew up in their mission orphanage. The girl was well educated and capable of teaching but was struggling emotionally over the prospect of leaving the haven of the institution.

She was the same girl who used manipulation to garner the favor of the orphanage director and his wife. With her privilege over the other children, she used her power to get back at girls she did not like, accusing them of all types of terrible things, even getting a few kicked out.

Although the director did not become aware of some of her lies until years after, he soon realized that her transition into adulthood was less than ideal. She could not cope.

At the time, Rebecca had no experience with people who'd grown up in orphanages or the trauma they experienced.

"When I met Tai, she lacked life skills, struggled with social interactions, and didn't have a strong understanding of some aspects of her culture. For example, her English was better than her Khmer. I began to wonder who was teaching whom about how to live in Cambodia?"

Rebecca described the next year living alongside the girl. "She didn't know how to interact with and respect adults and was constantly getting in trouble for being disrespectful. She was great at English and could teach but then she'd get her salary and not know how to handle it."

Tai completely unraveled in a local market. Overwhelmed, she'd panic and overpay or buy enough of an item to feed a hundred people. Her only experience shopping was going with the orphanage cooks once a month and purchasing food for the whole orphanage.

Rebecca said Tai starved or wasted food terribly because she had more than she could handle. Cleaning up after herself or doing laundry was another insurmountable obstacle, basic household chores were challenging for her. Her lack of life skills led to extreme meltdowns as even the most negligible task induced anxiety. No one had ever taught her.

Initially, Rebecca attributed some of this to Tai's personality, but over time she got to know Tai's seven other siblings and realized none of them knew how to cope with the basics of adult life. Rebecca also built a relationship with many Khmer young adults who had aged out of their orphanage, known as "care-leavers."

Tai was not an exception to the rule; every young adult leaving care struggled at some level. "They were fractured and struggled to negotiate the normal stressors and aspects of adult life. [The care-leavers] lacked discernment of who was untrustworthy and constantly got into bad situations."

In one such terrible situation, Tai's sister was promised work by some men a few years after she left the orphanage. She had no idea how to discern if people were trustworthy since she had no healthy permanent attachments in childhood to teach her, and she listened to them. They spiked her drink, raped her, and forced her into prostitution. The orphanage was giving the girl a full scholarship to attend university. She'd been doing well there, yet her lack of exposure to the outside world led her into the worst possible scenario. She became pregnant and had nowhere to turn.

Because the orphanage only wanted success stories from the

children in their care, Tai's sister knew going back to the directors was not an option. Instead, her sister came to Cathleen, who took her to Mother's Heart Organization (MHO), a crisis pregnancy NGO. Thanks to their incredible care and assistance, she chose to keep her baby and was prepared better to thrive as a mother. But it was a difficult start, having no family to fall back on.

Tai came from a desperately low-income family. Her father, a local authority, died in prison on trumped-up charges after getting on the wrong side of the new government. Her mother went out to work, leaving the children alone for days. When her baby brother died of malnourishment, their mother had to sell the house and possessions to pay the bills. Then, the children went to the orphanage.

Tai said that after about a week in the orphanage and getting enough to eat, she longed to return home to her mother. She missed her and would cry for her. However, orphanage staff treated them as if they were ungrateful for care if they missed their families.

Tai and her peers found that teachers and people in the community singled them out for not having families, a story that plays out all across Southeast Asia. The teachers made all the "orphans" stand up in class. The other children introduced themselves and told a little about their families, while the kids from the orphanage were labeled orphans. Tai wanted to scream, "I have a mother!"

She felt humiliated. Her peers at the orphanage often talked amongst themselves about wanting to go live with their aunties and uncles, even if they were true orphans.

Decades later, in an interview, Tai sobbed, "If I could have spoken to the donors who supported me [in the orphanage], I would have asked them to let me stay with my mom." She paused and then continued, "When I left the orphanage, I had nothing."

While her peers spoke poorly of Tai, Rebecca saw through

the veneer. Tai was a scared, traumatized girl without a mother. Much of her behavior was a product of being institutionalized. She became cunning and fought for favor in a sea of children because she craved to be seen and noticed. Children cope with powerful emotions in extreme ways. Tai learned to betray and lie to get what she wanted most: love. And for a while, it worked. The orphanage director and his wife rewarded her behavior with favor and let the other children know it. However, once her troubled mind started to reveal its inner workings, they removed her from their lives forever.

Tai shared that the culture frowns upon a single woman living alone without family connections; this was yet another negative consequence of aging out of an orphanage. Many people assumed that a young woman on her own was a sex worker, rejected by her family. "Good girls" stayed with their parents until they were married.

The same orphanage directors who let her live in their private home refused to speak to her or even make eye contact in her adulthood, leaving her screaming and weeping uncontrollably in a public setting.

When Tai married, her mother-in-law had to teach her the expectations of a wife and mother and how to act as a Khmer woman should. If it was not for the patience of this older woman, Tai would have likely become overwhelmed with parenting and abandoned that role.

"In Cambodia, people judge you by your speech and how you keep your home. I had no clue about how to do this," Tai said in an interview with ACCI.

Even with the support of her husband's family, Tai lacked instinct with her baby and struggled to bond.

This young woman made Rebecca take notice of care-leavers and the wake of dysfunction left by an upbringing in orphanages. She noted patterns amongst the young adults in their church. The same issues emerged consistently.

So, Rebecca started to do research. Did anything exist in Cambodia that could have kept Tai and her peers in their families?

As she asked about family-based care, she found it existed informally all over the place in Cambodia. It was natural for people to take in family members or care for an orphaned child in their community or even informally adopt.

Her research led her to the offices of the Ministry of Social Affairs, Veterans and Youth Rehabilitation (MoSAVY) and the District Office of Social Affairs Veteran and Youth Rehabilitation (DoSAVY).

Petite, blond, and in her early twenties, Rebecca walked into the government offices to find what existed in the way of family-based care. "I was the ignorant foreigner who just burst in," she laughed. "They were amazingly accommodating to me."

Because her command of the language was so impressive and her confidence appeared unwavering, she said, "A secretary brought me into a huge meeting that was in progress. The room was full of all these Khmer men in the government. I sat there feeling wrong and out of place, staring at my feet until the meeting was over."

The men continued their meeting around the ostentatious table with its high-backed carved chairs, almost ignoring her presence until it was over.

"The head of DoSAVY was there. I felt embarrassed and out of place, but he pulled me aside afterward and taught me etiquette."

Rather than be annoyed with her audacity, he took her under his wing and taught her. He invited her into his office, asking her questions, discerning her intent and background. After exhausting his own curiosity, he let her ask questions.

She asked about Cambodia's family-based care framework, wanting to know the legal framework, policies, and what existed regarding family-based care policies and children's rights. He explained there was no formal system. In addition, foreign adoption was currently on its way out due to corruption.

She found favor with this fatherly government leader, and he continued to meet with her. Soon after their initial meeting, he took her to one of the few government orphanages still in existence near Wat Phnom in the old part of the capital.

Rebecca said, "There were a few government orphanages still scattered throughout the country, but most were privately run. The government one in Phnom Penh housed mostly babies with HIV or disabilities. Caretakers did not want to care for them because they feared getting AIDS. Also, they feared inheriting the child's karma if they died."

Over time, her visits with DoSAVY and the orphanage director led to a deeper relationship. The woman in charge wanted her to foster young children with illness and disabilities, but Rebecca didn't think a young single person, let alone a foreigner, should be caring for the children.

"My idea was to get families from the church to foster these children. Many were desperately ill and in need of intensive care. I was shocked to find that none of the Khmer Christians I knew wanted to take them in. The stigma was just as strong amongst the believers as it was among the Buddhists. Everyone feared getting HIV."

Although it appears cruel, families did what they felt was best for their own. They believed that if a child was desperately ill or died in their care, the bad karma would end up on their children. So, it made perfect sense in Buddhist culture that taking in a child with a disease or disability came at a huge risk and danger. At the time, people did not understand HIV well, and many genuinely thought they could contract it through interaction.

After finding no one to help her, she agreed to foster several children and model this care for those around her.

"Cambodians emulate what is modeled. They do not innovate based on abstract ideas. You have to model it first. It is a traditional culture that uses the past as an anchor, rather than looking forward with abstract ideas."

Instantly, however, she hit a hurdle. There was absolutely no screening for foster parents.

"I went to DoSAVY and requested that they thoroughly screen me [before I took the children]. Then, I contacted a friend in Australia, a social worker, to get the procedures of my government."

She then asked the head of DoSAVY to screen her using the Australian process. The screening was slow; it started with her spending a few hours with the children in the orphanage several times a week. It built up to having them stay with her a few times a week. In the meantime, she arranged for medication and treatment for the children.

Even after receiving three children, the young, single Rebecca still worked on her project addressing communication systems. While working to develop a media company, she set up a meeting with a government TV station. A young TV director and photographer named Bandith met her. This Khmer professional was drawn to the strong and capable Rebecca.

The match was perfect. Bandith's family took in abandoned babies, so the idea of pursuing a woman taking on three children was a bonus, not a deterrent for Bandith.

His sister was a midwife in a nearby province. Her husband was a doctor, and together they had adopted two children whose families left them at his clinic. For years, the couple informally worked with local village leaders to get abandoned babies into families in their community. As a midwife and Cambodian, Bandith's sister's natural response to children without parents was to place them in families. It never crossed her mind to put them in a children's home run by foreigners.

//

Rebecca was busy with three foster children, a new relationship, and a full-time job. In the midst of all this, a mutual friend introduced Rebecca to Cathleen. The meeting was inevitable, since the two women had so much in common.

CIF was in its early years at this time. Rebecca said, "We clicked right away. Together we began to conceptualize the direction and work of CIF."

Not long into Rebecca's engagement to Bandith, CIF took on a baby who was very sick with HIV and who had no documentation, having been born to a Khmer sex worker living illegally in Thailand. According to the government, this child did not exist. The situation brought up all sorts of legal and ethical questions, and it forced CIF to figure out a framework for child protection. Since that time, thankfully, UNICEF and Family Care First (FCF) have done significant work around the legal framework for child's rights in Cambodia.

Early on, all children placed with Rebecca and CIF had special needs or complex medical issues. "It was a God-thing that CIF got these cases," she told me. "They were the most complex ones and not easy. Because of this, Cathleen and Anny built a strong foundation under the toughest possible conditions. All the cases that followed seemed so much easier."

"The orphanages did not want those kids," Rebecca said. By taking in children with disabilities and illnesses, they could show the community around them that they did not inherit bad karma. Rebecca regularly impressed upon the local church and neighbors that she was healthy and doing well.

//

As the Minister of Education at the time of the Khmer Rouge, Bandith's father was supposed to be taken to the killing fields or S21 Prison (now known as Tuol Sleng) in the heart of Phnom Penh and shot. But he wasn't.

Both of his parents have incredible stories of salvation from the Khmer Rouge.

After the Khmer Rouge fell, his parents worked outside

the city in a nearby province, setting up the schools. It was in this environment that Bandith grew up, appreciating education and seeing his family care for many children who were either unrelated or distantly related. For his family, it was natural to care for abandoned children. Rebecca had married into a family whose purpose and vision matched her own.

Although not on staff with CIF, she and Bandith joined the board of directors and were part of leadership in the formative years. However, they had their own projects. Bandith ran the media projects for Rebecca's organization; together, they worked to reduce corruption among the wealthy. People with money had one focus, their own families. Taking no one else into consideration, they oppressed the lower classes.

So, Rebecca and Bandith put together media targeting the younger generation of the upper class, trying to change the system and how they communicated.

In another one of their projects, they researched family separation and tried to figure out how to prevent family breakdown. By networking with local churches and other community-led development, they established grassroots processes that eventually reached ninety communities. Knowing no one can solve all the people's problems, they taught communes how to set goals, collectively map the assets in their community, and learn to address the psychology of poverty. Examples included farming co-ops, rice banks, savings schemes, and health and education initiatives. Each program was to become self-sustaining in three to four years.

//

After living in Cambodia for nearly a decade, one day in prayer, Rebecca believed God told her she would be taking all she had learned forward into something new.

For the next year, all the signs pointed to a return to Australia, but they loved Cambodia, so it was difficult to leave.

When the couple finally relocated to her home in Australia, they were both offered jobs with her mission organization.

Then, what God had spoken to her a year previously clicked into place. Her organization ran orphanages across the globe. She realized she had grown and learned so much about family-based care in Cambodia but had never taken her organization on the journey.

Her organization was perpetuating the same issues for hundreds, if not thousands, of children globally. She and Bandith also knew that what was true for Cambodia must be true across the world. Most communities naturally care for and take in children when they lose their parents, children do better in families, governments need frameworks to protect children's rights.

As she shared all that she had learned over the past decade, her leaders agreed with shifting away from orphanages to placing children back in families. They let her establish the Kinnected program.

The transition was far from peaceful. The missionaries running orphanages and the churches invested in children's homes became incredibly defensive.

She said, "Family-based care was very contentious as we started transitioning ACCI away from orphanages. I received daily calls and constant questioning. Some told me I was partnering with the anti-Christ. The process did not happen quickly."

Rebecca spent a significant amount of her time traveling across Australia and sharing. She was very intentional in educating the church.

Faith-based systems build an ideology around their work, which makes it harder to break. Rebecca was not just shifting social paradigms; her family-based programs were bumping into an ideology that the Christian orphanages were rescuing children on a spiritual and physical level.

She went into her work asking, "What scaffolding is holding these practices up? I had to look through human rights, law, and theology. I found there was a lack of theological framework for human rights. So, we needed a biblical theology to convince the church to change their practices [with orphans and abandoned children]."

She set about rewriting ACCI's theology of development, human rights, and care of vulnerable children.

"What aspect of the Gospel promotes raising Christians by separating families?" she asks. "We are told to go into the nations (go-out), not extract and take in, divorcing children from their social structure and culture."

"Why does it have to be either Christian and dysfunctional or emotionally healthy but not saved? Would you accept this practice in your own home?"

"We wrongly think that our good intentions are better than the customs that already exist in other countries." But good intentions can still lead to bad theology and harmful practices.

Although the battle for building Kinnected was fierce, the same woman who marched into a Cambodian government office and asked difficult questions was equal to the task. ACCI did transition their orphanages into family-based care. The field workers who took these steps now model family-based care in their countries and train others to do the same.

I asked her, "What would you say to people vested in orphanages?"

She paused for a while. "There are layers to this. First, respecting the dignity and equality of another person (i.e., children) is fundamental. It should never be stripped from someone, especially not in exchange for care. Second, orphanages will always take more than they give. Good education and food cost the child their family and community."

"Ask, 'Is what I am doing the least invasive way?'"

"If we intervene in the life of others, we have a responsibility to take our head along with our hearts. Intervene thoughtfully. There is enough information out there about what does and does not work. There is no excuse for not doing it well."

//

I had one final question during our interview. "What happened to your foster children in Cambodia?"

While many children flowed through Rebecca and Bandith's
home over the years through emergency care, three were with
them long-term.

One child got a simple adoption under the civil code,
which transferred guardianship without losing connection
with his family of origin.

Two of their children passed away. One, who was not supposed to live beyond infancy, died at twenty years old in a car
accident. He made it to adulthood through love and meticulous care, finally succumbing to a fatal crash.

"I was working in Myanmar when I got the news. It devastated me." Her prayer is that the legacy of these children
lives on through promoting better practices of care for children globally.

The Government Knows Orphanages Are Bad

"How can I be independent if I've never known freedom?"
–Young adult about to age out of a residential care facility

Children in Families could not exist without collaboration and partnership with other people and organizations. An essential part of doing family-preservation and family-based care well was having laws that protected the family and children's rights. Sarah Chhin's work in Cambodia was vital to the shift in these laws and policies.

"Over twenty years!" I repeated during the interview, marveling at how different Cambodia has been since Sarah Chhin moved here in September 2000.

"Why Cambodia?" I asked.

"When I was six years old, I became interested in Cambodia as a country," she told me, describing how she wore a Cambodia T-shirt to tatters as a child. Her fascination with the nation was intense as she spent time pouring over books and watching documentaries. However, life took her to West Africa and through many other studies before she miraculously landed in Cambodia as the country director for Cambodia Action, one of the first organizations to begin work in the nation after the fall of the Khmer Rouge.

Initially, Sarah lived in Phnom Penh where, at the time, wooden houses lined narrow dirt roads. Sarah settled into her tiny room in her landlord's wooden house and immersed herself in Khmer language for a year. She said, "It was so different. People ensured they were off the streets and home by 7 p.m. Any later was too dangerous. Traffic lights and cheese arrived in 2003. The markers of development!"

As of 2001, there was no regulatory framework to govern the implementation of alternative care for orphans and vulnerable children in Cambodia.

Amid language studies, she began work with a project called HOSEA, Helping Orphanages by Support, Education, and Advice. Sarah spent the first year researching the level of care and quality of alternative care in Phnom Penh and Kandal Province. "We surveyed all organizations that said they worked with orphans and vulnerable children to see the needs and service gaps. It was a gigantic task," she said.

At the same time, UNICEF started doing similar research. By the end of the year, HOSEA and UNICEF found that their respective reports shared almost the same conclusions and recommendations, the first and most important of which was drafting a governmental regulatory framework for alternative care in Cambodia. The two reports also clearly expressed that the capacity of orphanage caregivers to care for vulnerable children needed to be drastically improved.

After passing through countless gates of orphanages and anti-trafficking safe houses, Sarah felt a burden to make change. The conditions and care were abysmal. How did anyone think this was better for children than family? She pondered.

"Through these reports, we started a coalition to create minimum regulation standards in residential care for children and trafficking victims. The UNICEF representative and I agreed a lot more work was needed to create comprehensive, practical guidelines on minimum standards for alternative care," Sarah told me.

The group that first met began drafting sets of minimum standards for residential and community-based care, coordinated and organized by Sarah under HOSEA. Although the work was tedious, she had a detailed mind, thriving because passion met with her strengths in this. Gradually, the minimum standards took shape, using the UN Rights of the Child as the framework for the documents. "The vision always in mind was that we could offer these to the Ministry of Social Affairs, Veterans and Youth Rehabilitation (MoSAVY) as a new framework of policies to transition alternative care of vulnerable children in Cambodia towards family-based care and away from residential care."

In March 2003, the Cambodian government sent a delegation to Sweden to sign the Stockholm Declaration on Residential Care for Children, which stated that long-term residential care was not in children's best interest. Instead, residential care should be temporary and the last resort in the continuum of care, with family-strengthening efforts and family-based alternatives being the best and first choice for the care of orphans and vulnerable children.

This groundwork was necessary to establish Children in Families years later. Cathleen and Anny's vision for CIF aligned with the UN rights of children and the local legal framework recently built around the care of vulnerable children. They found Sarah to be a great resource and advocate for their work.

Later that year, MoSAVY had a big conference and workshop to explain the Stockholm Declaration that had been signed and to inform NGOs with MOUs who worked with children that Cambodia was shifting away from residential care.

The MoSAVY leaders publicly endorsed the minimum standards, beginning an action plan to implement regulations.

In 2004, the ministry set up what was called the Advisory Committee on Alternative Care. Committee members were officials from various ministry departments and representatives of UNICEF, Krousar Thmey (New Family), Hagar, Friends International, and Sarah herself. However, at that time, only a few people invested in the change toward family-based care.

Sarah described it as a painstaking process. "The representatives wrote all the documents in Khmer and English, so the advisory committee members spent a lot of time discussing them sentence by sentence to agree and check for accuracy. As a result, discussions grew heated as they reached a consensus on some of the more controversial issues."

However, they all agreed that the heart of their work was: *Providing quality and best practice services so that children can enjoy their right to live in a family through family reunification, reintegration, social inclusion, family separation prevention, and family-based Alternative Care,—and partnering with national and sub-national level authorities to actively support Cambodia's transition toward community-based care away from residential care.*

The process took a long time. Finally, in mid-2006, the organizations launched the Policy on the Alternative Care of Children and the Minimum Standards for Residential Care. They also finalized the Minimum Standards for Community-based Care later that year. However, it would take until 2011 before the actual implementation of these policies was enacted through the monitoring and inspection of residential homes.

I asked Sarah to elaborate on some of the findings as the ministry officials began to inspect residential care institutions. Her feedback was shocking and matched many of the stories from my interviews.

She stated, "Orphanages generally refused to deal with child-to-child sexual abuse claims in healthy ways. In one case, a director flat-out refused to work with us. The children were not safe. The director's response was, 'We prayed for them, so they're fine now.'" Other children were thrown out onto the streets to fend for themselves. Another orphanage was taken to court and closed for tying children up and force-feeding them with rice and vinegar.

Some of these cases arose years after the implementation of the new laws, showing that laws and frameworks are a start, but purposeful monitoring still needs to happen. Shifting to family-based care is a long, but necessary, process.

Creating Best Practices

Watching in horror as an orphanage director ripped two screaming children from their mother, Amy sat in shock. It was her first month in Cambodia, and she watched a documentary highlighting a Khmer orphanage with the intent to learn more about the nation. The documentary specifically followed an orphanage in Cambodia run by an Australian woman, but if the intention was to show the woman as benevolent, the opposite impression was taking place in Amy's heart. The two featured children were placed in the orphanage by their mother, a single factory worker. For two weeks, the children cried incessantly for their mother. Appalled, she wondered why no one was supporting the two children and their mother.

Amy had graduated high school passionate about serving street kids. She pursued studies in social work, family and child welfare, and primary school education, desiring to use her skill set overseas. Cambodia was her first destination.

"I was twenty-two years old. I came out of uni with a wealth of knowledge but had no experience anywhere, let alone Cambodia," she recalled.

Working with street kids in Phnom Penh, Amy said, "A lot of the kids on the streets and the children at risk in the community were related to weak or broken family structures and lack of social support."

She realized the street children's solution was rooted in the family. No one could solve it without an approach that included the whole family.

Several months into her work in Cambodia, she dug her feet into the sand in a coastal town and stared out across the expanse of water. As she listened to the waves, her mind wandered back to the woman she had seen at breakfast in her hotel. She could not shake the fact that she was supposed to meet that woman. Courage failed that morning when she felt God nudging her to introduce herself.

It was her holiday time in Kep, and she merely wanted to let the waves wash away the weight of her work and her many other concerns.

The next day, as she boarded her small boat to Rabbit Island, she saw the woman again. It was clear God was not going to let her out of the meeting that needed to happen. So, after they braved the choppy sea and disembarked, Amy introduced herself.

The woman's face lit up. Then, sticking out her hand, she said, "I'm Cathleen."

Their conversation quickly gained momentum as they exchanged the typical expat information. They asked each other, "How long have you been here?" and "What do you do in Cambodia?"

Eventually, Amy brought up the recent documentary about that orphanage. Still disturbed by it, she shared her heart with Cathleen.

Cathleen's eyes lit up as the young woman poured out a vision in line with her own. "My husband and I are trying to start something to support families to keep their children," she explained.

Amy remembered, "Cathleen gave me her address and phone number and invited me to their next meeting. At that time, about a year into the formation of CIF, it was just her and Anny."

The following week, craning her neck to look at passing street numbers, Amy bounced down the dusty roads of Boeung Tumpun in a *tuk-tuk*. None of the house numbers were in numeric order, making the search more difficult. Eventually, she opened the massive metal gate of the correct house. She stuck her head inside the front room of Cathleen's home, which had been set up as the office. Anny and Cathleen greeted her warmly.

Of their first meeting, Amy said, "It was an amazing experience. I heard about the initial stages of kids getting placed [in families]. From then on, I've been passionate about advocating for family-based care. I was blown away by Anny's and Cathleen's love of Cambodia and their ideas for integration."

Soon, they added Amy to their team. She sifted through Australian standards of care and found practices that would hold up in a developing country.

"Cathleen and Anny would go through what was left, and we all hashed out the cultural and contextual difficulties."

They forged something meaningful for the Khmer context between the three of them.

One of the deviations from Australian policy, for example, was vetting extended family, not only the parents. It is usual for a long list of relatives to live under one roof, so they were starting with questions like, "Who else lives in the household? Who is sleeping here? Who else will be taking on the care? Grandparents?"

It is even normal for multiple family members to share a bed. Parents, children, and cousins can all share their sleeping space into adulthood. What would be appropriate for a child to join the family? Not including them could cause feelings of isolation and alienation, yet it could also be a risk of inappropriate contact. They had to navigate these possibilities.

"On the Aussie forms," Amy explained, "questions were asking, 'Do you have a fire alarm system?' But, of course, in Cambodia, that's not possible. They're cooking over open fires outside and living in a wooden house with a thatched roof."

An example of adding in, rather than removing context, was that children must wear a helmet on a motorbike since that is the primary source of transportation.

The women had to take into account both city and village contexts when they wrote the CIF policies and procedures. It was vital to consider the village chief and authorities in the villages and the community as a whole. This was not just talking to one family. The wider community had to be on board with childcare and protection.

They made sure the documents aligned with the new Cambodian government standards. They also attempted to collect the policies and information other organizations in Cambodia were using and to get their input. However, most of the documents had to be created, as it was extremely rare to find any set standards or methods within the NGO community.

"There were not many kids going through CIF at the time; it was just starting. Only three of us were on staff, but we were looking to hire and figure out how to go about that. Cathleen and Anny were the trailblazers. I got to tag along and learn so much. They were huge mentors to me. I feel honored that I was a part of the journey [of CIF] for a while. I cannot speak highly enough of them."

A Foster Care Village

"The person who says it cannot be done should not interrupt the person doing it."
–Chinese proverb

Cathleen and Anny were on a path to healthy foster care but needed an anchoring point. So far, the program was small and included only a few families in Phnom Penh. They dreamed of a village where children could run free, where they could have a typical life, saturated in the local culture. A village where everyone knew each other and where there was access to a school and clinic. It would need to be safe. It also needed to be close enough to Phnom Penh that CIF's staff could travel there and monitor it. The roads at the time were still sparse and treacherous. No longer did bandits kill travelers, but heavy rain created craters, making the roads almost impassable.

At the time, Amy Sullivan was still volunteering with Cathleen and Anny and accompanied Anny on a visit to her home village.

As they neared the village, goose pimples covered Amy's skin. Something in her spirit told her this would be a good place.

About ten minutes into greeting some of Anny's family and paying proper respects to the village leaders, a young man with Down syndrome approached them. Smiles splashed across the village elders' faces; they greeted the youth by name and inquired about his mother. Amy and Anny looked at each other, both thinking the same thought.

Their time spent in the village allowed them to look in on the young man and his family. They found that he was treated well, and the community considered him a valued member. No one appeared to mistreat him. On the contrary, they accepted him without hesitation.

While the village lacked running water and electricity, the place felt safe and homey. It also had the connections and relationship ties to Anny that they needed.

//

CIF oversaw several local adoptions and kinship care families, but the foster care program, established for children to be cared for after all safe biological family options were exhausted, started with just a few volunteer families. One of the fathers became a CIF social worker. If they were going to expand to more than a few families, there needed to be intensive training.

"We had to do more than just place children; families needed equipping, so we brought Mick Pease out. (Mick founded SFAC, now known as Strengthening Families and Children, based out of the UK.) It was in the heat of April with no power."

Around 2007, Mick heard of the need for family care in Cambodia. He met Helen Sworn (of Chab Dai), who was on a visit to Oxford, UK. The bond was immediate. Mick, his wife, Brenda, and Helen grabbed a seat in the cafe and talked for hours.

"It felt like we were saying the same thing," Mick reflected. "She had concerns about orphanages, and there was no family care in Cambodia. Cathleen was just getting started, so CIF did not (officially) exist yet."

Helen connected Mick with Sarah Chhin, who had done the research on kids leaving institutional care. As young adults, they had been seriously unprepared for independent living. "Everything she [Sarah] said I completely agreed with, even though my experiences were in other countries. She was pretty brutal to the orphanages," he said with admiration in his voice. "Cambodia seemed so far behind [in family care]."

When Mick came to Cambodia, he met Amy Sullivan, who introduced him to Cathleen and Anny. Together, they traveled out to Anny's village. Overwhelmed by the extreme heat, they arrived to be met with about forty families interested in foster care. He describes all these faces staring at him in wonder and anticipation as he became flushed and drenched in sweat.

None of the families knew anything about foster care, and with no script or plan, Cathleen urged Mick to share. Quickly flashing through the files of his mind, he knew he needed to start teaching the most basic concepts.

Sitting on a wooden platform, faint from the heat, Mick shared about family care while Dale translated. Soon, the village chief appeared with a car battery. With deft hands they wired a fan to it and continued their discussion.

Mick, who has trained in family-based care across the globe, may have been saturated in his sweat, but he was unfazed by the conditions otherwise. This was his passion. Mick, Anny, and Cathleen encouraged the community. "You have the gift of time. You have the space. You can give these children love. You can teach them to be Cambodian."

They stared at Cathleen, unblinking. Most families had assumed the orphanages, with their cleaner clothing, basketball courts, and rotation of educated foreigners coming and going, would be better for children. Instead, well-intentioned outsiders had made Cambodians feel incapable and ill-equipped to care for orphaned or abandoned children.

Cathleen stood in front of the village and apologized. "I am so sorry for starting orphanages in Cambodia. I am sorry for making you feel like our model was better than kids growing up in a Khmer family. You have so much to give these children. They need you, your love, and your skills."

"We [foreigners who start orphanages] came to Cambodia and made a lot of assumptions about how you care for children. We were arrogant to believe we could do it better."

Mick did not just train families, however. He also worked alongside CIF to train social workers and those from collaborating NGOs. Initially, Cathleen taught willing people to be social workers, sending them to Chab Dai trainings and learning from people like Mick.

Mick has trained people in over thirty nations, and his organization has worked in at least fifty. A few things became clear from our discussions. The first is that family care works across cultures, religions, nations, and socio-economic spheres. The second is that, regardless of the culture, orphanages are not the best form of care for children. And the third is that children should only rarely be placed in residential care because they truly had no one to care for them.

"The concept [of family care] is simple. The outworking of how we do it is incredibly complex. Nothing is set in stone. We are dealing with people. Unique needs and problems. Some people are just more resilient. More than academia is needed. When you're in the midst of establishing and maintaining care, some intricacies need different responses."

"Cambodia had only new social workers. There were not many social workers who were older, who had family and life experience. With little life experience, making life-changing decisions for families and children is hard. Social workers need a strong reference point in their organizations and sound practices that hold the inexperienced in place. They need mentoring and coaching."

This was the basis for CIF's rule that no decisions would be made for a child or family without a team.

Whether in Cambodia or across the globe, an issue that often arises is that young people do not question their leaders. Untested social workers and staff do not know how to ask due diligence questions with a family. They don't know how to go deeper because it's not cultural. This can be especially true for young women. Mick shared about guiding them to learn how to investigate families or programs while honoring the culture.

"They need to learn that you cannot take people at face value. Always go behind and beyond. Of course, do it in the least offensive way possible. The progressive nature of SFAC is training people to do this." SFAC has the tools and practices that help social workers and family care staff members grow in these areas.

As Cambodia developed, people were graduating with social work degrees. They had better theoretical knowledge, but still needed the practical practice.

Later, Mick reflected that orphanages would not give children to CIF. He explained that taking children out of their orphanages undermined their funding and excuses for what they did.

Not long after he left Cambodia, he received an email from Cathleen sharing about the children who were finally handed over. All of them had a disability.

"One was blind, another little girl had lost an eye, and the final girl had cerebral palsy. The village chief took one of the children," Mick said. He was delighted at the news, even though he knew the orphanage's motives. "Basically, they gave Cathleen their most difficult kids to prove family care would not work. But it did work!"

//

Amy and Anny went to a local orphanage to pick up the first children CIF officially placed in foster care.

"Anny was the caseworker for the first cluster of children placed in her home village. We didn't just place kids in a family; we placed them in a community," Amy recalled.

A foreign woman ran the orphanage. It looked picture-perfect, and inside it was cute and well painted. The shiny murals were a veneer for the lack of care. Amy remembered rows of babies in beds just lying there.

The orphanage staff did little to interact with any of the children or babies. She and Anny came across children with disabilities of which the staff members were unaware because they had spent so little time caring for them.

With the first few children in their care, they left the orphanage. Situated in the back of the car, the little girl clutched at Amy's side. Soon, the boy began to bang his head violently on the car's floor. Startled, she attempted to stop him. Unfortunately, due to neglect, this was his way of communicating that he was hungry at the orphanage. Finally sitting in her lap, he calmed and felt her face.

The stress of the ride made her wonder how the foster mother would cope with this child. He had so many special needs, and his behavior was shocking.

Her worries evaporated as the car rolled to a stop. A group of villagers stood by a house, waiting for this moment. Anny gently lifted the boy from Amy's lap. As the young children arrived, one lady ran up and whisked the boy out of Anny's arms, hugging and kissing him repeatedly. It was his new mother. She had been waiting for him. Smiles erupted on everyone's faces, and some villagers even clapped with delight. It was a special moment.

Later, the mother told Anny and Amy, "Our family is so poor, I thought I would have to leave and work in a factory to support my family. But I love being a mom, and being a foster parent finally makes me feel valued for the work I can do as a mother."

She thrived on being a mother to the children and found that CIF's support changed her life. The village was on board to take many children with disabilities. The initial foster families were Christians. Amy explained that many Buddhists saw disabilities as a result of bad karma for the kids. However, they watched as Christian families loved these children, and nothing terrible came back on the families. The fear of karma did not rule them, and their families did well. It was a witness to their neighbors, and slowly paradigms about disability shifted. It was the beginning of breaking down cultural stigmas.

Whereas he once banged his head to communicate hunger and was unable even to chew solid food, the little boy developed impressively in his family. Soon he was riding bikes and communicating. He is now beloved in his village, a young man who cracks jokes and brightens his community. Everyone talks to him. Eventually, when he was ready for school, CIF worked with the leaders and teachers to accommodate his needs.

"I cannot imagine his life in the orphanage versus what it is now," Amy said.

His family has since taken in another child and even upgraded their living conditions. They put in a toilet and improved their home to accommodate foster children.

//

Although the first placements in the village were a joyous success for Children in Families because they were breaking new ground, many questions surfaced. Amy, Anny, and Cathleen sat around Cathleen's dining room table, meeting to address these important details. Cathleen read out her scribbled notes as they worked through each. "How much money should a family get?"

The team wanted to value the extra work and expenses additional children made. Yet they didn't want to give too much money; they didn't want families to choose to foster for the economic benefits. They also wondered what the appropriate financial support would be for children with disabilities, especially the severe cases.

After painstaking hours, they agreed. Kinship care, biological family members, received less money; however, they got enough to help the family keep their children and educate them. There were a lot of discussions in the team to find the right balance.

//

After a few years, Amy returned to Australia, profoundly impacted by her time in Cambodia. Her favorite memory was placing a little girl with cerebral palsy. She was first taken into short-term care in Phnom Penh to receive physiotherapy, but then they found a home for her in the village. She thrived, and her family's love was incredible. The placement greatly improved her quality and length of life by being in a family rather than an institution.

In Australia, Amy began working with children whose behavior was so violent they could no longer be placed in families. She contrasted her experience in the Australian foster care system to that of Cambodia.

"The kids in the system in Australia came from severe trauma and abuse. The West has so many support systems around them that when children are taken away from their families it is due to much worse circumstances like severe abuse. Many of the families we worked with in Cambodia were not abusive. It's more a lack of social support and poverty that breaks up families in the developing world."

As time passed, Amy married, had a family, and worked with refugees and in the school systems. But her passion for family-based care never wavered. She shared about CIF all across Australia at churches and missions conferences. Then, she and her husband started an organization to fund and support family-based care[5] overseas. They invest the money given, and the dividends from the funds go to the organizations. They found this approach more sustainable in the long run than constant fundraising.

She explains that the smaller amounts over the long term help them lock in how many kids they can help each year. She is amazed at how far finances can go for families in Cambodia.

The Growth of CIF

*"If I were worried about offending people,
CIF never would have started."*
–Cathleen

As they hired more staff, CIF outgrew Cathleen's home, and they moved into a tiny rental house, paying minimal rent. Soon they expanded again into a Khmer house called a "pteah lvang."

At the same time that Anny's village welcomed eight disabled children into families, a neighbor of the foster children approached Cathleen. "You know, I could care for a child. I am not sure I could take one with a disability, but I know I could care for a little one who needs a home."

So, they placed the first child without a disability or chronic illness. "Before we knew it, half the village had their hand up to foster," Cathleen grinned.

Orphanages were bursting with healthy children who needed families, and local people were approaching Cathleen with a desire to foster. But when Cathleen began meeting orphanage directors hoping to match children to families, they were only willing to give up the sick or disabled ones.

Amy reflected, "Despite being offered family placements for their children, the orphanages needed to keep their beds filled to keep donors happy and to justify their existence."

One orphanage director reached out to CIF. Cathleen was excited as his voice crackled over the phone, he jumped at the chance of emptying his orphanage of children. "This is won-derful!" Cathleen thought initially.

She said, "Let's set up a meeting so we can evaluate the children in your care and match them to families."

Soon, however, there was a caveat. In his conversation with Cathleen, he referred to the children with chronic illness and disability as "leeches." Those were children he was eager to be rid of. These children were at the highest risk for aban-donment, yet these same children were unwanted by the orga-nizations claiming to exist for the most vulnerable.

Another hurdle was the local medical professionals' bias against children with disabilities. Many convinced the parents to abort or allow the child to die without offering support or solutions. After children with disabilities were placed in Anny's village, people began to see how they contributed to the love and life of the family. Often, as personalities emerged and they developed, their parents grew encouraged, and attachments formed. As their neighbors began to take note of this shift, more people realized they could care for these chil-dren who required unconditional love.

Many developmental delays were attributed as much to lack of care and attention as to an actual disability. Healthy and loving interactions transformed many.

CIF's waiting list for children grew exponentially.

At one point, an orphanage asked them to place a healthy baby girl. Anny picked her up in a tuk-tuk. It only took a cou-ple of minutes for Anny to realize that the baby could not see. Even though it was a smaller Christian children's home, no one had figured out that the baby was blind.

However, there were other cultural issues at play that needed addressing. Most orphanages will tell you they have more boys than girls. Anny and Cathleen explained that Cambodians have the "pampered prince" mindset. They do not punish their boys; they give them everything they demand when they want it. So, the boys grow up to be tiny tyrants. At their wit's end, the parents put these naughty boys into orphanages between eight and ten years old. The boys are very unmanageable. Cambodians think raising boys is more complicated, not realizing that the behavior arises because they parent boys and girls differently. So, culturally, families believe boys are brats and girls are wonderful.

It is for this reason that CIF has always focused on parenting classes. These classes help change parents' desire to put their boys in orphanages for behavioral reasons.

The Cluster Model

When I bring up the work of Children in Families, many expats respond that Cambodians only choose to foster because they are poor and want money or that they will treat the child as a servant rather than a family member. This is a common misunderstanding.

I have heard these stereotypes too many times to dismiss them. While many of our families are from rural areas (partially because CIF chose to start in a village with known and trusted leaders), we have several families who are well educated, middle class, and even wealthy. Whether they want a child due to infertility or feel their family is incomplete, Cambodian parents are like all parents around the globe. Many people love children and enjoy parenting.

Once domestic adoption opened again in Cambodia, many CIF foster families immediately placed their names on the list. Adoption would mean the loss of financial support from CIF, but these parents did not care. What mattered more to them was having their children put in their family books, a place of permanence and legitimacy. In just a few years of domestic adoption opening again in Cambodia, nearly forty of CIF's foster children were legally adopted. Others who were above the age for official adoptions were made part of the family through a more informal yet legal adoption process, while others, although not legally adopted, are considered equal members of their households.

//

When CIF places a child with a foster family, the paper signing and placement happen with pastors, village leaders, and other essential community members present.

"We [CIF] work with entire villages. So, it's not just our kids and families who benefit. If a non-CIF family is struggling in one of our communities, we also support them."

A child's well-being should not only fall on the foster family's shoulders but also on the whole communal unit. It came to Cathleen through prayer. She got a picture of a cluster of grapes, and it clicked in her mind that foster care should exist in clusters. CIF prefers a minimum of three families in the community to be foster parents so that they have support and encouragement. It also helps for social work visits because they all lived near one another.

CIF's initial "cluster model" of fostering grew into the Communities of Care model used today. On a social work visit to the village, groups of ten parents meet once a month. Sitting on a large wooden platform under a house or on the cool tile floors, they use this time to develop relationships, discuss issues arising with foster children and their families, and encourage one another. This model helps the staff save time since they can meet with many at once. But the most significant benefits are for the families rather than the staff. Collectively, they can solve problems much quicker than on an individual basis. In addition, longer-term foster families can offer advice and experience to others with new struggles and concerns.

As a foster mother to a toddler brings up her potty-training struggles, a murmur runs through the group. A veteran to the potty-training battles speaks up. Her third child was just as stubborn, so she offers advice. Another cuts in to agree and offer further tactics. A timid father, sitting a little outside the circle, asks a clarifying question. Usually, laughter mingles with advice as the time wears on. The new foster mother begins to realize her struggles are similar to so many parents. She knows the older children of the woman giving advice are good kids.

The social workers listen and observe as families share and open up. It allows them to take in what is not working well. If issues arise with multiple families, CIF learns they need to adjust their approach.

Before communities formed these clusters, parents would hide their issues until they compounded out of control. In the meetings, they realized they were not alone. Some felt they faced impossible odds, but through sharing, they found other parents who were walking through similar issues.

"Staff can share theory, but the most effective learning comes from creating space for families to share [with each other]," Leak, the foster care manager, said.[6]

The cluster meetings reinforced learning. Families learn best through role modeling. They absorb the information better when it can be tangibly seen and heard. It also allows CIF to respect the parents' rights to make their own choices.

"When they talk, we listen," Anny said. "We let them know we are part of the solution but not all."

The social workers cannot show judgment. Instead, they need to remain calm regardless of what is shared, earning trust and gaining a fuller picture of what is happening in homes.

When parents can share openly, child safety improves. It lets the staff members know where their focus should be. The families also hold one another accountable. Another benefit is placement security. If families get too stressed, they give up, but clusters prevent this.

Another benefit of the cluster model is sibling groups. Often it is difficult to find one family who will foster an entire sibling set, but CIF has found placing siblings in the same community or extended family is a good alternative. While they will not grow up in the same home, they live near to one another and attend school together with their foster parents meeting up regularly. The children can maintain relationships with each other while living in a safe family.

I met our first foster family when I visited the village. The couple who took in two children with disabilities also fostered several others. I noticed an incredibly tall young man for a Cambodian, obviously well nourished. He was one of her adopted children, although she never made the distinction between him and her biological children. I got to interview the young man with his mother at his side. The looks exchanged between them told me of a bond deeper than DNA.

The Village Who Gave Away Their Kids

What do you do when two sets of people tell you opposing information about what is best for children?

The boat created ripples across the dark, glassy surface as they navigated through the shallow waters to the villages. Cathleen and the small CIF team were heading there to advocate for family-based care. Her goal was to explain kinship care and foster care.

A week earlier, she'd had a heartbreaking conversation with a pastor who was attending training with Dale.

"Bong Cathleen," he spoke with her across the food placed on the woven mat where they were all sharing a meal, "Brother Dale tells me about the work you are doing for Cambodian families. There is a village not far from here. All of the families have put their children in the church orphanage."

Cathleen looked at him, unsure if he was exaggerating the number of children. Then, probing further, she was shocked to hear that a foreign missionary in the area had convinced the families their children would be much better off in the orphanage.

Soon, she, Anny, and Dale found themselves in a room full of adults eager to learn about family-based care. When they taught the third group of villagers, Anny nudged Cathleen and whispered, "Do you notice how we have not seen a single child over four?"

The silence of the village felt odd to Cathleen. Dogs, chickens, and toddlers were numerous; however, the town lacked school bells and children clad in uniforms walking or biking in groups to and from home. Only the sound of the breeze and local animals stirred the air. It felt unnatural.

All the families wanted to foster children, so they clamored to sign up. After inquiring, two things became clear: these parents missed their children, and they wanted financial support to raise foster children.

Cathleen and Anny poured out their hearts. This model of care was not the best for the community's children. They, the parents, were the best for them. Food and education are essential; however, Cathleen stressed that love and belonging matter more.

The families were conflicted. The foreign missionary had stressed all the opportunities their children would benefit from if they lived in his orphanage, one cut off from the village by water during the wet season. Their children learned English and were cleaner and fatter than ever. What could a generation who had starved and lacked so much do with this new information?

Brokenhearted, the CIF team left the village. There was no way they would be placing foster children here.

How could they begin to dispel the myth that to be a successful pastor or church planter, an orphanage needed to exist as well? Institutionalizing children remains a lingering lousy theology.

Cathleen and Anny wavered between anger and sorrow. All those children were cloistered away from their families and raised by strangers from another culture. Their families missed them dearly, but held a false conviction that this was the will of God.

It smacked of spiritual and cultural abuse as well as control. Cathleen's heart ached at the unnecessary cost. This system was the opposite of God's heart and design. What false gospel preaches the love of God while simultaneously ripping children away from their mothers and fathers?

Family-based care advocates refer to this style of mission work as the "Unholy Trinity." The formula for foreign Christians across Southeast Asia has been that a successful pastor needs a church, a Bible school, and an orphanage.

The Highest Honor

Cambodia is an honor-shame culture. Leaders, government officials, elders in a family, and Buddhist monks are all highly honored and treated as such. Honor is so interwoven into the culture that the Khmer language involves an entirely different vocabulary for kings and monks. One must address a position of honor with the correct phrasing and body stature. There is a proper way to stand and sit around leaders. There is also an appropriate way to greet them with hands pressed together. Not doing so can bring incredible shame and even punishment.

CIF operates within this culture. Working closely with the government involves knowing how and how not to speak to and treat leaders.

In the organization's early days, a government official joined Cathleen and Anny to inspect their foster care and tighten up the MOU. NGOs pay the official for their time and are responsible for providing all meals and transportation.

A particularly pompous official joined that day, along with two young people from the ministry. Anny and Cathleen had never met this man. Not long into the journey, the government official began to rail against them. It was clear he felt the trip was a waste of his time. Anny and Cathleen's eyes met as they sat packed tightly into the car, exchanging wordless pleadings for prayer.

This man had the power to destroy all that CIF had built.

The official sat on his cell phone, raging loudly against CIF. Anny tried to speak kindly and respectfully to him, explaining the programs. A cold, derisive snort was the only response he mustered. Cathleen frantically sent emergency prayer requests over text.

Finally, the SUV halted in front of a stilt house in a humble village. It was their first stop, and the tension in the vehicle almost tumbled out the door when they opened it.

They approached the home of a foster baby with microcephaly, a congenital disability in which a head is smaller than expected. It often results in a smaller brain, and the baby may not develop properly.

The family's traditional wooden home was clean and simple. Soon, the foster mother descended the stairs with the baby in her arms. Though the child had an obvious physical disability, she held her as if she were the most precious treasure in the world. The infant wore a frilly dress. Calm, almost silent, the woman approached the government official, holding the baby gently for him to see.

A miracle unfolded before their eyes; the official melted as he gazed at the baby. All his grandeur and pomp faded, replaced by a tender, fatherly look. He reached out and put his hand softly on the baby. Then, he started to ask the mother questions.

All of a sudden, he was attentive, listening. The love of the mother for her child transformed him.

In awe, he kept asking Anny in disbelief, "This isn't even her child?"

They reiterated to him that she had chosen to foster this baby.

The stop was short. When the group rose to leave, the official placed his hand on the foster mother's arm. Then, he pressed his hands together, holding them to his forehead. A person in Cambodia would know that sign as highly respectful. It is one of the highest signs of honor one Cambodian can give another.

As they met with more foster families, those caring for

children with disabilities, he chose to honor each this way. On the drive home, he raved about the fantastic work that CIF was doing.

He is now an advocate for children with disabilities in Cambodia. He uses his government power to find families for each one who crosses his path. Love broke through that day.

"The government advocates for CIF," Cathleen and Anny shared. "Our experience has been positive. They've wanted to learn from us because CIF has put into practice what they know in theory."

Reintegration with Hannah Won

Hannah Won has accumulated vast experience in reintegrating children from orphanages back into families. But her journey to reintegration work is a long one.

The rate of people who come on short-term mission trips to Cambodia and who return to serve for a more extended period is low. When I spoke with Hannah, we laughed when we realized that this was the path to Cambodia for both of us. I told her, "I led a team of young adults here for six weeks. You know, the annoying pack of foreigners who think they can save the world in a few weeks? That was me."

Our laughter was seasoned with experience and humility as we admitted how naive our past selves were. Hannah had come on a short-term visit as a teenager and continued to return every chance she got. Those brief visits were filled with village life, hosted amongst a high concentration of lepers. Hannah taught English and violin. She cracked up as she said, "Violin! It was such a useful skill."

Because of her close contact living in a local family, she was immersed in the language and culture of Kampong Cham. "Like sleeping on a solid wood frame without a mattress and living with the cockroaches, the things only a seventeen-year-old likes to endure," Hannah described.

Of course, her immersion was much more holistic than sleeping conditions and insects. She loved Cambodia and wanted to leave college and move to the Kingdom of Wonder forever. Her mother convinced her the wiser path was to finish her education and train in something that could benefit the people she served.

Around 2006, amid her studies, she volunteered for a short season at an orphanage in Siem Reap, the seat of the ancient empire of Angkor. Back in America, she used her studies to learn about alternative care policies and reintegration. She was unable to get a full-time job in Cambodia right away, so she worked in California with children in transitional housing. It was a place for rape victims and women who had escaped domestic violence alongside their kids. While it was a good experience, her heart remained in Cambodia. She moved when she was offered a job at the orphanage.

The one she worked at had one of the highest standards for orphanages possible. It was beautiful with fantastic funding and special programs for the children. The caregiver-to-child ratio was about one to six. Many houseparents remained consistent over the years, living with the same small set of children, only rotating out when it was their time off. Some had children of their own who lived with the orphans. "There was good consistency with the caregivers," Hannah shared.

Welcoming oversight, the orphanage was one of the few that was adequately registered. It even requested regular inspections by the government to keep it safe and up to the best standard of care.

Traditional homes were built on extensive grounds with soccer fields, schools, and access to excellent care. The other positive of the orphanage was the strong gatekeeping standards in place. Unlike most orphanages globally, many children in their care were true double orphans: both parents had died. The director carefully vetted the children who were referred. Other organizations had attempted to track down family members but had yet to be successful. Toward the end, some of the standards were relaxed due to funding, and they began to take in kids from single-parent families. It was a model orphanage that had a close relationship with the Cambodian government.

Hannah's role would be the education care coordinator. Working closely with the director, she worked to improve the orphanage. While she had researched reintegration and alternative care options for orphans, she initially felt it would not apply to most of the children in their care. The Khmer and European organizations that funded and oversaw the orphanage also had no intentions of reintegrating kids.

Once settled in her role, the idea failed to subside. She thought she could try reconnecting children to their extended families. Not necessarily to leave orphanage care but to give them community and identity. The minimal international standards for orphanages state it is the minimum practice to put kids back into their families when safe.

The charismatic European leader of the foundation was against it, however. His statement ran along the lines of, "Why would we send these kids back to their poor, dirty families when they can live here?"

After all, why would they have that state-of-the-art orphanage if they were to get rid of all the children? The idea of supporting a whole community with these incredible resources was lost on him.

His Khmer counterpart was even less supportive. It was all about the money, and some status, but mainly the money. By reintegrating children, his income source would dry up.

"On both sides, I was met with resistance," she explained. "It was very stressful; I would not advise doing it that way without buy-in and protection. But I pushed forward with it anyway."

Although the Europeans controlled the funding, they were not on the ground. So, Hannah raised the money for reintegration outside of their jurisdiction. Explaining what deinstitutionalization would look like and providing the evidence that children placed in families thrived in a way that even the best orphanage could not boast, donors came on board with her vision.

"I felt successful in changing many minds with the donor base," she reflected.

She also had the support of many of the Khmer staff on the ground, especially those in leadership. "The lower-level staff," she explained, "did not care either way; they just wanted to get paid. On the other hand, the caregivers were more on board because they had relationships and invested in the children. They desired the best for the children."

The Cambodian director caught the vision after one family visit. A four-year-old boy was allowed to spend time with his single mother. She was a mess. With multiple children from multiple relationships, she abused alcohol and was rather neglectful. Despite her many shortcomings and dire circumstances, the child still wanted to be with her. It was a moment where the director realized how vital family is for kids. He saw how much they need connection, even when their families are imperfect.

Children ran away despite the glowing stamp of approval from the government and the highest quality care. Kids begged to go home, even though their home was much poorer.

The director had grown up in residential care. He lost both of his parents to the Khmer Rouge and understood the longing for family. Despite the backlash from the foundations supporting them, Hannah knew he and other leaders were on board. They wanted what was best for the children.

Little could she foresee just how much that support would be needed. By the end of their project, the European leaders threatened to sue Hannah. In a more extreme response, the Khmer foundation leader said he would poison all of the children and burn down the residences.

He was furious when they had put child-protection policies in place that required him to give notice before he came rather than strutting in unannounced. His aggressive behavior further proved that orphanages exist for those running them much more than for the good of children. Thankfully, nothing serious came of his threats.

In the two years Hannah served at the orphanage, the staff reintegrated all but a few children. Of fifty-four, they could not find a single family member for four of them. These were all children found living on the streets by other organizations. Their initial rescuers had spent resources and time trying to track down their families before placing them in residential care, so it was unsurprising that no one could be traced.

There were a few children who had mild disabilities and whose family homes were unsafe to live in, so in the end, about six children remained at the orphanage and were placed in a tiny group home with a consistent caregiver.

The worst part about institutionalization is the harmful sexual behavior. Hannah explained that regardless of the size of the institution or the quality of care, caregivers cannot have their eyes on that many children all the time. Kids came from abusive situations and sexually abused other children.

ACCI's research states: "Having non-related children of varying ages and both genders, who come from troubled backgrounds and are all living together exacerbates this. Orphanages are often positioned away from community and therefore out of sight. This provides little protection for children as abuse can go unreported and unseen. People naturally think children are safe in orphanages; therefore, they don't scrutinize practices within orphanages. All of these factors in combination place children in residential care at risk of being abused."

"Young kids, older kids, girls, boys, I saw it all," she said. There was no set pattern except that it was rampant.

They got permission and funding to address the issue during her time there. First Step, an organization based in Phnom Penh, did training with their staff and children. Management was supportive, so they could get counseling and help for many children who had been sexually abused or for those acting out harmful behavior.

All their good intentions and all their hard work, however, failed to stem the behavior. Children continued to be victimized.

Despite all her best attempts, a cloud of guilt hangs over the ending. Some of the placements could have gone better. Worse still, in their anger over the reintegration project, most donors immediately pulled their funding. Three of the children in their care were re-institutionalized and placed in one of the worst orphanages in Cambodia at the time. This happened after Hannah had left, but the pain of knowing three children were re-traumatized has stayed with her.

Donors aren't always interested in the transition process or in family-based care, but funding is still needed during the transition. It takes time to place the children in safe families, and during that time, they still need residential care. Other times a transition will fail. Therefore, funding needs a grace period.

Although the process in Siem Reap was less than smooth, Hannah's passion for deinstitutionalization grew. She decided to help other orphanages transition into family-based care. She started the Residential Care Network in Cambodia. Advising different orphanages, she connected with those interested in improving their standards of care and reintegrating children into their communities.

She got to know Cathleen at CIF and Rebecca Nhep with ACCI through her work and connections. By 2015, her work had expanded into Thailand, Myanmar, and Cambodia. She was hired to consult a peer-led initiative in Myanmar. All the programs focused on getting children out of institutions and back into families and communities and helping during the transitional time.

Cultural Abuse

Government authorities were shutting down an orphanage because the living conditions and reports of trauma were extreme. They called upon CIF to help process the youngest children and transition them into families. The orphanage operated for decades with little oversight or accountability, and they later found that the director was an alcoholic and went on regular drunken rampages. Eventually, a foreign journalist exposed the truth behind her bright, muraled walls.

CIF brought all the babies and toddlers into the office to sort out paperwork and decide which families would be suitable for placement. Cathleen, Anny, and the small staff at the time juggled caring for the children while working through logistics. All of them were little girls dressed in cute and frilly outfits. However, when the tots needed diaper changes, it was a shocking revelation that half the children were boys. Even some of the older children turned out to be males dressed as females.

Investigation showed the orphanage director preferred girls. Photos and sob stories of little girls raised more money from foreign donors. So, the staff dressed them all as girls. Some former staff members stated they did this so the children would receive better care. But the director treated the girls much better, and the staff worried about the boys, so they hid them.

The older children in the orphanage gave statements of brutal beatings, especially when the director was drunk.

One child, in particular, was the strangest case of them all.

At about six years old, he spoke baby talk in English and acted like a toddler. This is his story:

Jacob was confused. Who were all these new people?

One day, people in uniforms came. They rounded up the staff and children. He was in the orphanage when it happened. He usually lived in the house on the property. Momma Judy told him he was special. But he went to the orphanage during the day. However, he did not like the other children because they were different. They were Cambodian. He knew that from how Momma Judy talked about Cambodia, it was better to be like her than to be Cambodian.

He got better food and his own room. Although Momma Judy rarely talked to him, the staff pampered him. From his earliest memories, the faces of his birth parents faded. When he began to form and speak words, she would slap him.

"No Khmer! You speak English!"

Momma Judy never said so, but he knew she preferred the tiny children. The adorable ones. So, Jacob tried to keep himself from growing.

Curling himself into a tiny ball, he made statements like, "I am small. Jacob is small."

After the people took him away, they placed him in a family. They had children who all looked different. The family spoke English, but they also spoke Khmer. He despised hearing Khmer. He would scream and wail. He knew it was bad.

Yet as the days went by, he began to see that the family liked to speak both languages. No one ever got punished for it. He waited for a swift smack from the parents or a drunken rage, but nothing like that ever happened.

They sat at a big table as a family, eating rice and curry. They laughed together. Sometimes the kids argued but always found a way to be friends again. He wanted friends.

Jacob soaked in all of it. He was not special here. He was just one of them. He did not know how to feel about that.

Sometimes, he would grow angry and cry until his lungs gave out. He never got in trouble, though. The lady would come to hold him and speak Khmer softly to him. If he pushed back, she'd talk to him in English. In either language, they were kind words.

She would tell him all about family. How one day they would find the perfect mother and father for him. But he never asked about Momma Judy. He was afraid to ask. She could be scary. The longer he was away, the more he wanted to stay away.

One week, she explained that he would stay part-time with another family. They were very kind too. He met them when they came to dinner sometimes. The Cambodian lady had older children, and Jacob liked the big boy. He was funny and played games.

Jacob also realized he did not need to be small around them. They liked him the size that he was. They encouraged him to eat and grow.

One day, the foreign lady took Jacob into a new home where the Cambodian lady and her son lived. Hesitant at first, he saw there were no small kids there. Good, he could be special.

They ate, sitting on mats on the floor. Piles of rice with fish soup and cooked vegetables were the main meals. Or grilled pork with a fried egg on top. They mostly spoke Khmer. He understood it well now. Yet sometimes hearing it still made him rage. That's when the big boy would explain things in English to him. But, again, he never got in trouble in this home. He had not been slapped or screamed at in months. So, while he still feared it, his fear grew less.

Sometimes he dreamed that Momma Judy found him. She would drag him back to his room and lock him there. In his dream, he had forgotten English. He could only speak Khmer. Momma Judy would scream in his face. She would call him scum for speaking that language.

"Have I not taught you anything!" her face contorted as she reached out to pinch him.

He woke up crying. The kind Cambodian lady would sit next to him, the faint light from the hallways spilling into his room. She would pray for him softly until his heart stopped racing and he drifted back to sleep.

"Momma Judy cannot find you," she promised him. Yet for days after he dreamed of Momma Judy, he feared speaking Khmer.

Finally, the lady explained they had a forever family for him. He would have a mother and father to call his own. He trembled as they drove into the village.

Would they like him? Would they want him to be small or be a girl?

Pulling up to a cleanly swept lawn with chickens strutting about, a couple and their daughter stood in their best clothes with another woman who had paperwork. They were his family.

Before he could process any more internal fears, his mother embraced him. She smelled good, like lemongrass. Kneeling on the ground with her cheek pressed against his head, he felt her warm tears. Then, shyly, the girl approached.

She gave him an awkward greeting that he returned with equal awkwardness. Then, handing him a teddy bear, she looked at her feet and said, "I picked this one just for you."

Finally, he looked at the man who was his father. Those eyes reflected such warmth. He was a skinny man with a wide smile. He learned they were teachers. He had never been to school when he lived with Momma Judy.

Soon the days turned into months. Jacob liked his sister. She was musical and sang all the time. His mother made the best food with just the right spice. But his father, he adored his father.

Like a shadow, he followed every move the quiet man made. He was a gentle, soft-spoken man who knew so many wondrous things. He would show Jacob books, teach him how to ride a bicycle, and walk with them to school daily, telling him all sorts of information along the way.

Years later, Jacob heard the voice of the foreign lady with all the kids. He turned around to look at her, and his old enemy fear rose. His throat closed. She had been one of the people who took him away from Momma Judy. Was she here to take him away from his family?

She spoke to him in English, and he froze. Heart pounding, he understood her but did not know if it was safe to answer. Maybe she would think he was bad and not take him if he did not speak English?

Father and Mother were there, but they seemed happy and at peace. Jacob slid beside his father, clutching his arm as if life depended on it. He could never leave Father!

Then the foreign lady's eyes softened, and she addressed him in Khmer. She asked him how he liked his family. Still afraid to answer, tears choked him as he responded feebly, "Please don't take me back to Phnom Penh! Please don't take me from my family!"

Realization dawned on her face. Very gently, she responded, "Of course, I won't take you from your family. You like them very much, don't you? I am only here to see that you are happy. Are you happy?"

He believed her. Looking at his father's face, he saw his father trusted her.

The floodgate opened, and words of joy poured out. He told her about his school, the three-legged dog down the street, and his new clothes, exhausting every topic his young mind could conjure. She mostly listened and smiled.

By the end of the day, he liked the lady. After she left, he climbed onto the seat next to his father and rested his head on the man's side. This was his home. He never had to leave.

//

The investigators discovered that the orphanage director had set Jacob aside as a child for herself. Most of the time, he lived in her private home, but she used the orphanage as a day care. He isolated himself from the other children. It was clear he had significant trauma. The director taught him that being Cambodian was wrong and that he would be punished for speaking his native language. He was treated superior to the other children, yet not like their child; he was not sent to school and was so underdeveloped in his speech that it appeared he lacked interaction.

Jacob's case was so extreme the government was adamant they should place him in a Cambodian family, and his whereabouts and identity were kept secret so that the woman could not track him down.

At the end of Cathleen's first visit to check on Jacob in his family, the boy earnestly looked into Cathleen's face and asked her to promise never to take him to Phnom Penh. He saw the capital city as an evil place where he endured a lot in his early years at the orphanage.

Cathleen explained that she was thrilled to see him seek shelter behind his father. It is a natural sign that a child has bonded to a caregiver when they look to them for safety.

"He's big now, and he's doing well. He struggles a bit in school, but that's natural with his delays in development due to neglect and language confusion."

Cathleen referred to the orphanage director, who claimed him as her child and demanded they return him to her. "If you love a kid and intend to spend your life with them, you speak to them, play with them, and send them to school. And you do not put down their culture. It's their identity."

Investigators found little about Jacob before his orphanage years, so CIF staff guessed his age. Unfortunately, there was no documentation of him at the orphanage. What little documents existed of the children were handwritten notes ripped from a school notebook. They only knew his year of birth.

"We have no idea where he came from or who his family is."

Cathleen asked a doctor to look at the teeth of one of the boys to guess his age based on his dental development.

The orphanage had not followed laws or protocols, let alone common sense or professionalism.

"It is common for orphanages to destroy traces of these kids and their lives. As a result, even after 2010, many orphanages still have no biofields or documentation of the children in their care."

While Momma Judy's orphanage was secular, a missionary orphanage director took children regularly without paperwork or proper government referral. "I do it for the Lord," she declared to Cathleen, "so I don't need documentation."

Sadly, she is one of half a dozen people running orphanages or children's homes who I've heard say the same thing. "God told me" or "I do it for the Lord" is a common excuse for bypassing laws, disrespecting a culture, and not heeding what decades of research shows are best practices for children.

The Golden Rule

"Do unto others as you would want them to do unto you."

While CIF values its donors, one of the guiding principles was to give their families the most ordinary lives possible. One way to do this was to limit donor exposure. Although it's wonderful when people can experience the programs up close, that exposure cannot come at a cost to the families. Families and children are not secondary work, they are the most vital. Cathleen and Anny never wanted families to feel like they were on display or exploited.

They worked hard to lump all visitors into one group and limit visits with families.

When Anny took donors out to the villages to see the projects, she would let them scan the field of children playing, and then ask, "Can you spot the foster children in the group?"

The donors never could. Her response was, "Good. Because all children should look and act the same. They should be happy, loved, and have someone to care for them. They should never be treated differently." Especially not as victims or charity cases.

It was a value Cathleen brought from the orphanage days when she felt like the children in her care were on display, like zoo animals, to evoke pity or to please the visitor rather than being given a normal childhood.

This mentality fed into communication about CIF's families. Consent is required whenever a staff member wants to take a photo or tell a family's story, including tracking their progress. The family can refuse exposure and still receive the same care and support from the team. Even Cathleen and Anny are required to ask permission.

During the rare visits allowed, CIF banned donors from taking photos.

It came down to asking the fair question, "Would you want foreigners showing up at your home and taking photos of your life without your permission? Or come to your child's school or day care, play with the children, and take pictures without background checks or consent?"

When one woman complained about these rules, Cathleen asked, "Did you teach your children about 'stranger danger' while they were growing up?"

"Yes, of course," the woman responded.

"Well, when you go out to this village, YOU are the stranger. So why do you think you should have full access to these children?"

Her jaw dropped. Blushing, she responded, "I never thought about it from that perspective."

The same respect and dignity are owed to the children and families in CIF's care. Their socioeconomic status does not negate their human rights.

//

Perspective at the root level is a core value of CIF.

A donor emailed Cathleen a proposal to dig ten wells, so when Anny returned to the village to do assessments of recent foster families, she met with the village chief and commune leaders. With heads bent together on a balmy afternoon, the leaders identified those most needing clean water access. Per Khmer custom, the village chief maintained authority to lead and ascertained where the wells should go.

"One well should go in at the school," the chief said as he

pointed out the merits of benefiting all the school children. "We'll have fewer children home sick with diarrhea and dehydration."

Of the nine families chosen, most were not in CIF's program. Anny left the meeting content that the project would positively impact the whole village by raising the poorest families' living standards and improving the school children's hygiene standards.

Cathleen shared, "Later, we had water filters donated, so we went to the community to bring clean water to every home. Initially, the village chief thought we wanted something in return because we provided for everyone in need. But all we wanted was to provide training at the school, so the kids would know how to use the water filters in their homes. We wanted to love everyone. That is the Gospel!"

Wherever CIF has families under its umbrella, training will be accessible to everyone in the community, including "Good Touch/Bad Touch," sanitation, nutrition, positive parenting, and more. While families in CIF's programs are required to attend, all parents in the village are welcome to join. A healthy, informed community benefits everyone around them.

Another value Cathleen and Anny agreed on after a lengthy discussion was credit. After seeing spray-painted NGO and church logos across the country on all things donated, they wrestled. "I think there's a difference between being accountable for the wise use of donor money versus putting your stamp and name on everything," Cathleen said to Anny.

When Anny faltered a little with indecision on this, they both went to the Bible to see what Scripture says about giving. She realized it was strange that so many Christians expected a plaque or photo. The desire for credit and the habit of putting up plaques contributes to the issue of poor development work from the church. These practices can create inferiority, dependency, and favoritism.

If someone were to enter communities where CIF operates, other than the gate at the local office, they would not find the logo on anything. In fact, they would have absolutely no idea who in the community were beneficiaries of any projects, nor which children were in foster families.

//

Children in Families did their best to maximize the impact of their budget. After meeting with the board of directors a few years ago, the leaders applied for a UNICEF grant and submitted their care budget.

UNICEF promptly responded, "Can you please check over your numbers? These seem too low."

They thought CIF had made a mistake on its budget sheet when they saw it only cost CIF $170,000 for hundreds of children in the programs. UNICEF thought a few zeroes were missing from the ends of numbers.

A decade earlier, when Cambodia's cost of living was much lower, it took about two million dollars a year to care for the one hundred-plus children in the Joneses' orphanage. Children in Families was able to provide social work and services to more than double that many children for significantly less money.

While donor transparency is vital, many grants and large donors require so much paperwork and red tape that it almost seems not worth it. In addition, most large donors do not want to fund program maintenance; they want to give to something new. Yet what CIF was doing was fruitful. A small amount of money was making an enormous impact.

//

Once CIF started functioning well and local staff took on more responsibility, Cathleen realized that she had to address advocacy. Like Rebecca, she realized she needed to bring people along with the vision of family preservation. If CIF could not get children out of orphanages, they could try to prevent kids from flowing into orphanages.

"How will they know better if we don't tell them?" she thought.

She started meeting with anyone willing to hear about family-based care, including individuals, short-term visiting teams, donors, churches, pastors, people wanting to adopt, board members of orphanages, prominent NGOs, Peace Corps, ambassadors, and embassy staff. In addition, Cathleen and Sarah Chhin met with foreign ambassadors looking at reopening international adoption.

Advocacy took place through conversations over coffee as well as large-scale training. With mixed audiences waiting in rapt attention, she began educating others about her journey to create CIF and the Cambodian government's process of shifting policies and practices to care for children's best interests. For example, many people were unaware of child protection laws. They also did not realize that family-based care already existed in the nation.

At a training with Peace Corps volunteers, a young man raised his hand. "If I can't serve in an orphanage, where do I help? You're saying that I should not volunteer to teach English in the orphanage, what should I do then?"

This is a valid question.

"You want to help kids, right?" Cathleen questioned and he nodded in affirmation, so she continued, "I have just shown you how nine in ten children in orphanages aren't even orphans. Do you want to reward parents who give up their kids and punish the poor mom who wants to keep her family together? She doesn't get the same opportunities for her children because it's only for the orphan or the orphanage. Consider opening up a free English class for anybody's kids. Make sure you get the word out to poor and vulnerable families that it is a free English class. Reward the struggling parents and help their kids."

//

A crucial sphere of society that needed to be addressed was large NGOs and Christian funding organizations pouring millions of dollars into orphanages annually. Through meetings, she helped them shift their focus to the children's best interests. She encouraged funding for family-based care and preservation.

Her training involved a series of questions.

"Who here have children? Grandchildren? Nieces and nephews?"

Hands went up.

"What would happen to your kids if you passed away? What if you did not have money to care for them?"

"What if you were facing divorce? Crisis?"

"Who would you go to for help?"

The responses always began with "Family. Friends. Church."

Not once did anyone suggest an orphanage as their option. Cathleen concluded, "If you would not choose an orphanage for a child you loved, why would you choose it for someone else's children?"

//

Before CIF even began, the government shut down avenues for foreign adoption due to the corruption involved. In the big picture, international adoption is a business. It became about money, not helping children. Americans and other Westerners looked to developing nations to adopt because it appeared to be a less stringent process. Which should have been a red flag rather than encouragement.

Adopting from foster care in their own countries also came with the risk of children being taken away.

On a regular basis, foreigners have come to CIF, wanting to foster or adopt. But Cathleen and Anny decided that CIF had to be a Khmer-only program. The priority is supporting Cambodian families.

Despite it being illegal, many orphanages and NGOs are adopting children out to international families. Adopting children to foreigners bypasses the laws of a nation and the rights of the local families and the child. International and Cambodian law dictates that all local resources and family of origin need to be exhausted and thoroughly investigated first before a child is internationally adopted. To bypass those laws not only deprives children of their family, community, and culture, it also opens the door to unscrupulous practices by adoption agencies.

In fact, the amount of money poured into those adoptions could be used to support disabled children and their families within their country's context. There are children with great needs; however, pouring money into local solutions is more cost-effective and has greater social reach.

There is no reason a foreign family should be taking Khmer children. Linguistically and culturally, it's better for children to grow up in their country of origin.

The rare exception to international adoption is a child with a massive medical need who will not thrive or survive if left in their home country. Recently, Cathleen and Sarah Chhin evaluated the conditions for children in Cambodia and concluded that each year about fifteen children exhaust all local resources and meet the requirements for international adoption, meaning there is no Khmer family available with the medical training and ability to meet the demands of their illnesses or disabilities.

//

After a session teaching a short-term team about family preservation, Cathleen poured herself into bed, exhausted. Despite her passion, getting out of bed each morning became more

difficult. More than a decade of late nights up with sick children, advocating, pushing for better laws, and championing
Cambodians compounded into pain and weariness.

Children in Families had grown from a tiny operation
to a medium-sized NGO, positively impacting hundreds of
children. Cathleen had already stepped down from most of
her responsibilities when her medical test results came back.
Diagnosis: cancer.

CIF was always meant to be locally run, but this was not
the exit she had planned. Yet she had laid a very solid foundation of family-based care that could be built upon, expanded,
and improved as Cambodia developed and the needs of the
people changed. While her future was uncertain as chemo-
therapy ran through tubes and into her body, she had peace
about the future of CIF.

An interim director, Jesse, stepped in to help until a long-
term solution could be found, while Anny maintained her role
as the Cambodian national director.

Meanwhile, the same determined drive that led Cathleen
to pioneer CIF was poured into battling her disease.

In late 2016, Jesse made way for a young Cambodian leader,
Lynny. After seven years in leadership, Lynny made way for
CIF's current executive director, Sam Ol. The goal remains
excellence at every level of caring for families.

A Westernized Khmer Kid

I purposely interviewed Atith for the book because he has been the poster boy for foreign Christians in Cambodia to applaud orphanages. I also interviewed him because I had heard mostly good things about Richard and Lori, the orphanage directors.

Those who are pro-orphanage would point to Atith and say, "If this is what we get from Christian orphanages, then how can they be bad?"

As I spoke with Atith, however, I got a different impression. Atith is a born leader with brains and cunning. He is a survivor. I think no matter what life had thrown at him, he would have found a way. But I wanted him to be blatantly honest with me and I am grateful he was.

"My orphanage experience was positive," he told me. "It helped preserve me. I became a Christian. I received an education. It was a haven for my sisters and me. I met some of my best friends, whom I consider family now.

"Given the time and the situation [in Cambodia], I feel like the orphanage is what I needed. But that was about twenty years ago. Now, I would lean into more of a family-based care model."

On our first meeting, he was excited to find out I worked for CIF. He and his wife wanted to foster and adopt more children. He admitted that abandoned and orphaned children need a healthy family and home. However, there are things that large groups of children cannot get, even in a smaller children's home model like Richard and Lori's.

In later years, the directors debriefed with Atith and the others, wanting their thoughts and opinions. Many of them gave feedback that they had lost their Khmer identity. While they believed the orphanage directors did the best with the knowledge they had, they still regretted the loss of their cultural ties.

//

Atith's eyes shot open. Sweat beaded on his face, and the images began to fade as he became more fully awake. In his dream, he was squatting in a rubble-filled villa, hunting small animals with a slingshot, dodging through dense trees, and trying to remain elusive on the outskirts of the village. He always woke up just before his uncle caught him to drag him out of hiding.

But he was not there anymore. That was a past life far from the tidy bedroom with other boys sound asleep around him, fans humming in a futile attempt to stave off the city heat.

Atith had lived in the orphanage for about six months. Although only thirteen, he felt a hundred years older. His life had consisted of surviving in the village and surviving on the streets of Phnom Penh with a few good moments mingled in between.

Sometimes he dreamed of his life in the province. Sometimes even darker memories of life in the street gangs of Phnom Penh surfaced. It was a short-lived experience but marked by fear and dread. God, Atith believed, had pulled him out of the street gangs just in time to escape drug addiction or a severe beating.

On his sister's birthday in the orphanage that year, she stared into the lit candles and dissolved into inconsolable tears. Her only wish was for her sister and brother to be with her. Even though they lived in the same city, Atith had not seen his sister, who was tucked away in the orphanage, for several years. Though she was surrounded by other children, they did not feel like family to her. The orphanage directors had promised to track down her siblings and try to bring them to her. So, because of his sister's pleas, in 1999, Atith's life took a sharp turn for which he is grateful. He moved into the orphanage.

Situated in the north of Phnom Penh, the American couple Richard and Lori had taken over from previous directors. In a large, old villa, they attempted to make a family out of the thirty-some children they inherited. Previously, they had split up sibling groups and would only take one child from a family in order to alleviate the financial burden on their family. But realizing it was harder on kids to separate them from their siblings, Richard and Lori attempted to track down sibling groups and bring them all in. They believed in equal opportunities for all children in a family, not merely one.

In the early morning hours, with his sisters sound asleep in another room filled with girls, Atith lay back on his pillow and allowed himself to remember. To remember what life was like with parents and a home.

//

He was a tiny child living the village life. His father was a three-star general, having spent his younger years fighting the Khmer Rouge in the war. Atith never knew that strong, brave young man. His earliest memories were of an old man riddled with shrapnel and war injuries. After achieving success and money, his father left his first wife for Atith's young mother. Atith is the firstborn of their three children.

At the time, the community looked down on divorce and second wives. So, despite living near many family members, they were pariahs.

His father was a big shot with a substantial new home contracted for them, so Atith skipped out on the actual school time. Barely in elementary school, he already had the attitude that his father would bail him out of anything.

However, the man he called Father was older, reserved, and distant. Primarily memories of a sick man linger, a sick man who told the teachers to fail his son at school to teach him a lesson.

Atith grew up close to an uncle who took him fishing and had conversations with the small boy, who had an overinflated self-importance. However, his uncle was one of the few who made Atith feel like he was merely appreciated for being himself rather than the outcast son of scandal or the wealthy general's kid.

Due to their financial and social status, their home was bursting with friends. Despite rejection from family and the fact that his cousins and relatives were considerably older, friends were in the home constantly, taking advantage of the overflowing pantry. His memories of his mother centered around the kitchen, entertaining and caring for his younger sisters.

Atith remembers running wild with the village boys. He was popular despite the extended family's ire toward him. It was a carefree time.

Atith's world quickly crashed down. While their home was still under construction, his father succumbed to his litany of illnesses and injuries. After several visits to Vietnam for surgeries, they were told the doctors could do nothing more. Shrapnel riddled his spine and body. Atith recalled memories of the funeral pyre as flames consumed the body while Buddhist monks chanted mournfully. The young boy stood in a daze near his little sisters, not realizing life would soon strip him of all that was familiar.

His mother's cultural state of shame as the mistress and second wife left her incredibly vulnerable. Powerless, the relatives stole the inheritance and land, selling it off and leaving the widow and her three children without a stick to share. When his loving uncle passed away shortly after, Atith fell off his throne faster than he could process.

Atith had not realized how much his father had shielded them from the abuse of their aunties and uncles.

Cast out, Atith's mother fled with his youngest sister. His aunt was supposed to care for him, but she never did. Abuse from uncles and cousins kept him far from their homes. He only returned from time to time for food. He lived on the streets for two years. Each time he got desperate and went back, his extended family used him as a servant, forcing him to get up at 3:00 a.m. to help with their business.

He made the fire and deboned fish for their curry and porridge. He no longer attended school, and after years of slacking off, no one felt the need to track him down and force him to go.

In his time of running away, he squatted in their abandoned, half-built villa on the edge of the river and a nearby forest, away from the abuse.

Most of his old friends shunned him as he was no longer useful to them. However, a few middle-class boys who needed diversion occasionally met with him. They brought him food, and in exchange, he took them hunting.

"It wasn't a real friendship," Atith reflected. "They were just looking for something to do."

Just as he drifted off to sleep again, a pillow smashed into his face. Laughter followed as the boys in his orphanage room rudely awoke him. It was morning, and he was late to get up.

It was chore time, followed by breakfast. Thirty-odd children, along with the Khmer caretakers and Richard and Lori's family, filed into the dining room to eat after they cleaned up the grounds and the building.

"We had a set schedule but were treated like family," Atith shared. "There were always extra people staying with us. We lived in a ten-bedroom mansion, but it was old. There were always plumbing issues, and the power was frequently cut off."

After eating, they piled into vans as drivers took them to their respective schools. Atith could no longer sluff off his work. Being treated like one of the family meant he had to work hard. He was so far behind in his education that they changed his age to a few years younger so he could attend the proper classes. He got to pick his birthday, not knowing his real one.

Pulling at the starched collar of his white uniform shirt, he stared out the van window. Sometimes he missed the freedom of squatting in a half-built villa, playing in nature. Yet he liked life in the orphanage. Although school could be tedious, he was a decent student when he tried. And he liked knowing he'd eat three times a day, have a place to sleep, and, most of all, have his sisters with him.

//

Atith remembered living on his own in the village until his mother's sister found him and brought him to her house in Phnom Penh. Soon, he was tracked down by the orphanage and living there alongside his sister.

Years earlier, when the orphanage took in Atith's sister, his auntie, who worked at the orphanage, had lied that she was a true orphan. She said the same when they took in Atith. The kids did not know their mother was alive until years later when she showed up at the orphanage gate to visit her children.

However, Atith grew accustomed to life in the orphanage. The leaders attempted to get him caught up academically and forced him to study practically day and night.

Public education in Cambodia was poor, and the teachers required bribes for good grades. So, Richard and Lori pulled all the kids from public school and began homeschooling them. They also banned the Khmer children from speaking

Khmer to get them to think, eat, and sleep in English for their Western homeschooling curriculum.

The program expanded to become a school. There was a mix of Khmer orphanage kids and missionary children. Each year the school added on another grade until they offered all grades.

While lauding Richard and Lori, Atith feels there were weaknesses in the setup of both the orphanage and the school. "I feel they pushed Western culture on us. We had to speak English in the children's home. They molded us to become American. Later, we realized we were bicultural."

It was and is difficult for these Khmer kids to fit into the world of Cambodia.

"The vision was that we would all go to school in America. In some ways, it was a positive," Atith explained. Richard and Lori thought highly of the kids and knew they were capable of more than what the Cambodian education system could give them. However, their choices damaged the children's Khmer identity and made them misfits in their own nation. Most young men who grew up in the orphanage married foreign women because they fit better with French, British, and American wives than Cambodian ones.

True to their vision, Atith moved to the United States in 2007 to finish high school in an exchange family. It was Richard and Lori's vision for each of the kids in the home to get an American-level education and use their skills for both the church and to return to Cambodia and help their nation. "Their goal was to raise leaders for Cambodia," Atith explained.

They wanted to provide good care for the small group of children they believed God had given them and to close the orphanage once they were all successfully living on their own in adulthood. The Atith of America was a far cry from the fight-fixing street kid of his early years. He was no longer the stuck-up, school-skipping little boy who looked to his wealthy father to get him out of trouble. His encounter with loving people in the orphanage and having a haven to grow led him to God. He truly was changed as he experienced Christians who lived out their faith consistently.

After high school, he attended Master's University in California, studying biblical languages.

"I loved university; it was a dream come true." His home-school Latin studies paid off as he delved into dead languages, learning to translate and read ancient texts. He worked hard, pored over his studies, and made a multitude of good friends. Atith draws people to himself; he's a born leader. Perhaps some of his biological father's leadership DNA was written within him, even though he hardly knew his father. And living in a college community with many young men and women was natural for an orphanage kid.

//

Before he had flown out to America, his biological mother had seen him off at the airport. In his final year at university, Atith tried to maintain a relationship with her, using Skype to communicate. In the end, however, her constant calls at all hours and her usual plea for finances infuriated him. It disrupted his learning and was difficult when he had little money of his own.

She had abandoned him as a child, and now as his life seemed to be in its best phase, he felt used and manipulated. She consistently ignored his requests to call only during certain hours and not to talk about money.

Eventually, he lost his temper with her. He had every right to feel angry. His mother had not been good to him but cutting her off did not make him feel better about it. Not speaking to her might have been a healthy boundary; however, the hole where his parents should have dwelt lingered.

He felt like Richard and Lori were more parents to him

than his Cambodian family. But despite the broken relationship with his mother, Atith graduated and returned to Cambodia to serve his nation. Life was not so simple, however. There were gaps in his maturity, and he wrestled with finding his place back in Cambodia.

"We had a lot handed to us," he explained. "They paid for all of our needs. I never had money on hand except for a little pocket money. Many of us struggle with budgeting because we did not learn to do it."

He continued, "We grew up weak in Khmer because we had to do everything in English [at the orphanage and school]. It's just different learning things with thirty-five other kids versus in a family. People treated us like foreigners, not like local kids."

He explained that he was mainly with other institutionalized children or foreign missionary kids during his formative years.

"Thankfully, we did not have many foreigners coming and going from our orphanages; however, it still impacted us. A negative point of view is that my 'siblings' [the kids at the orphanage] feel excluded and do not fit in either culture."

Atith reiterated that many Khmer orphanage kids married people from Western nations. While there is nothing wrong with cross-cultural marriage, the orphanage kids relate more to outsiders than to their fellow Cambodians, which speaks volumes about the cultural identity and values that were instilled in them by the orphanage directors.

Atith began to work in a local church but attended an expat church alone. After a while, friendships with the expat and missions community became difficult. Atith felt constantly abandoned as people in his community came and went often. Due to his translation skills and education, he also felt many foreigners wanted to take advantage of him, poaching him for their work and projects rather than just being his friend or fellow Christian.

He said most of the people he considers siblings, those from the orphanage, did want to return to Cambodia and invest in their nation. They have influential positions with good jobs; many lead in NGOs, working at high levels.

But just like Taevy, who grew up in Dale and Cathleen's orphanage and returned to work in an orphanage because life outside the institution felt daunting and foreign, Atith and the others almost need to be part of foreign NGOs and institutions to find their place in their nation.

//

After working in Phnom Penh for a while, Atith met his wife when they both were teaching a course at a Bible college. They married and started a family. Having a family and a daughter changed Atith in profound ways. God had already challenged him to forgive his mother; however, life as a husband and father opened him up to pursuing a better relationship with his mom.

"It took a long time to forgive her completely," he admitted, yet he felt God gave him the ability. With a stepfather and new siblings in the picture, their relationship is still tricky to navigate. But his mother visits her granddaughter, bringing eggs from her chickens when she stops for a visit.

Having his own child, too, has shifted his ideas of who should raise someone's child. The idea of putting his daughter in an orphanage versus having a good friend or family member raise her if she were orphaned caused his mindset to shift. He wouldn't want his wife to lose his daughter if he were to die. He would prefer a loving community to come around her with help and support.

"There are more Christians in Cambodia now. There were no churches to care for communities when I was on the street. It [the orphanage] was God's grace in preserving us. Now there is not a need for more orphanages," Atith continued to explain.

Despite the positive impact of Richard and Lori, I still pondered the moral implications of their choices. Was it right to take in a group of Khmer children and purposely raise them all to study the Bible and require them to get American educations to "help" Cambodia? While their goals seemed to work out well for most, the kids had no say in the futures being built for them.

I wondered how Americans would feel if a group of Nigerian Muslims, Indian Hindus, or even Cambodian Buddhists came into their community, taking in poor and vulnerable children and sending them to their religious schools, forcing them never to speak English.

And although Atith's experience in the orphanage leaned more positively, many years later, it was revealed that several of the children experienced sexual abuse in the home. It mainly was child-on-child abuse, a by-product of housing many children together who had experienced trauma and abuse.

Richard and Lori's orphanage model was small and one of the better examples, yet it was still riddled with flaws and robbed over thirty children of their cultural identities and place in their community.

Family of Origin
as First Priority

Following Menghong, the kinship care manager's motorbike, on my own *moto*, we wove our way through Phnom Penh to visit a family. After Menghong and I parked near an open sewage ditch, we found ourselves in a crowded sliver of a building parceled off to countless families, each with a small dark room and a single window. Here I met two sisters who lived with their grandparents. The girls had different fathers; one was a foreigner who returned to his home country and was not involved in her life. The other was a local man who disappeared before his daughter was born. While the girls were still young, their mother tragically died.

Sitting on plastic chairs outside their family home in the narrow walkway between buildings, I could see why the grandparents felt their only option was an orphanage. Despite a deep love for the girls and sorrow over the loss of their daughter, they had a meager dwelling space. The grandparents were older and ran a small drink cart in the city, earning most of their money from selling snacks or cell phone credit.

They had no financial margin to take on the costs of feeding and educating two young girls.

Brokenhearted, they set up a meeting with a nearby orphanage to place their granddaughters. It felt like they were giving up their world after losing their daughter. Thankfully, the meeting never took place.

At their local church, a friend told them about CIF. Hope

glimmered, and they contacted Menghong. This is the type of family situation CIF loves to support. The grandparents were healthy, kind, and striving to scratch out a living. They loved their granddaughters but they were poor. They only needed a little support to keep the girls.

Delighted to stay with their grandparents, the sisters thrived in the years since their mother's death. So close in age, they are best friends, giggling and sharing homework. Their grandfather picks them up from school daily on his motorbike while their grandmother watches the drink cart for customers. While small and dark, their home is clean and near the business, so the grandparents are always close.

As I spoke with the grandmother about their struggles, the girls returned from school. Then, without compulsion, they clustered around her, arms draped over her shoulders, leaning into her with the ease and comfort of natural attachment.

I did not know the state of the orphanage that almost became their home. However, I did see that the girls have a bond with each other and with their grandparents that no institution can manufacture. Despite the trauma of loss, both grandparents and girls found healing in one another.

//

Before a child is considered for foster care, CIF does extensive research to find a child's relatives and place the child with family members instead. Other times, CIF supports a family so that they are never separated to begin with. Originally known as kinship care, this effort is now known as Family of Origin as First Priority (FOR-1).

Menghong led the project from 2017 to early 2023. He helped staff with case management, conducts supervision, leads case meetings, and oversees both staff and family training.

The journey to CIF began for him as a child and linked directly to his faith. From a young age, God showed him that he has a strong mind; therefore, he can use it to help people. He likes to use his skills and education to promote family and help others in Cambodia. He said, "I am not perfect, but the love of God has helped me love people better."

Many family stories are memorable to him, so he shared a few.

Widowed and sick with HIV, Bopha had eight children. Because Bopha was so ill and caring for the family alone, her oldest daughter, Maly, dropped out of school to work in a garment factory and support the family. It broke Bopha's heart, yet they had little choice. Either Maly worked, or the entire family would go hungry, and none of the children would get an education.

At fifteen, Maly's life stretched before her as endless days of climbing into the back of a large dump truck, packed in, standing shoulder to shoulder with as many garment workers as possible. Driving through bumpy roads, choking on dust, she traveled an hour each way to spend at least twelve hours stitching details into clothes, only to get up and do it again the next day with the only respite being a few weeks of holiday a year.

A local government leader intervened and asked Menghong to monitor the situation. As he sat across from Bopha, who was frail and thin with lines of worry that aged her beyond her years, Menghong asked carefully worded questions about their life that would give him a better understanding without shaming the woman.

Then he asked directly, "If we can help, do you want your daughter to return to school?"

She responded, "Yes. I want Maly to have more opportunities. I want her to finish her education."

Although medication for HIV is free in Cambodia, many people do not always have the time or ability to pick it up from the hospitals in the city. With so many children, Bopha rarely gets a chance to do basic things to care for herself, yet she knows that not taking the medication will ultimately leave her children orphaned.

Maly cried tears of joy the day she returned to school, along with her younger siblings. CIF's intervention allowed her to be a kid again. As well as consistent access to medical care and enough food to eat, her days became filled with studies and fun with friends rather than exhausting labor.

CIF's staff works hard knowing hundreds of children each year benefit from the love of a family because the Kinship Care program walks alongside those at risk of separation, helping them stay together and grow stronger.

Menghong explained, "The work of CIF is to promote child protection, child rights, and participation. We take a holistic approach."

This holistic approach has to consider a list of factors and see each family as unique. It takes partnerships from the community, active participation and willingness from the families, and collaboration across programs within CIF to improve the lives of children, families, and communities. The team recognizes that struggles within family units are rarely due to one facet of life. CIF's other programs frequently overlap since there can be additional factors that make a family vulnerable to separation.

//

Families often have other layers of problems, like alcohol and gambling. Alcohol and gambling can get out of control, spiraling into extreme debt and abuse. In those cases, the children may be removed and placed into emergency care or with relatives until the parents can show they are getting help and are stable enough to get their children back. This involves collaboration with organizations equipped to deal with specific struggles or problems like alcoholism or drug abuse.

//

Another family lived in the city's poorest region, near an old garbage dump where people scavenge for things to recycle. They had only one child at home, but because of the mother's chronic illness, they became indebted. Tuberculosis caused her to cough until she nearly passed out. Her body was weak, and she could no longer do the backbreaking labor of walking the city streets to collect recycling every day. So, her husband did it alone, making mere dollars a day.

With frequent hospital stays, their debt grew. Their young daughter, nearing her teen years, would stay alone at home for many days at a time in an unsafe environment. Sweet, shy, and very beautiful, she was at risk from unscrupulous men in the area. Loan sharks were not above taking out high-interest rates in human flesh.

The family was at high risk of separation, if not worse. The social workers at CIF spent time assessing their situation. They were able to help the father increase his earning potential, take the mother to get medical treatment, and find a solution so their daughter would not be home alone. With the father earning more money, he could be there to pick her up from school and help her with homework. They also made the home more secure by installing a locking door.

None of the solutions cost much money, but they shifted the family's situation from being one step away from complete ruin to hopeful. They were able to pay down debt, gain margin, and spend more time together as a family.

For now, they still need support and monitoring, but as things improve, they may become self-sufficient. If not, as their daughter grows up and finishes her education, she will have many more opportunities to gain safe employment. She is on a trajectory of breaking the poverty cycle.

//

Helping families with their earning potential is one facet of the FOR-1 project. For example, a widow with two teenage daughters who have chronic health issues, Soriya sold home-made soya milk and treats made from ground rice. She traveled a long distance daily, waited in a queue to get the soya and rice ground, and had to pay three thousand riel (about seventy-five cents) for the service. Each day, this process took her away from her daughters and cut down on time to make and sell the food.

CIF helped her purchase her own grinder. As a result, she doubled her daily earnings. In addition, they addressed her daughters' health issues. With regular care and medication, they not only began to feel better but also to attend school more frequently. As their mother's financial stability increased, their family became more sustainable, and they needed less support. The mother's burdens began to lift, and she became less angry and reactive since she worried less about her family's future.

Having a relationship with social workers and local church leaders also meant Soriya did not have to carry her burdens alone. If problems or concerns arose, she knew she had trustworthy people who would walk alongside her and the girls.

Family preservation can be as simple as improving upon existing skills, supporting the business, or helping people save for essential equipment that makes their work more efficient.

The Charis Project is another family-based care organization in Southeast Asia. Charis runs financial classes and savings groups for families on the Thai-Myanmar border. After receiving some training and seed funds, families combine their meager wages and set aside small amounts each time they earn money.

In the past, many refugees and displaced families on the border placed their children in orphanages because their labor could not feed, clothe, or send them to school. Yet after a few months of attending the savings group, most of these families realized that having a basic budget and setting aside a percentage of their income made the difference between abject poverty and being able to care for their children. Many have reached goals that felt impossible before.

When an emergency arises, they can tap into their savings or get an interest-free loan from their group pool that gets paid back over time. They're able to avoid accruing even more debt with insane interest rates from loan sharks.

//

Menghong explained that, in more complex cases, severe mental health issues in the parents need to be addressed. The consistency of other family members can help manage many of these cases, such as grandparents stepping in to care for the children and their adult child. CIF will work with the parent with mental health issues to get them help while the extended family members become primary caregivers to the children.

In one such case, the grandparents received chickens to raise and sell the eggs and meat, so they could remain home to care for their sick daughter and grandchildren.

There is a broad spectrum of solutions for children in poverty or difficult home situations, and rarely is separation from their family of origin a long-term solution.

One of the most memorable children Menghong helped with CIF was a thirteen-year-old with a severe disability. The girl, Vy, was to live at an orphanage because her mother did not know how to care for her.

Menghong said, "Even though Vy cannot speak, we could tell

through her nonverbal communication that she understood her mother was going to leave her at an orphanage. She understood everything that was happening."

The girl was completely panicked.

Thankfully, working closely with the local leaders and CIF's ABLE Project, Vy remained with her mother. He said he has seen the relationship improve and that the family's joy has grown. "It was extraordinary to help keep Vy in her family."

Foster Care

A dozen CIF staff sat packed in a large van as the driver navigated a maze of streets that led out of the city. With only a month of experience on staff, I was excited to head a few hours away to villages where we worked. I was fighting a cold, but I didn't want to miss my first opportunity to visit the villages and see our work firsthand. The departure time was early, but half the staff arrived thirty minutes late, and a few forgot their keys, so we waited.

Finally, we were on the road, and enthusiasm replaced my exhaustion. I nearly groaned as I realized we were stopping again. Our foster care manager climbed in, clutching a baby, and we started moving through traffic again.

Sitting next to this blanketed bundle, I looked into the unblinking eyes of an infant. A toothless smile formed on his chubby face. Had I not been sick, I would have picked him up and squeezed his pudgy cheeks.

Owing to my lack of good Khmer language skills and our manager's lack of good English, I could not ask much about his story.

A few hours later, we stopped at our first village. In a green-tiled church building with plastic chairs stacked in one corner, our staff met with parents who filtered in and out quickly. CIF distributed money and supplies, ticking names off a list. Near the group's rear, I saw a lovely woman with a long, thick braid of dark hair. Although not wealthy, her clothing was tidy and clean. Beside her, a slender, older man stood. Weatherworn from a life of labor, his face was pleasant. Soon only the couple remained.

I watched as our staff entered the room with the baby. Both man and woman clutched at each other expectantly. It was as if they were awaiting a promise left unfulfilled, both hesitant and joyful.

Our staff met them halfway into the door as the woman reached for the baby. I felt like an intruder in a very private, emotional moment, yet I could not peel my eyes off their faces. It was as if the mother melted into the baby. I watched as her greatest dream came true.

Yet it was her husband's face that made tears slide down my cheeks. Love radiated from his eyes, and he was captivated. His hands shaking, he reached out and touched the baby. I could almost read his thoughts. "My boy. I have a son."

I learned later that they had been married for over five years and hadn't conceived. Not only was it heartbreaking for them, but there's still shame and stigma around childlessness in Cambodia.

The baby had come from our partner, Mother's Heart Organization, an NGO working with women in crisis pregnancy. For whatever reason, his birth mother felt unable to raise him, so she gave him up for adoption.

How I wished his birth mother could have witnessed the union of the baby to his foster parents. Although this couple could not give him material wealth, they would love him.

//

From the inception of CIF, a primary goal was stability, permanency, and solid family units that would minimize trauma and attachment disorders. Rather than shuffling children through a system and repeatedly uprooting them, the process Cathleen and Anny formed—one CIF continues to build on—is intentional from the first step and seeks to ensure the best possible outcomes for the children and the foster families.

Before a child is even considered for foster care, CIF looks for relatives who could care for the child. In the beginning years of CIF, Cathleen and Anny primarily focused on foster care due to the higher death rate of adults and the challenging circumstances from which children came. However, it was always their dream to reverse this trend and keep more children with their biological relatives.

As of 2022, nearly three times more children in CIF's programs are cared for in families of origin, kinship care, rather than foster care. Yet a biological family is not always an option. So, CIF has a stringent process for children to end up in loving foster families.

In late 2018, the foster care project manager, Leak, walked me through the recruitment and monitoring processes for foster families. Follow the Cheang family's journey:

First, CIF hosts an event in a location, usually a village or city where they work or hope to work. This happened in the Cheang family's village where all the village authorities, community leaders, police, NGO partners, and local churches were invited to join. Next, the staff members shared about our Foster Care and Kinship Care projects and explained their policies.

If anyone is interested in becoming a foster parent, CIF's caseworkers start an application process, which is how the Cheangs signed up. The caseworkers also encouraged those who attend the event to share the information within the community. Since not everyone was clear about the process, the staff followed up with interested families.

Once the Cheangs filled out the application, their village chief, commune leaders, and police reviewed and signed it. This step ensures that local leaders are also involved in the monitoring and safety of each family and child. In addition, community leaders are witnesses to the family's day-to-day life and have intimate knowledge of behaviors not necessarily noticed in shorter visits.

After the application was complete, the foster care project manager, Leak, reviewed it. Then, he met the Cheangs at home, conducted an interview, and took notes. Assessing the family home gives the case workers an idea of the home's safety, the family's financial stability, and the family's responsibility. Families also need to be equipped to deal with children who come from trauma, not only for the health of the child entering their care but also to keep their family safe.

The staff checked with neighbors and village leaders to ensure there is no gambling or drinking among the family members. This is followed by an interview of village leaders and extended family members.

Once assessed as a safe, healthy family, the staff begin to discover what role the Cheangs can play in fostering children.

CIF uses several different assessment tools to filter families. Staff asked the Cheangs questions like: "Would you be willing to take a child long-term or short-term? Why do you want to be foster parents? Do you prefer a girl or a boy? What age groups would work well with your family? Are you willing to care for a child with a disability? And is there a school and hospital nearby?"

These questions help to identify which children would be a good match for the family and what support the child would have in the Cheang family and their community. The children in CIF's foster care project are referred via the Department of Social Affairs, Veterans and Youth (DoSVY), other NGOs like Mother's Heart or anti-trafficking organizations, and hospitals, primarily due to abandoned children or those with disabilities or illnesses left in the hospital.

Cambodian law only allows married local couples to be foster parents and requires that neither foster parent has a chronic illness. This law is to ensure the family can look after a foster child. It also helps prevent children from becoming attached to an ill foster parent and tragically losing them.

Social workers explained the monitoring process to the Cheangs. They learned the protection policies and that the staff will regularly visit, working with them to support the child as they grow and form attachments.

Finally, CIF leaders and social workers meet to decide whether the family is approved. They always make this decision in collaboration. The structure of CIF involves multiple people's input, especially for children's big decisions. It is not foolproof, but it adds a level of accountability and helps remove favoritism from the process or overlooking something that could be problematic in a home.

CIF finds it better to be thorough in the beginning than to put a family and child into a less-than-ideal situation and have to hurt them by removal later.

Once approved, the Cheangs were put on a waiting list. In the meantime, children enter CIF's emergency care, in which a trained family takes in children at short notice for a short time. The reasons a child may enter care range from abuse, neglect, and risk of trafficking to losing their parents. Leak and the team prioritize finding a long-term solution that is both safe and loving.

While they wait for this long-term family, the emergency care families and staff screen the children for health concerns. Many enter CIF's care undernourished, traumatized, and potentially having illnesses like HIV. CIF addresses their medical and emotional needs and arranges the proper care for them. The screening helps the team assess potential long-term needs so that families taking the children will know what to expect.

When a child who is a good match for the family needs fostering, CIF staff let the family know. The husband and wife must both agree to take the child. They have time to decide, so it is a smooth process.

//

In addition to training and monitoring, CIF generally pays a monthly stipend, though situational needs may mean adjustments happen here and there. The allowance covers a child's medical, education, and food requirements. Often, families take pride in caring for their children and turn down the money; as long as they can remain financially stable, CIF allows their financial independence.

Placing a child into their foster family is an event. Local authorities and pastors join the process. Beyond a single-family unit, fostering is a community's responsibility, ensuring the child belongs. Leak said the idea that it takes a village to raise a child is foundational for Cambodian society. This philosophy imbues a child with great value and ensures they are cared for by everyone.

CIF staff work with the family and local government witnesses to process guardianship documents with DoSVY. DoSVY is the legal guardian of any children placed in foster care. This is similar to how state governments in America or Australia have guardianship of children who enter the foster care system.

//

"On rare occasions, a family is a bad fit, but we try to work with the child and family to find a solution," Leak told me.

He explained that these situations require patience, but many families heed the social workers' advice. As a result, they receive more regular follow-ups and training. Social workers support the parents in working with the child's problematic behavior. Once the child realizes they have a consistent family who will stand with them, their behavior almost always improves. CIF only ends placements when circumstances become dangerous for the child or the family.

While ongoing training is fundamental, so are regular visits from social workers and project managers. These visits can be unannounced or scheduled, and they help the team gain a more accurate picture of their home life. The children receive individual visits from the social workers so that the staff can assess an honest portrayal of treatment and care. Children also gather in informal meetings with CIF staff to relate with one another and learn about other foster children's home lives.

While there is always room to improve, CIF's foster care project has seen incredible success. Since domestic adoption became legal in 2018, many foster families have adopted their children.

The staff members are very vested in the families they serve. Several adopted and fostered their own children before joining staff at CIF. Leak continues his job as foster care manager, despite the exhaustion because he finds it so fulfilling. He lost his father at ten years old and knows what it feels like to miss the love and warmth of a parent. While his mother did her best, he knew the value of being a good husband and father and he wants children to experience the love and stability of two parents.

In a previous interview with CIF's communications team, Leak said, "I get to see kids in foster care growing up healthy and happy. They are loved and get to go to school. It makes me so happy to meet with these children."

Sometimes children make such significant improvement in their foster families that he hardly recognizes them when he sees them again. Consistent love helps them overcome health issues, attachment disorders, and even trauma.

One such child was Sreynear. After years of extreme abuse, she went to live in an orphanage at the age of three. However, her mother took her back when she needed money, planning to sell her to address mounting debt. This beautiful child knew nothing but pain and sadness.

A local anti-trafficking group, in conjunction with local police, rescued her in time. She entered CIF's emergency care and was treated tenderly for the first time in her life. After

CIF found a foster family for her, she entered a heartbreaking transition. While her family was patient and loving, the only way she knew to control all the difficult emotions within her short life was to lash out in rage.

Constantly angry, she fought the children at school and struggled to socialize with both children and adults.

At their wit's end, her foster family needed intervention. CIF increased their support and encouragement and planned more frequent visits. Despite the challenges, Sreynear's new parents never gave up on her. Once she realized what it meant to live in a safe and stable environment, she gradually improved. Letting her guard down, she slowly changed, making friends and learning to listen. The foster parents showed incredible faithfulness and endurance. And when Sreynear realized this, she was transformed into a creative and loving child who thrives.

Abortion Baby

What was that sound? Anny slowly roused from her sleep and realized the noise was coming from her phone. What hour was it?

Her home was dark, but as she opened her bedroom door, she realized a faint light shone outside. It was early morning. Pork vendors heated their grills and set small plastic chairs in front of their roadside stalls. Old aunties swept in front of their homes. The air was still thick with the night's humidity.

The phone rang again, so Anny answered. It was a hospital with an abandoned premature baby. She tried to keep up with the voice on the other end but all she could discern was, "A botched abortion." Then, grabbing her bag, she swept out of her home, locking the gates behind her and flagging down a moto driver to take her to the hospital.

Concern welled inside. How badly botched was this abortion? Was the baby suffering?

That year, they had had several premature and unwanted births referred to them, but never an aborted baby who survived the procedure.

Upon arrival, the story became a little clearer. A premature but healthy baby boy had been born due to a late-term abortion.

//

A few days earlier, Thida feared the worst. Her peers were starting to send her sideways glances. There was no more hiding it. With her breasts swelling and her slight frame putting on weight, people would guess. Two years into her university studies, she fell headlong in love with another student, Soklim. Their parents had no idea they were dating. Despite her education, she knew little about anatomy and biology. Pregnancy was a risk of sex, that much she knew, but little else.

Soklim was kind and fun. But he was young like her, and they both panicked when they realized she was pregnant. They were scholarship kids from the village. While neither came from an impoverished family, they were far from wealthy. If she had this baby, their lives would be over. They discussed their families and their futures, knowing a baby would jeopardize all the hope their parents had placed on them to lift their families out of village life.

Knowing little of abortion or even the stages of pregnancy, Thida resolved to take action before it destroyed her life and shamed her family. Soklim still loved her, but he was afraid too. His father was stern and would not respond well to the fruit of their relationship.

Soklim dropped her at the clinic in the evening. Neither of them had peace about the situation, yet their circumstances left no other choice. He watched Thida disappear through the doors. He dismissed a twinge of guilt for leaving her to do this alone and drove away.

The doctors did not explain anything and asked pointed questions about timing. Thida was unsure. In a back room, on a cold metal table, she felt humiliated in the compromising position with her feet up, exposed as nurses looked on. They injected her and waited. The waves of pain and nausea were excruciating. Panic coursed through her veins.

After dressing and signing a few forms, she stood on the road outside the clinic, waiting for Soklim to pick her up. Although the Phnom Penh night was balmy, she shivered and hugged herself. Her body ached. Her breasts ached. But more than that, her heart ached.

Soklim arrived, hardly making eye contact; he returned her to her shared dorm wordlessly. Restless, he paced outside, worried about her yet unsure what to say or do.

Soon the pains came quicker. Thida's body was pushing. She ran to the bathroom. In shock, she heard the wails of a tiny baby. Thida knew little of the abortion process, but she knew the baby should not come out crying. The staff had told her she would pass blood and tissue; instead, there was a baby, not much larger than her hand, lying on her bathroom floor. No one told her it would be a baby.

Soklim knocked on the door, hearing her sobs and the tiny wails.

Thida could only respond through breathless, choking words, "A baby. Soklim, help. Oh, help!"

Soklim pushed open the door and reeled at all the blood on the floor and on Thida. Shaking, he grabbed a piece of clothing and bundled up the boy. A million thoughts clouded his mind, but he knew they needed to get the baby to a clinic. He wrapped the baby up and ran out into the night, hailing a passing *tuk-tuk*. Next thing he knew, he was standing at the entrance to an all-night clinic, handing the baby to a nurse. Detached from his body, he answered their questions but felt like it was someone else's voice.

A few hours later, he stumbled back to Thida's place. Silent tears slid down his face. She wanted to ask if the baby would live, but feared the answer. She both feared his survival and his death. The two did not speak but lay down with their backs to each other, desperately wanting to sleep. They could not.

Unbeknownst to Thida and Soklim, the clinic took the boy to a local hospital, and in the early morning, Anny stood over the tiny infant, looking down at his shriveled little face and black tufts of hair. He weighed only 1.1 kilograms. His survival hinged on receiving the proper care in the coming days and weeks.

//

Anny wanted more information on the baby and what had happened to him, so she traced the clinic and spoke with the doctor involved. In less than a day, she was knocking on the door of the young mother. A pale face and sad eyes met hers. The girl's eyes widened as Anny announced she was there about the baby.

Dissolving into tears, the girl poured out the whole story.

Soklim soon sat in the same room. Anny made them aware of the state of their son and his desperate need for care. She also managed to convince them their parents needed to know everything. Although Anny agreed to act as an arbitrator, the two young people were terrified of what the day held. They would start with his family. The young woman was too sick from the previous day's abortion.

Soon, Soklim's family arrived in Phnom Penh, and the group met. Anny prayed through the storm of emotions. To her surprise, although the parents were shocked, they were not angry. The tsunami of information about their children had engulfed and rendered them unable to register strong emotions. No one even knew the young couple was dating, let alone that a baby was involved.

The hospital demanded a caregiver and the provision of milk for the baby, so Anny took the young man's mother to see the baby. "The grandmother took one look at the baby and fell in love," Anny recalled. "CIF paid for all the supplies and milk. The boy's mother cared for her grandchild in the hospital."

Soon after, Anny notified Thida's family. Her mother was in such great shock that she fainted over the phone. Later, they came to the hospital to meet the baby. Anny sat with the families as they worked through their options.

"We could have just taken the baby, but the right path was to get the family involved and do what was best for everyone," Anny said firmly.

She remained a mediator; arrangements between the families needed to be negotiated. Anny let them know CIF would help, but the baby would be better off staying with his family. In those meetings, the family decided the two young people should marry. However, Soklim's family had no money for the bride price. So, Anny became the broker for the wedding as well. They figured out finances, and the young man borrowed two thousand dollars to make the marriage happen. Both sides decided to chip in for the event.

What began in tragedy had turned to joy. The two young students loved each other and wanted a marriage. The groom's mother was utterly smitten with her grandson and hardly left his side.

By bringing the relationship to light, all the fear, shame, and guilt bound up in the secret relationship, unwanted pregnancy, and abortion washed away. Anny worked hard to join the two families, and amidst the circumstances, she shared the love of God with all of them. God's heart for children. God's heart for a healthy relationship. God's desire for the family to forgive and love one another.

The young man's parents became Christians, and they both fell in love with the little boy. Once he was healthy enough, they moved him to their village home and raised him, this time with more grace and less firmness than they had raised their son. Thida and Soklim regularly visited on weekends and holidays.

Both families wanted the newlyweds to continue their education, so the two returned to their studies after the wedding. A few years after the incident, Thida called Anny. She was angry because she and Soklim wanted their son, but his grandparents refused to relinquish him.

"Well, what do you want to do with your son?" Anny asked pointedly.

The young woman explained that she and Soklim were working in the city, but they wanted him back.

Anny explained about healthy attachment to them, realizing they would shift him into daycare, and he would rarely see his parents.

"Leave him where he is if you cannot care for him yourself. You will hurt him more if you take him away and cannot be with him," she said.

He was part of CIF's kinship care program, and the value of permanency is vital. If the child is safe, loved, and thriving, there is no value in removing the child. So, Thida and Soklim left him in the village. They still see him regularly, but they love him enough not to bring disruption into his life.

Slowly, CIF left more of the finances to the family and checked on the boy less. His grandparents are still raising him. And, as a result, he is growing and happy. The entire family got to experience grace and redemption through the failed abortion. Because of the experience, the baby who lived was raised in a loving, Christian home.

Flawed Agendas

Dy's head spun. She stared into the bucket, vomit in the bottom. Each morning, it was the same.

Trembling, she tried to stand as tears slid down her pale face. Soon, she stumbled into the doorway of their home, and her mother looked up at her from stirring the breakfast porridge. She nodded at her mother as the older woman gave a knowing glance back. Their fears were confirmed; Dy was pregnant.

She had not known her rapist. Passing through their village one day on a job to do electrical work, he had caught her gathering firewood in a nearby tree grove. Before she knew what was happening, she was face down in the soil, her skirt violently pulled up.

Thirteen, she was only thirteen. Terrified by the violence and knowing what the man did to her was shameful, she lay in the dirt alone until it was dark. Her mother found her there. Twigs and dirt tangled in her long, thick hair. Saying nothing, her mother sobbed as she cradled her young daughter's head in her lap, hands shaking as they brushed Dy's hair from her face. Memories of an uncle from long ago crept back into her mind. No one ever knew.

As the sadness wore off, hot anger coursed through her veins. She would not allow anyone to submit her daughter to a life of secret shame. It was not the girl's fault.

"Do you know who it was?" she finally asked in a choked voice.

Dy could only look down and shake her head. "No."

"Let me take you home. I will get Oum Ly to come to help

you. You must be brave, my dear."

They stood together and slowly walked back to their house. The following days were a blur. Oum Ly, a local community worker who specialized in caring for women and children, had come that night and gently questioned the girl. More authorities were alerted, they told Granny. But Dy's mother and Oum Ly sat through all of it with her. Oum held her hand at the doctor's painful examination. More silent tears slid down the girl's face.

Authorities quickly caught the man. People from the city in several organizations were going to put together a trial against him. He currently sat in jail, having been roughed up by the local police.

Still, it all felt like she would never wake from this bad dream. Not even old enough to drive a motorbike to school, the girl was more interested in her plush animals and hair accessories than boys.

Her father had died of tuberculosis when she was very young. Had he been alive, she wondered if he would have defended her. She only remembered him as a frail and sick man; however, the wedding portrait in their home showed a handsome, kind-looking man. Would he be proud or ashamed of her?

Now, even showing her face at school was impossible. She was with child, and soon everyone would know.

One day, Oum Ly stopped by with a very kind social worker. She came from the city and worked for Mother's Heart Organization. Oum Ly and her mother had been discussing this for a few days, so Dy was not surprised when the young woman in a crisp, ironed shirt appeared with her bag full of notebooks.

After so many interviews, Dy was exhausted, but this woman was the most gentle and compassionate of all the people. Together, they would make the best decision for Dy and the baby. The girl had options. They told her all about the care she and her mother would receive through the coming months; there would be midwives to teach her about the phases of pregnancy and parenting.

If she wanted to keep the baby, she could. If she wanted to give the baby up for adoption, she could. They would give her time to process it all. She did not want to process it all. She wanted to escape and return to a life where her biggest concern was the semester exams.

Although supportive, Dy's mother became busy with her younger siblings. There were seven of them in all. Life didn't stop for the pregnancy.

Granny, who was still rather young and spry, lived in the same area, and all parties agreed that Dy would go live with Granny for the remainder of her pregnancy as the woman could focus solely on the girl. Granny was a better cook than her mother and could make a person laugh until their belly ached.

The birth was terrifying. Despite the midwives' best efforts to prepare Dy, the fear of a baby and a new life to care for compounded with all of the pain and trauma of the last nine months. The girl thought the pain would never end.

Yet as she held her daughter for the first time, fear seemed to vanish. This little girl was like her brothers and sisters at home, who had all come in a tiny, perfect package and grown into lovable little people. Dy marveled at the intricate hands and fluff of hair.

"She's mine," Dy thought. "I made that."

Soon, Dy was getting into a routine with Granny and the baby, whom they called Rita. She was happy to return to school, which she loved, although she felt a million years older than her classmates now. Children In Families took over her case for kinship care and made regular visits to help the three of them adjust and provide essentials like the formula Rita needed.

Dy had heard little about her court case over the months, but she knew it would proceed soon. One day she arrived home from school and was shocked to see a large SUV in front of her home with a group of staff from the legal team, some of whom she had met a year ago, gathered under their home on stilts, chatting with Granny and her mother. Packed bags sat near the car. Before she could take it all in, they informed her that she and the baby were being taken to a safe house in the city for better care.

Dy wanted to protest and cry, "But I'm safe here!"

However, it was not cultural to disrespect leaders and elders, so she refrained. Her mother looked sad, and Granny gritted her teeth. This team of professional, intelligent, well-dressed people had convinced Mother that Dy could not fully recover from trauma and get the counseling and help she needed without going to this place in the city. Neither did they believe it was safe for her and her child to remain in the village.

As Dy climbed into the vehicle with baby Rita, Granny, who rarely expressed physical affection, grabbed her hand and squeezed it tightly. Dy held back the tears, knowing Granny's touch was both a sign of love and admonition to be strong.

In the city, the barely fourteen Dy stared up at the walled house with never-ending barbed wire strung around it. The courtyard had a few sad potted plants and shaded benches. The house was full of women and girls from all walks of life, many of whom were former prostitutes, using crass language and speaking of men in terms that made Dy turn a deep crimson.

Baby Rita was taken from her almost immediately and placed downstairs in the baby room where a house mother looked after all the women's children. Dy would reside in a room with three other girls, all victims of rape or sexual trauma. Their routine became counseling, parenting or life skills classes, group meals, schoolwork, and visits with her daughter twice a day, all behind high walls and barbed wire.

It took Dy a while to quiet the inner shaking that started again. She felt exposed and vulnerable despite the razor wire.

The feelings that had eventually worn off after the trauma of her rape now resurfaced after being wrenched away from Granny.

Here she had no privacy. No one hugged her like her siblings or stroked her hair as Granny did. Nights were the worst; used to snuggling up on the mat with Granny and Rita, she slept much worse in the safe house. Nightmares and fears kept her awake at night, and she could not feel the reassuring warmth radiating off Granny or even Granny's instinct to awaken and silently run her hand up and down Dy's arm until she fell asleep again.

Little did she know the day after the NGO took her, Anny found out from the grandmother. Irate, she called Cathleen, "The anti-trafficking organization just showed up and snatched her and the baby away into their residential home! I made a few phone calls. Our hands are tied; they convinced her mother this is the only way she'll receive healing."

It was true. After the initial call from the grandmother, Anny called every possible person involved in the uprooting of Dy to find out what happened and why they took her. The anti-trafficking organization staff was fully aware that CIF and Mother's Heart Organization were involved in helping the family and monitoring Dy and Rita. Over a year after the incident, they could not understand why the organization suddenly felt the girl needed rescuing.

The answer came less than a week later when the anti-trafficking organization posted all over social media, "Pregnant Thirteen-Year-Old Rape Victim Rescued by Our Team."

They plastered Dy's story across the globe through press releases. Sure, her name was changed, and there were no photos of her face, but it made a great sob story. Not one mention of partner organizations like Mother's Heart or CIF or the work of the local community worker, Oum Ly, was listed in the process of rescue and restoration of the young girl.

Anny paced their office in restless anger after seeing the articles.

"They did it for fundraising! They uprooted Dy and her baby because she makes for a good story!"

Dy never did find out how hard Anny fought to get her and her baby out from behind those gates and back with her loving family.

A few months later, however, Dy's mother called in distress and told them, "Rita is not doing well. The NGO staff fear she might die. They said she has failure to thrive."

After a few more phone calls, Anny stood outside the gates of the safe house, demanding entrance. The staff of the anti-trafficking organization would never forget that encounter because Anny gave them such a stern tongue-lashing on their failing Dy and Baby Rita. Dy was languishing as much as Rita, but sadly, Anny could only secure the release of the infant from their care. She felt like she drove a nail in Dy's emotional coffin as she left in the *tuk-tuk* with the morose, underweight baby in her arms, looking at the young girl's face.

After a brief stint in the hospital with Dy's granny by her side the entire time, the baby began to gain weight and become more responsive. Soon, baby Rita comfortably settled back into a routine with Granny, and her health improved remarkably.

Eventually, the NGO reintegrated Dy home with her mother but not before years of living separated from her loved ones, having guests and international teams shuttled through the safe house regularly, meeting her as the young rape victim. She went from a girl in her community who faced a terrible trauma that not everyone knew about to forever being labeled "the rape victim."

The anti-trafficking organization successfully prosecuted her rapist, but the cost to Dy was high. Sadly, Dy missed out on the early years of Rita's life. Dy also missed out on several years of her siblings' growth and development. She developed attachment fears, thinking at any moment, someone could show up at her home and cart herself or Rita away again.

Cathleen reflected, "I do not understand why these organizations cannot provide counseling and social work to these girls in their own homes. Why do they have to be uprooted from all that they know to get healing? Labeling them victims in the process. Dy was safe at home, and it was a random act of violence, not a family member."

CIF has served a few other young girls who have been raped, but no others became pregnant. Another famous international anti-trafficking organization also took these girls away from their families, despite CIF handling their cases initially.

"In one case, the mother's boyfriend did it, but the woman immediately kicked him out. She was incredibly supportive of her daughter, yet they still took her away."

Cathleen and Anny begged the organization to bring the counseling to the girls rather than take them away and put them in residential care. The other girls did not stay in care for long, however. Determined mothers who loved their daughters nearly pounded down the doors to take their children back. One of the girls ran away from the safe house back to her mother.

The girls healed much better in the loving embrace of their families, attending school with their friends and living a somewhat normal life.

As in other countries, some parents in Cambodia abuse and exploit their children for selfish gain. But these parents are the rare exception. Most love their children and are devastated when they are sexually assaulted. They may not all have the tools or understanding to give their children everything needed for healing but they are willing. Yet the anti-trafficking organizations often paint the parents as negligent or indifferent. A more accurate depiction should be a lack of knowing where to find support, not a lack of care. And then, when they do find support, their children are stripped from them and punished for seeking care.

The flashy documentaries of men kicking down brothel

doors and pulling children from pedophile rings make up a tiny percentage of the finances and needs of nations battling sex trafficking. Most people in Southeast Asia who are victims of sexual assault, rape, and even trafficking are not kidnapped or held against their will. Neither are many of them in constant imminent danger.

Poverty is the major contributing factor. The issue is similar to the orphanage crisis and at times overlaps. Rarely are the roots of poverty or the holistic care of communities considered. The "victims" are isolated from their circumstances. Meanwhile, nothing changes in the community and society as a whole. Their parents' lives have not improved or changed, and their peers do not receive better opportunities.

//

To combat this problem at one time, the CIF staff picked up the idea of counseling on location the girls harmed by sexual abuse. The idea came from the physiotherapy our ABLE program provides for families throughout Cambodia.

Once a counselor came from overseas to train CIF's staff in trauma counseling. After going through CIF's visitor and child protection policy, Anny took him to the village. He and his wife signed the policies and went to meet with the girls.

After the first visit, the staff saw his social media plastered with photos of the girls and the village. He did not respect the boundaries and breached confidentiality from the start.

After only one month in Cambodia, they had to ask him to leave. Once in the country, he threw out all his training and professionalism as a certified counselor. CIF had to give up the idea and refer trauma cases to other organizations instead, which still ran the risk of repeating Dy and baby Rita's story.

Accepted, Belonging, Loved, Empowered (ABLE)

On a gray spring day in Geneva, Switzerland, a slender Khmer woman, barely in her thirties, stepped up to a lectern and began to speak to the United Nations Human Rights Council about family and community-based care for children with disabilities. She cleared her voice, her hands shaking as she leaned into the microphone.

"Good afternoon. My name is Srey Ny Sorn, and I am from Children in Families in Cambodia.

"Children In Families is an organization that supports family-based alternative care for children who have been orphaned or abandoned by their families. We developed the ABLE Project because we believe in the fundamental right of all children to be part of a family and a community.

"That includes children with disabilities.

"There will always be some children who cannot remain in their birth families. We know that the next best option is family-based alternative care. Unfortunately, many organizations that support kinship care and foster care say that they are not equipped to help children who have disabilities. Or they cannot find suitable families who are willing to care for a child with disabilities.

"It is wrong for children with disabilities to be excluded from family-based alternative care only because services are not available. It is discrimination and a violation of children's rights.

"The ABLE project allows children with disabilities to be placed in CIF's kinship and foster care projects, just like all other children. It equips and supports families to provide for the special needs of these children, so that they do not grow up in institutions and so that they can be a part of their communities.

"People with disabilities often face barriers which prevent them from participating in their communities. The ABLE project helps remove these barriers by making family-based alternative care more inclusive.

"To date, CIF has been able to support more than fifty children through the ABLE project toward achieving full inclusion in family-based care and community life. It is possible to include children with disabilities in family-based alternative care. We know it. Many of you know it. Let's keep working toward it.

"My name is Srey Ny Sorn, from Cambodia. Thank you for your time today."

//

Almost seven years before the UN Human Rights Council, an amicable, gentle-natured woman named Lisa landed in Cambodia, leaving her successful career as a physical therapist to children with disabilities in the States after learning that Cambodia had the highest rate of physical disabilities in the world. She thought about her skill set and her desire to make a difference and felt the budding of a vision to empower and bring better care for people with disabilities in Cambodia.

She had met Cathleen during a visit to scope out work options. When Cathleen shared about the work of CIF, it seemed like the perfect fit for what Lisa wanted to do for people with disabilities. Little did she realize the depth of what she had signed up for: the sleepless nights, prolonged power cuts during heat waves, a litany of health issues, cultural blunders, and the tragic loss of family members back in America while she worked across the world.

Lisa settled into language and culture acquisition in Phnom Penh. She set to work learning everything she could about programs and services available in Cambodia and what the most immediate needs would be to start.

"I was not building the ABLE program out of nothing," Lisa later explained. "CIF always had the heart and perspective that children with disabilities should not be left out. They were inclusive from the beginning. ABLE exists because there was already a recognition of the need to include children with disabilities, who are more vulnerable and who are at such a high risk of separation."

After all, the first children placed in families by CIF were orphanage outcasts who were disabled and who had been neglected by their caregivers. These children required more care and did not present the orphanages with publishable success stories that made donors flock.

Lisa explained that although creating ABLE was a long process, CIF provided a solid starting point. "If you [programs and organizations] don't start with inclusion, it's tough to get to inclusion." And CIF already had a framework of inclusion.

After intensive language studies, Lisa began traveling to the villages to meet the CIF families caring for children with disabilities. In her eagerness to help, however, she made a significant cultural blunder. At a group meeting in the province, Lisa saw an auntie caring for a child with disabilities. Lisa's eyes lit up, and she sought to connect. Excited to learn more and hear from them, she pulled the auntie aside and began asking questions.

"I immediately sensed her shame and internal retreat," Lisa shared. In her zeal to help, she had publicly singled out the woman, and everyone in the room took notice.

"I had to realize that I needed to learn to understand how families affected by disability felt about others' perception of them. There is a sensitivity that needs to be considered. I had unintentionally made them feel shame. So now, I would meet them in a more private space. Especially for our first meeting."

Racked with guilt and mortified by her blunder, Lisa vowed to watch, learn, and understand the real challenges that families caring for children with disabilities had.

"To address the child's needs, the biggest thing to start with was learning to address the family's needs. CIF strives to make the family aware that they are the parent or primary caregiver; we are there to support them as they care for their child.

"Building the relationship is critical before you can get far with anything else. They [the caregivers] have to believe you are on their side, that you care about them, and you're not just there to tell them what to do or cast judgment."

For the first several years, Lisa not only spent time getting to know families but also sought to find what was available in Cambodia. She explored the environment, working to find people already in the field of disabilities. There was not a centralized system to find help for specific needs and situations. The few services available to families with children with disabilities or chronic illnesses are difficult to track down. In addition, if you wanted to access one of these programs, you needed to know someone with connections. So, Lisa began to catalog the options and the contact people.

"Even if there is a service, Cambodia's context is different. What I was used to having available in the US does not exist here or is vastly different. As a result, I needed to lower my expectations. Services like wheelchairs may not be customizable to the lifestyle, terrain, and accessibility of families."

In the beginning, the overwhelming need threatened to bury Lisa, yet the strong foundation CIF provided the passionate team she would soon build and the families who cared deeply for their children all kept her from giving in to despair.

//

Lisa shared that after she began building her vision of the ABLE program, she sought out a local physiotherapist to hire. She knew she could not do this alone; she needed a solid team. Physios are challenging to find in Cambodia as the role is highly misunderstood and even looked down upon. Srey Ny shared that some people think of it as only slightly more admirable than being a massage therapist, a front for many brothels in Cambodia.

At the time of Lisa's search, Cambodia had about one physiotherapist per ten thousand people.

The role, however, required more than just a degree or skill; it required a passion for children with disabilities. Srey Ny stood out immediately. Her mother worked with people with disabilities, and some of them lived with her family. As a result, from a young age Srey Ny and her sister had exposure to their lives and struggles. Her sister pursued work in Khmer sign language with the Deaf Development Program, while Srey Ny studied physiotherapy specifically to work with people with disabilities.

Lisa interviewed several candidates, but when she met Srey Ny, she knew she had found the perfect fit. Lisa said, "She [Srey Ny] shared the same heart and vision for children with disabilities. It was in her DNA to champion these children. We are kindred spirits in this."

In a culture where disabilities aren't well understood and people with disabilities are easily marginalized, Srey Ny stands out. "My mother worked in an NGO that cared for children with disabilities. We lived on location with the children. I genuinely love them."

Srey Ny's passion shined through as she continued to explain how difficult it is for people with disabilities in Cambodia. "Lisa and I care about each other and understand each other. It is difficult to find Cambodians who care about people with disabilities. A lot of it is a lack of knowledge, as well as survival. People need to make money, and children with disabilities may be unable to provide for their families. I want to see this change and for people to value them for who they are. I want to help them get jobs."

//

During Srey Ny's first week of work, she crashed the motorbike carrying Lisa into deep mud. Rather than get angry, Lisa flailed in the mud and laughed until she cried. Lisa's reaction sealed the beginning of their work relationship and built a solid personal bond that would carry them through some profound struggles and sorrows but also incredible joys like the birth of Srey Ny's daughter.

As the two struggled to breathe through the giggles of sharing their story, their cheeks glistened with happy tears. Their relationship reminded me a lot of Cathleen and Anny. Deep mutual respect and admiration mingled with sisterhood.

The two women's relationship grew, and they added a staff member in the province who could regularly follow up with families in the more remote areas.

Lisa never wanted to be the lead but instead to support Khmer physiotherapists and social workers. Srey Ny and Lisa worked closely to develop a documentation system. They created natural assessment and care plans for everyone to walk through. Together they also set a triage plan for kids and families and how to address the needs of each. Early on, Srey Ny took over as the program manager, while Lisa became the technical adviser.

//

On one of Lisa's first trips to a village CIF operated in, she followed a social worker through rice fields to a traditional wooden house. Paint peeling from the weather and tropical sun, it was the home of the auntie whom Lisa inadvertently shamed at their first meeting. Seeking to rectify her mistake, she met the woman in her setting and comfort zone.

In this shabby farmhouse, surrounded by water buffalo, a little boy with cerebral palsy dwelt. Once his mother realized her son was severely disabled, she panicked over his life prospects and absconded. Her sister, mother, and grandmother stepped in, taking Rithy into their care.

While they were well-meaning, they lacked basic knowledge of his needs. As a result, he remained motionless for the first several years of his life, lying flat on his back and staring at the ceiling. Fed, clean, and regularly changed, his basic physical requirements were met.

Rithy's world was a tin ceiling. His eyes could sometimes hover to view the occasional face of his caretakers or a fly buzzing overhead. This view was the only world he knew. No one interacted with him outside of being fed and washed.

Lisa immediately took to Rithy. Gently picking him up, she showed his family how to move him in order to practice gripping and building neck and back muscles. Looking him in the eyes and speaking to him, she showed them how to interact with him, and the child came to life. His world opened up as he was moved outside and carefully propped up to watch the chickens and livestock.

"His family did not know how to connect with him or the potential he had to improve. When we started working with him, his personality came out. I watched his auntie and grandma see it too. They were doing the best they knew how to do, but did not understand what it meant to have a disability. They could only see what they saw [until they learned to look deeper]."

"Children with disabilities are on a different trajectory. People know what to expect from healthy children in development and progression. The families and caretakers need to learn about the potential and trajectory." That's what the ABLE program is designed to teach.

Not only did Rithy begin to develop incredibly well, but his family also found hope. A more profound attachment formed as they realized they were not merely serving the physical needs of a human shell. They were caring for a soul with his own character and personality.

Lisa fell in love with his enthusiasm for life and entertaining personality. Now that he is up and people engage with him, he's excited to be included in what is happening.

Rithy's whole person began to develop under the new understanding and care. He loved Lisa from the beginning. When he saw her, his eyes would light up and a grin would spread across his face, indiscernible gurgles emanating from his lips. During my first year working for CIF, I took a photo of him and Lisa playing with blocks. Rithy is looking at her with pure adoration.

His world expanded even further when CIF gifted his family a specialized wheelchair. It's designed for rough terrain and is narrow enough to stay on the single-wide tire tracks. As a result, Rithy can go out with his family and spend time with neighbors.

In the developed world, hundreds of years of thinkers, investigators, doctors, and scientists have shaped our knowledge, assumptions, and worldview. But people do the best with the knowledge they have until someone shows them a better way. So, Lisa's job, in the beginning, was to find out where the gaps were and to make achievable goals to train and assist families and to help them access the help that was available.

//

In a neighboring village, a young mother took her child with cerebral palsy to the doctor. Her child had a rash that was not clearing up. By the end of the long ordeal, she left with her head hung low, visibly shaken.

After returning home and depositing her young child on a sleeping mat, the mother stood nearby and vomited in a copse of bamboo. She was so upset from the doctor's interview that she could not keep food in for days. Every time she rubbed salve on her little one, she felt a rift of shame tearing at the fabric of her bond with the child.

The culture tells her the little one's disabilities were karma for a sinful past life. When she asked for help, medical professionals shamed her for her child's low weight and her lack of progression.

It was significantly more complicated to raise this baby than her past ones. After all the love, ministrations, and attention she lavished on this baby, her child was still skin and bones and could only stare into the distance. No one taught her how to feed her child or how hard it was to keep this little one clean in an open-air home with rats, bugs, and animals running around. That was in addition to the other children she needed to care for.

"A lot of medical professionals do not understand what it is like to care for a family member with disabilities," Lisa explained. "Rather than being supportive, they are critical. These actions make it harder when families take their children for visits. They fear the doctor might think they do not take good enough care of their child, but the doctors do not know what it takes to care for them."

Lisa continued, "It takes enormous empathy to serve these families. Empathy is one of the ABLE team's core values. We recognize that families with children with chronic illnesses or disabilities find it challenging to care for their children, even though they love them. Their environment lacks the necessary support."

Caring for children with disabilities is complex but also rewarding and life-giving. However, when not supported but criticized, discouragement deepens. It is no wonder many discouraged parents leave these children at hospitals and disappear into the night.

//

As Lisa and Srey Ny wrapped up a visit with one of CIF's families, a neighbor reluctantly inched her way into the yard. Hat clutched in her hands, she twisted at the frayed ends while waiting for a polite moment to catch the attention of the two.

The woman looked familiar to them. On several other visits, she had lingered in the periphery, observing their work. Srey Ny greeted her very gently and invited her to join them before they got on their motorbike.

The woman stammered through a vague story about a child who seemed to be in need. Eventually, Lisa and Srey Ny followed her.

Hidden behind the main roads of the village was a shockingly dilapidated home. It leaned to one side, and the roof appeared to be missing chunks of palm fronds used as shingling. Except for the pot of rice sitting nearby and the evidence that a wood fire had recently burned, the home would have appeared abandoned.

As the woman beckoned them closer, their eyes followed her outstretched arm to a form on the ground. An audible gasp escaped Srey Ny. Lisa was too stunned to make noise, but tears welled up despite her efforts to control her emotions and appear professional.

Laying in a bed of filthy rags was a shriveled and starving child. Hundreds of ants crawled over his body, biting him indiscriminately. Without thinking, Srey Ny snatched him up, attempting to brush off the gruesome little creatures. Sadly, he had soiled his pants, and his skin appeared chalky from dehydration.

The neighbor knew his granny, who cared for him. Granny loved the boy but was desperately poor, even by Cambodian standards. When the grandmother was with the boy, she did all she could, but her support system was nonexistent.

Lisa stayed behind with the boy while the neighbor and Srey Ny drove around the area. As soon as the two left, massive tears slid down Lisa's face. This child would die without intervention. Meanwhile, Srey Ny and the woman tracked down the grandmother, who was collecting recycling along the roadside.

Holding the frail body in her arms, Lisa cried out, "God, how can this be? Why do some people have so little?"

CIF worked with Granny to help her keep her grandchild. First, medical care was arranged to deal with his immediate physical needs like hydration and antibiotics.

Then her living conditions were cleaned up and improved. The roof was patched, and a door was installed to create safety for the two. CIF also provided clean water and filtration systems. Granny could no longer leave him to work all day, so a livable stipend was determined. It was enough for the two to do well without creating dependency or taking away Granny's work ethic. One way to do this was to find something Granny could do at home with the little one nearby.

During the initial days of care, it became clear he had unregulated epilepsy. The doctors also thought he had cerebral palsy, although they determined no formal diagnosis. Without the benefits of early intervention, his delays were extreme. With early detection, the brain can learn to rewire itself; however, he lived without care for nearly six years, so the damage left a permanent, irreversible mark.

"He was in such bad shape. Once he received proper medication, his epilepsy was regulated, and he improved immensely," Lisa told me. "It is clear his grandmother loves him and is committed to him. She needed a lot of information and a little support."

More than four years have passed since their initial meeting. At that time, he did not have the strength to roll over or sit up. But now the boy can walk with assistance and eat normally. He throws a ball and plays with his grandmother. Although still nonverbal, he understands what those around him say and can communicate in his way.

"In his initial situation, many people would have said, 'He's better off in an orphanage.' But if you saw where he is now, you would never make that choice for him. Not to mention, his granny finds joy in him, and he gives her purpose."

//

Caring for a person with a disability or illness is a job that runs all day, every day. People need to be aware that burnout is a reality for families caring for these children. Respite is not available to most families in Cambodia. Early on, figuring out a respite plan for the families in CIF's care became a priority for the ABLE team. Their aim is to support the families well enough that they can care for their children rather than CIF becoming the carers.

Lisa and Srey Ny built up a group of families trained to care for a child with disabilities or illnesses for a short time. There is no set schedule for the families who need breaks, but they are aware of the availability of respite care.

In the future, the ABLE team plans to set up a respite home where children can spend the day. Typically, healthy children attend school, but since local schools usually lack accessibility for children with disabilities, their families never get a break.

Now, the local schools have started including more ABLE children. Since the program began, there has been significantly more awareness of the rights of children with disabilities.

//

Born with severe cerebral palsy, Kanika had feeding problems. The older she got and the larger she grew, the harder it was for her foster family to keep up with her nutritional needs.

In infancy, she had been placed with one of CIF's very first foster families. A Christian family with strong values, they had other healthy foster kids and a few older biological children. They were one of the first in their community to invest themselves in caring for children outside their DNA. Brimming with compassion and patience, the mother had pulled many hurting children from the cusp of self-destruction and given them a strong sense of love and acceptance.

Kanika's CP limited her mobility, and as she grew older, feedings became difficult. When she ate, food got into her lungs, which meant it took hours to feed her. With the risk of infection too high in the countryside and no option for surgery, a feeding tube was not an option.

Day and night, her mother's life revolved around feedings. The family pitched in to care for the home and each other, doing their absolute best for Kanika, but it was not enough. Repeatedly, she got chest infections, ending up hospitalized in Phnom Penh. The hospital staff would put in a nasogastric (NG) tube, and she would slowly recover.

The cycle continued with Kanika losing vital body weight due to infection. Infections became more and more frequent. The NG tube also carries the risk of aspiration, food entering the lungs, or regurgitation.

Sitting by her daughter's side in the hospital, her mother grew weary and disheartened watching the girl languish. With each infection, Kanika grew less responsive and engaged less with the world around her. During each cycle of hospitalization, she lost resilience.

Lisa lost sleep. Kanika's parents lost sleep. Torn between the fear of losing her and the fear of holding on too long and prolonging her suffering, they wrestled with their choices, constantly questioning themselves.

The what-ifs piled up in her mother's mind. It reached a point at which the team began to question if this cycle of hospitalizations was in her best interests. Was it only prolonging her suffering?

Kanika never really improved. Hope glimmered with a feeding tube at one point, but it was not enough, and she relapsed soon after.

"How aggressively should we treat these infections? We

kept losing ground, and eventually, there was no hope she would ever get much better," recalled Lisa.

The team, alongside the family, came to the heartbreaking decision to no longer take Kanika back to the hospital. She would be fed as best as possible, loved, and surrounded by family, but she would die.

At nine years old, in her bed, in her home, next to her mother, Kanika breathed her last breath. As tears slid down the woman's face, she and her husband stood side by side and murmured all the words of love they had. Her siblings were there too.

Not only were those siblings fostered into love, but they also learned to care for, play with, and love a child rejected by many in society. As a result, Kanika's life was not wasted.

Kanika's older brother, Pisey, who now towers over his parents, looked at his foster mother with deep affection as he shared with me a life of abuse and neglect before she took him in at six years old. But that former life was merely a shadow to him. Most of Pisey's memories started after he was in this home filled with laughter and care. Despite his mother's time spent nursing Kanika, he never felt ignored.

In 2015, in reflection on Kanika's death, Lisa wrote, "How do you determine the value of human life? Of course, the answer is clear for those of us with a biblical worldview. Every human being is precious, having infinite value, based on having been made in the very image of the Creator. This inherent worth of human life is further declared by the price that Jesus was willing to pay on behalf of these image bearers, giving up His own life for us. Others, however, have their own points of view . . . In many cases, people are valued for what they contribute or devalued based on the perception that they have nothing of value to give. In a cultural setting where many people are struggling just to get by, this tendency to value people based on their earning potential or their capacity to contribute to the work can seem like a practical necessity from a purely human perspective."

Lisa wrote about how Kanika's family saw her intrinsic value and treated her with as much compassion as their healthy children. Although Kanika was nonverbal, her experience with the genuine love of a family showed through her bright eyes and personality.

At her funeral, her parents broadcast Kanika's testimony to everyone gathering out of respect for the family. Their adult children traveled a day to attend because she was a significant part of their family.

Kanika's mother's open and unreserved grief spoke the loudest to their community. Her mourning ripped at the hearts of those in attendance. A strong woman of deep faith, her neighbors knew her gentleness and bright smile the most. But to watch her weep relentlessly over the girl imprinted the costliness of the loss upon them.

Lisa summed up Kanika's funeral, "It was readily apparent that her life mattered; in her brief time on earth, she had made a positive difference in the lives of others. And that's why we do what we do at Children in Families. Because these little lives matter, every single one, and they all need to know the love and affection of families who will affirm the value of who they are and help them develop into the people they were meant to be. Not because the value of human life is a nice idea, but because it is true."

Equipping To Serve People with Disabilities

Just as Cathleen and Anny never made decisions without the other person's input, the ABLE team communicates closely and consults each other for every decision. Although Lisa felt a weight of responsibility for Kanika and the other children in the program, there are other factors in decision-making. The families, government, policy, and the team's input are all important.

Lisa and Srey Ny built the program together. They found kindred spirits in each other, a bond beyond coworkers. Their shared experience growing up with children with disabilities and their passion for using their gifts to help these children made it an easy match.

Early on, Sovann was brought on to the team as the provincial physical therapist. Although she hadn't received much training in treating people with disabilities, she was dedicated to learning and has played a key part in the program's success. Lisa and Srey Ny can only travel to the villages occasionally, whereas Sovann is always there.

One CIF social worker took the personal initiative to push for a child with disabilities to get into the local school. He refused to be deterred by the initial lack of willingness of the school directors. As a result, some of the school programs now offer braille and include our blind children, an achievement that would have felt impossible in the early years.

//

Not only is keeping children in families better for the child, but an unintended consequence of keeping children with disabilities in a family, rather than placing them in residential care, is that the society around them becomes more inclusive. When removed from society, people with disabilities or chronic illnesses are not present in people's daily lives. It robs a whole community of growth. It is through proximity that people become more familiar with interacting with people with disabilities. Exposure is a massive catalyst for understanding and empathy.

In the beginning, personal relationships were how the staff could find families to care for children with disabilities. Yet as people in the same community were exposed to families caring for these children, more and more people showed willingness. As a result, the idea of caring for a child with disabilities or chronic illness became less intimidating. Cambodians just needed to know it was possible and an often joyful experience.

Community exposure and inclusion also help children get early intervention for their needs and encourage new parents who may have an ill or disabled child to keep their child and work through the initial struggles.

//

What happens when a child with disabilities turns eighteen in the ABLE project?

It hasn't happened yet, but CIF is on the cusp of reaching this point. Relationships with other organizations will be essential. A few group homes with work environments and schooling are available for adults with disabilities. There is even an organization in Kep that gives them an occupation.

It is a farm that sells tea and vegetables. Adults with disabilities live there and learn life and job skills. It is all done ethically and monitored. Their goal is to have these young adults eventually move back into their communities and contribute, but for now, it is residential.

There are limited spots for these residential programs, and the option only exists for people with less severe disabilities. However, they try to focus on family and ensure that the young people do not lose connection with their communities. There is also a community of artists and people who make crafts and serve in a cafe called Epic Arts in Kampot.

Some families, the ABLE staff anticipate, will be able to continue as surrogate families. CIF will not cut off their support as their child becomes an adult if there are no other avenues of care for the person with disabilities.

"An emphasis currently is on advocacy, making people aware of services for adults with disabilities. However, an essential key for family-based care to be a success is that parents need to know there are options for when their children reach adulthood. Families need to know that their child will grow up, move out, and potentially contribute one day."

Families of adults with disabilities will need residential and nonresidential support. In addition, more recreational and job opportunities are needed. Lisa continues to survey those in the field who have more specific expertise. She wants to hear from them and get their input to help build the best possible programs.

//

"If my 'then-self' knew in the beginning what this program would become . . ." Lisa said, Srey Ny going to Geneva for the UN Human Rights Convention was something she could have never imagined.

Lisa still pinches herself at how the vision of being in Cambodia herself, serving people who serve those with disabilities, has come together in such a beautiful way. Her passion and reality are being able to positively impact people who are working to empower people with disabilities. With the ABLE project on a small level, she has witnessed a widespread rippling effect not foreseen in the early years.

With ABLE in the capable hands of Srey Ny and the team, Lisa is expanding to a broader geographic area in Cambodia. She is not precisely replicating ABLE; instead, she is building on its foundations and existing programs in other organizations.

"We know what families who care for children with disabilities need to succeed. Cambodian government policy states children should be in their own families, so how do we make this possible throughout the nation?"

Rather than relinquish them to residential care, there are several different touch points to address. First, there are awareness and advocacy. There are resources and availability. Lisa's new project addresses service needs by building the capacity of staff working with people with disabilities in community roles. Then also, it is building relationships with national and local authorities, educating on awareness of the needs of children with disabilities and their families. The project also helps connect authorities with what resources are available locally and regionally.

"People are much more willing to help if they know how to help. When empowered with knowledge, they have a greater willingness."

Outsiders come to Cambodia and nations like it, and often they make the false conclusion that society is apathetic to the needs of the vulnerable and marginalized. Yet scratching below the surface reveals not apathy but a lack of knowing where to start. Rather than passing judgment on the culture, Lisa and ABLE seek to give people tools to know how to walk alongside those with disabilities.

When "Calling" Lacks Wisdom

I had gone to Australia for a year to do an intensive, inductive study of the entire Bible. I returned to Cambodia in late 2017, resuming my work with CIF. When Lisa and I met for lunch, she was so excited for me to meet Alicia, a new member on staff. "You will absolutely love her," Lisa told me. "She reminds me a lot of you. Big heart and incredibly passionate."

I did meet Alicia, and I immediately took to her. I was blown away when she and her husband, Samuel, shared their story with me.

//

"The truth is, my brokenness and desire to create a family to fill a hole in my life fueled the orphan industry."
–Alicia Taylor

As of 2006, it was illegal in Cambodia to open new orphanages, and those in existence were expected to slowly phase out. However, even as family-based care and family preservation began in Cambodia through CIF and more child protection laws were created and enforced, orphanages continued to open throughout the country. Millions of dollars continue to fuel the orphanage industry, despite laws, and over 400 orphanages operated across the nation.

With a mere three months between her undergraduate and graduate studies, Alicia felt the lure from Christine Caine's A21 Campaign. She wanted to cast off her privileged American life and go to Southeast Asia to make a difference. The only problem was her lack of experience and the short time window.

The rejection emails stacked up, and for good reason. Most organizations found short-term volunteers to be a drain on their time and resources rather than a help. As she browsed social media, she found an orphanage in Cambodia seeking volunteers. She clicked through photos of poor children with lush vegetable patches and a swing set.

Working with orphans could be an incredible calling. Hope rose in her chest; perhaps this was where she should be. She would gain experience and could learn from the directors. Who would begrudge a summer spent with lonely children in need? The orphanage accepted her volunteer request.

A few months later, the red and blue metal roofs of Phnom Penh appeared as her plane drifted past the Mekong and Tonle Sap rivers. Skeletons of new high-rises dotted the landscape. It was a far cry from the bullet-ridden brick piles of the early '90s.

A taxi took her about two hours south of Phnom Penh. As they pulled into view of the orphanage, the shouts of excited children rose; she watched them kick up dust in packs, running toward the gate to greet her. Clamoring and shouting, they vied for her attention. Stepping into the glaring sun, she laughed out loud—what bliss, where calling meets fulfillment.

After a whirlwind of greetings from about fifty kids, a middle-aged American man sauntered toward her from what appeared to be the office. His hand extended in a warm welcome.

"Hello, I am Lawrence. You must be Alicia. How was your journey here?"

Just as she opened her mouth to respond, a diminutive Khmer woman with a few gray streaks in her hair stepped out from behind Lawrence.

"Excuse my rudeness," Lawrence interjected. "This is my wife, Tieng. She's been your main contact through messages."

Two young women approached quietly and were introduced. Barely twenty years old, they were the houseparents for the girl's dorm. The room housed twenty girls, with these young women as the primary caretakers; there were about the same number of boys in another dorm room with one young man supervising them. The children crowded around, watching and waiting for the introduction.

"Sophear, please show Alicia to her room," Lawrence said to one of the young women. She nodded and motioned Alicia to follow her toward the main building. This place would be home for the next two months.

In many ways, Alicia was nothing new. Vans of foreigners pulling up for a few weeks were routine for the children. Then, as quickly as they came, the teams would pile into the van and barrel off down the road.

Most of the year, they attended public school down the road. After a light breakfast of borbor (traditional rice porridge), they traipsed off down the road in their crisp uniforms. Kicking up dust in the dry season and navigating puddles in the wet, they walked to school together as long as there were no visitors.

But then, with little notice, vans full of visitors would unload, and candy and new soccer balls would appear, bringing in much-needed funding. But each time a team or donors came through, the directors took the children out of school, putting their learning and futures at risk, so the teams could play with the children. It caused many orphanages to groom their younger children to act even more childish and needy. Predictably, they did not vet volunteers.

"Make the strangers like and take pity on you" seemed to be the unspoken mantra in the institution. Teams preferred the cute little ones, toting them about all day, lamenting their "parent-less" status. It taught the kids to be brazen in their interactions with strangers and to remain childish.

Church services, songs and dances, crafts with colored paper, and games abounded. Their only responsibility was to show up, look cute, and hold hands with the tall, sweaty white people wearing baggy clothes.

The children liked the teams for more than just getting to miss school; the food portions were significantly better when foreigners were around. All the children slept better and ate better during those times, and they quickly learned to perform for the visitors. The little ones always got the most attention, climbing into laps and pulling arms tightly around themselves. Visitors would shed tears over the small ones as they left. Sincere hearts ached on behalf of fabricated stories and a romanticized glimpse into the lives of poor, rural Cambodians.

"I wish we could take him home," they lamented. "Poor motherless child."

Good thing the child could not understand English well enough because he was not motherless. His mother's home was a twenty-minute walk from the orphanage. He recalled his mother's sorrowful eyes as she gathered him in her arms and carried him to the institution's gates. She had put him there to save him from his abusive father, hoping her situation would improve one day. But he did not understand. Several years passed, and he would still sleep at night with a prayer in his heart that she would return.

He did not need a stranger's arms to cart him across the globe to a strange home and stranger culture and language. Instead, he needed his mother to be safe and capable of caring for him.

Alicia remained blissfully unaware of most of the children's real stories for that summer. Simple communication played up the magic of her experience. It kept her safe from the responsibility that comes with deep knowledge of the children's lives and made room for assumptions.

Each child strove to make the absolute best impression on

her. Sitting in the dining hall on her first day with the staff and kids, they ate a simple meal of rice, pork, and overboiled greens. Then she explored the grounds with a trail of children following her. It was beautiful with vegetable gardens and a large fishpond. Swings and slides sat under a voluminous tree nearby.

From all accounts, the grounds were delightful and would make any donor proud. The children's environment seemed to lack nothing. "How wonderful," Alicia thought as she surveyed the grounds, "that these poor children have access to an abundance of opportunities."

Lawrence and Tieng invited her to their flat for dinner that first evening. It did not cross her mind to question that the director, his wife, and three children ate in separate quarters. That evening, sitting at a proper dining table upstairs from the compound, Alicia marveled at the steam and delightful scent emanating from a stack of grilled hamburger patties.

The following day, she rose with the sun. The children were preparing for a school day, yet made the time to greet her eagerly as she left her room. While short-term teams elicited the chance to miss school, Alicia was their visitor who stayed the longest. Therefore, the children's schedule was less interrupted. The young dorm mothers promised to teach her some Khmer after the children left.

The directors emerged from their upstairs apartment after the children were gone. Lawrence made his way into the office for paperwork. Tieng went to the kitchen to review the food budget with the cook. Alicia learned within her first week that they would be less available. Tieng seemed to be in constant motion between her small children and the logistics of the orphanage, while Lawrence was more reticent. Their children rarely interacted with the orphanage kids. There was a clear distinction between the director's family and the orphans.

A daily routine developed. The children went off to school, and the staff began their tasks. As Alicia's relationship with the three main caregivers grew, so did her unease at their age. They were noticeably young to care for so many kids. They had no families of their own and were barely older than some of the children they looked after. Lawrence and Tieng had met them all at a local church and enticed them with their role being a "calling from God."

There was a small, niggling voice inside of her that sensed the staff were under spiritual manipulation; however, recognizing she knew little of the culture and the orphanage, she brushed back her doubt and served with joy.

The remainder of the summer sped past. Before she knew it, Alicia had fifty tearful children huddled around her. Finally, she slid into the back seat of her taxi and left. Her heart was torn between a feeling of satisfaction with her work and grief over the loss of those relationships.

//

After settling into grad school, Alicia remained in communication with Tieng. She convinced a group of friends to return to Cambodia over the coming summer for two weeks. The group included a guy named Samuel who was bright and good-natured; by the end of the trip, Alicia and Samuel were more than friends. They left hand in hand, dreaming of a life in Cambodia.

The visit was fun, however, Alicia couldn't help but notice the new houseparents. None of the previous staff were there.

A whirlwind of years passed. The completion of grad school and physical therapy training. Engagement. Marriage. She and Samuel were standing together, ready to take on the world.

Just as the Taylors prepared to return long-term, an email from Tieng arrived in their inboxes. She and Lawrence hoped to focus more on a private school they started. Then, in a shocking request, they asked Samuel and Alicia to consider taking over the orphanage. It was not the direction the

Taylors had planned, but perhaps it was the direction God wanted them to take.

"It struck us on all kinds of emotional and spiritual levels. What if our calling was to be a family to these kids?" Alicia reminisced. "There was a clear gap in the kids' lives. They had attachment issues and a heartbreaking lack of care. We had good intentions; we wanted to help. We were not aware they had families. In fact, we would find out later that they all had families. Most lived about five minutes away."

In 2016, the couple moved to Cambodia. Within the first week, it felt different. Abnormally different. Alicia had known Tieng and Lawrence for about six years and had been to the orphanage twice, yet for the first time, she was there as staff, not a donor. Without visitors, the magic evaporated. A sad weightiness hung in the atmosphere.

As they trained to take over, inside information made them quickly reevaluate their dream of being "Mom" and "Dad" to these children. One of their first tasks was to deal with child-on-child sexual abuse.

Lawrence's sweeping decision to kick the perpetrator out of the orphanage shocked them. Then, he merely told the victims to move on. The boy, clearly a victim of sexual abuse himself, had nowhere to go and would never receive the help he needed.

While the Taylors agreed that the threat of abuse needed to be addressed and neutralized, they were left uneasy about removing him. He would return to his community even more vulnerable than before. Would his history of sexual abuse lead to harming more children, or would it make him more at risk?

They balked when nothing more was said or done.

Samuel and Alicia only saw the directors sporadically. The kids referred to Lawrence and Tieng as "Mom" and "Dad," but they didn't play the role of mother or father to these children. They worked in their offices during the day and then spent time in their upstairs apartment with their own children.

The institution boasted all types of innovations as well as gardens, a basketball court, and bright murals and walls painted countless times to entertain visiting teams. It worked to draw in donors who would celebrate the opportunities for the children.

However, there were glaring areas of neglect. For all the extracurricular activities, the food was abysmal. The Taylors ate dinner with the children. It consisted daily of soup, rice, cabbage, and cow bone. There was no meat and only small leaflets of vegetable remnants. Both clutched their empty stomachs and sometimes cried themselves to sleep from hunger pangs. Within the first month, Samuel and Alicia dropped almost twenty pounds.

Funding was inconsistent and usually allocated for a unique feature. Food, a basic human necessity, was the first budget line to be cut. When teams came, the children and the Taylors ate feasts. Real meat with sauces and flavors graced their plates. When teams left, so too did the culinary delights. It was window dressing.

The Taylors had concerns about the lack of oversight. The umbrella of accountability quickly deteriorated. The churches and donors who helped start the orphanage faded out of the picture. So, Lawrence and Tieng held responsibility for the budget and running of the ministries, plus the children's livelihood.

Often, orphanage donors are told and shown what the directors want them to know, believing it's safe and working well. Under the surface is another matter. However, when that shallow layer of accountability evaporated, the directors went completely unchecked. All decisions and responsibilities flowed through them, concentrating power and setting them up for corruption.

To the Taylors, it began to feel like the whole setup existed to please the visiting teams and the directors. In absolutely no area were the children put first.

As the magic of the orphanage dissipated, Samuel and

Alicia's language improved. Their cute little phrases and play-time with the children suddenly grew into deeper conversations. During these conversations, they slowly unearthed the truth that many of these kids had parents. Throughout the year, many adults stopped by the orphanage, some looking shockingly like the children in their care. They were usually accompanied by other children, siblings to those in the institution.

One day Alicia sat with a girl as she did her math homework. All of a sudden, the girl looked up from the pages and poured forth the story of her mother's recent visit to the school. It was neither a lament nor a plea for help, but a simple statement of fact. Alicia asked for more details. The girl took her hand and walked her to the orphanage gate. She pointed down the road and described the corner shop a few streets away, her home.

As Alicia and Samuel were preparing for bed that evening, she brought it up.

"Did you know Chanta's family lives nearby?"

He stared at her, toothbrush dangling from his mouth, and blinked as if he did not quite understand her statement. Then, after he spit out his toothpaste and rinsed his mouth, he engaged more fully in the conversation.

"That's interesting," he replied. "Just last week, Rith indicated his father lived in the next village. I thought I heard him wrong. What did Chanta tell you?"

"She told me her mother stopped by the school today to check on how she was getting on with her studies. Her mother is illiterate but cares very much that her daughter becomes educated. It is why she is here. She's the oldest and will be obligated to care for her parents later in life, so her best chance of attending school was to be put into the orphanage."

Samuel pulled back the mosquito net and hopped into the bed. Absorbing Alicia's words, his thoughts drifted to the youngest one, Bora. The kids all teased him and called him a "naughty child." It was clear to anyone that Bora struggled in the orphanage. He had no siblings there and lacked consistency. His behavior ranged from endearingly cute though emotionally stunted to full rage and a desire to aggravate the older children. Those traits in an older child would make them insufferable and disliked by society. Samuel knew Bora needed a family.

After Alicia turned out the light and crawled into the net, Samuel voiced his thoughts on the little one. Then, after a lengthy conversation, they drifted off to sleep, determining the following day to dig into his history once the kids were at school.

The children raced off, and the Taylors began tidying the campus and running over budgets with the kitchen staff. Just as Alicia was about to track down Tieng to ask about Bora, an email from a donor caught her eye.

The donor, having been made aware that most children across the globe who dwell in orphanages are not truly orphans, raised a valuable question. What was their plan for reintegration? He outlined his concerns for long-term residential care and indicated his funds would come to them as long as they used it toward working the orphanage out of a job. These kids needed to return to their community.

Alicia's heart sang. The timeliness of this message was providential. Perhaps she and Samuel were not placed in the orphanage to create their own family. Maybe they were there at such a time to help with reintegration.

It was the confirmation she needed to address Bora head-on. After sifting through his files, she learned his mother lived in a nearby village. She pulled aside one of the dorm parents for further questioning. Another young woman from a local church knew who Bora's mother was. His mother came by regularly for the past two years, asking for him back.

"What?" Alicia asked the girl to repeat herself, this time in English, to be sure she understood.

Alicia processed this. She had heard correctly that his mother wanted him. She and Samuel decided to meet the woman. There must be some misunderstanding or danger they were unaware of for the child to still be in their care when his mother longed for him.

A few days later, the village chief and a dorm mother sat in the woman's stilt house with them. She offered Samuel and Alicia a cold Coke she purchased for their honor, handing them a plastic straw.

Her story poured out. She, herself, grew up in an orphanage. Unaware of her vulnerability, she married in haste at a young age, quickly regretting her choice. She detailed the abusive husband, the threat to Bora's life. Glancing at her snoozing toddler, she smiled and continued her story. She had remarried a kind man. The village chief interrupted at this point to share about her new husband and his merits. Bora had a family, a safe family who wanted him. How wonderful!

They proceeded cautiously, ensuring they gathered as much information as possible from the mother and the village chief. Putting the boy into any sort of tumultuous situation could be his undoing. Still, they were excited to return to discuss the case with Lawrence and Tieng. This transition would be the perfect opportunity for the directors to shift their focus from the orphanage to the school. Reintegration was a win-win solution for everyone involved.

Their meeting with Lawrence and Tieng was shocking. Alicia and Samuel could not have been more wrong about the director's response. Their months of hard work, tracing families, investigating, and meeting with local authorities was met with outright rejection by Lawrence. They left feeling disoriented.

All of Lawrence's reasoning seemed circular and unclear. He was an American who came to rescue kids; who was anyone to question his tactics? Who were these children's parents compared to him and his overwhelming sacrifice and compassion? Didn't he know better than they did?

Samuel and Alicia were astounded by his arrogance, and both spiraled a bit in the emotional upheaval. The Taylors returned to their daily drudgery, feeling gaslit. Initially, Lawrence appeared to like the idea of reintegration, yet when they put it into practice, he shut down their forward momentum. It did not make sense.

//

The orphanage was drowning in dysfunction. Amid the reintegration dilemma, they realized many of the children were sick.

One girl, Srey Mom, came to the orphanage after her parents died of TB. She was the only real orphan of the entire bunch. She failed to gain weight, and her lethargy and chronic cough caused concern. The Taylors highly suspected she also had TB.

If she received no care, it would be her eventual death sentence. In addition, living in close quarters with other children made her illness another cause for concern. TB is contagious. Yet Lawrence refused her medical care.

Maslow's Hierarchy of Needs categorizes the needs of human beings and places them in order. Physical conditions form the base of the pyramid, like food, access to clean water, and medicine. These needs must be met first. The next need is safety and security, followed by love and belonging. These are the relational needs, and they are most often met through family and local community. At the top of the pyramid, after all the other needs have been met, are the spiritual and psychological needs for esteem and self-actualization.

This orphanage had flipped the pyramid. Basketball courts and fishponds (leisure) took precedence over the physiological needs for food and medicine. The need for a child to experience love and belonging was considered last of all.

Srey's Mom's condition was concerning for both her and

the others around her. Several of the children had worms. One child had such a bad case that he had vomited worms. After several rejections of medicine due to budget constraints, Samuel lost his temper. He marched to the director and called him out. But Lawrence remained steadfast. He did not believe the children's condition warranted a hospital visit or even deworming medicine.

The Taylors felt their favor with Lawrence and Tieng wavering and decided to address everything. The food, the health care, and the reintegration. Alicia pressed Lawrence on his refusal to reintegrate Bora. She did not let the vague deflections throw her off course like before. She dug and dug until he gave an honest response.

Bora could not return to his mother because Bora kept donors interested. Teams fell in love with him. He was the poster child of the institution.

Lawrence's statement not only incriminated his character, it incriminated the entire model of orphanage support. The truth stared Samuel and Alicia in the face.

For an organization or people to be worthy of attention and donations, they had to be cute, vulnerable, and entertaining. There had to be an element of poverty and need. Distant, brown-skinned people were neglecting their adorable children; in turn, sacrificial and benevolent outsiders would swoop in to rescue those precious children. The smaller, cuter, and more vulnerable the children, the more the donors gloried in their role.

Bora played his part well. If he had not been a victim before entering the orphanage, he was certainly being exploited now. They didn't know what to do with this information, but what came next nearly broke the two of them.

They'd been working with another couple in the community on curriculum for "Good Touch, Bad Touch." They began to teach the children about sexual abuse and set up a reporting system. Lawrence seemed angry about it, but they'd just had the big fight about reintegration, so Samuel moved forward with the program.

It did not take long. Through tears, a young man revealed the touching and the sex acts. But it was not child-on-child. It was Lawrence.

They had seen the play wrestling and the preferential behavior toward young men, but now the pieces fell into place.

The boy Lawrence had kicked out of the orphanage had not learned the behavior outside the orphanage, but rather from within. This explained his hesitancy to get a counselor to help the children and the boy's immediate dismissal from the premises. Lawrence would have been exposed.

When Lawrence became aware of the accusations, he talked Samuel into circles. After all, it was cultural to play with penises. Samuel's jaw dropped at this confession. Tieng looked as though she were about to slide out the door. They suspected that she was aware of her husband's preferences.

A nauseating few days followed as the Taylors alerted the US Embassy and Homeland Security. The FBI joined in the investigation. The boys clammed up during the interview and made no direct confession. After all, it was confusing. The man they knew as Dad was also an abuser. They knew it was wrong, but fear, trauma, and abandonment wrapped around their hearts. What would happen if they were kicked out? He had groomed them well.

The home churches and donors were alerted and immediately pulled funding. Overnight, every dollar dried up. Everyone abandoned the kids. The Taylors also knew they were insufficient for the task at hand.

After a providential encounter with Lisa from CIF, Samuel and Alicia found their answer. CIF stepped into the fray and reintegrated the children into safe families.

Since there was no direct evidence of sexual abuse, the government institutions monitored Lawrence but never could charge him. He and Tieng and their two children seemed to vanish entirely from all the ministries.

Samuel and Alicia's organization moved them to Phnom Penh for debriefing and healing. Less than a year after landing, their whole world was spinning. They could understand why so many people slinked away from abusive organizations without raising alarms. The aftermath of setting off this bomb, even if it was the right thing to do, was devastating. God seemed to carry them, but the costs were high and the wounds ran deep.

In time, Alicia and Lisa's friendship blossomed. They both worked in physiotherapy and had grown up with disabled sisters. And they both wanted to see family-based care take over institutions.

Not only did CIF help the children, but it also became a balm to the Taylors. Here they found like-minded people and an organization that focused not only on the best interests of the children but also on the best interests of the parents and communities. They discovered a staff, composed primarily of Cambodians, who were passionate about family-based care.

Over time, Samuel and Alicia found themselves almost seamlessly knitted into the CIF community. They joined the team. That first year in Cambodia was a painful catalyst for the passion they have found now.

During her healing time, Alicia allowed God to search her heart deeply. She dug into "calling" in Scripture and saw that it did not point to a location or career. Instead, it pointed to character, long suffering, and a call to love. It was rarely a direction or occupation.

A feeling of peace and freedom grabbed her soul. "He [Jesus] wants me to be like Him. It's not about what I am doing, but who I am.

"I wanted to use calling to justify our decisions. But I made a mistake. I had a selfish desire to be important. 'Calling' kept us at the orphanage despite the issues," Alicia reflected.

Rather than become embittered or broken by their experiences, Samuel and Alicia leaned into their failings. They openly admitted their wrongs and worked to learn and make things right. They are a model for those of us who want to work for a better future for vulnerable children and families.

An Advocate for Women and Children

Ing is a community children and women's advocate. Since 2009, she has worked closely with CIF, helping to vet families for the programs. The role is both an honor and a challenge. Living in the community gives her direct access to the people. She has insight into their behavior, ability to raise children, economic situation, and family history. Ing is aware of past violence, substance abuse, and gambling issues, key identifying factors that would raise flags about taking in a child. She also watches how the children behave.

Rarely do the placements of foster children fail; however, Ing recalls one family whose situation did not work out. They had accepted all the conditions and gone through the training, but not long into the foster child's placement, Ing discovered relatives caring for the child.

While it is common in Cambodia for extended families to share in child-rearing, CIF's policy is clear that the parents with whom we place the child must be their primary caregivers. After inquiring, Ing found that the foster girl had overwhelming behavioral issues with the foster parents. CIF works to keep children in one home, however, they found the girl to be a poor match for her family, so she was placed in a new family. She had been sexually abused and sadly the only way she knew to bond with adult men was expressed in sexualized behavior. Her new father learned to only reward her appropriate behavior and set healthy boundaries. Soon, she realized she was loved and safe, her new father treated her like a child, not an object to be used. As healthy relationships grew, most of her behavioral issues were resolved.

It takes time to overcome cultural assumptions about raising families. The majority of families who foster want to change and grow. However, traumatized children act out, and at times the parents want to give up. Ing and the social workers step in to assist families in solving the problems. And as foster and kinship families learn, their neighbors also learn.

Having known the commune families for her entire life, Ing was aware of the difficult living conditions, lack of nutrition, and sanitation issues. The work of CIF has raised the quality of life for all her community. Ing worked alongside organizations and teams who installed wells or dug toilets.

Ing is also vocal about the rights of children with disabilities. She advocated for CIF's ABLE children to get access to local schooling. "I want all communes to do what CIF does," she told me. "CIF does not just put children in families. They educate the parents. The good fruit of this is that the whole environment improves. Things are cleaner, health improves, and living conditions get better."

Consistently, she has seen the families who take in children experience holistic growth. In turn, they influence the community around them.

I asked her if she thought this was only something for Cambodia or if it could work in other cultures.

Ing responded with a resounding, "Yes, of course, the world needs to know."

The difference between family-based care and institutionalization is stark. These same children could have been placed in a children's home and maybe gotten food and cleaner water, and their education would likely have improved. But their families and communities would still have the same problems. The children would exist behind a gate, separated from their neighbors and relatives. Instead, whole communes have learned from one another and received access to sanitation, parenting education, and better health care.

Institutions cannot honor the leaders of the community the way CIF does. Ing and other village and commune government officials have key roles and input in the work of CIF. The organization could not have access to the community without their partnership, nor have the scope of understanding to help make wise decisions for the children in the area. While CIF brings programs, education, funding, expertise, and social workers to the scene, the local leaders get their people's buy-in and active participation.

Aging Out

"I would sit by the wall, gazing out at life beyond the orphanage compound, wondering when I could get out, wondering when I would be free from this cage."
–Chrisda, who lived in an orphanage for three years.

In 2008, Sarah Chhin launched Project Sky. The project would eventually become M'lup Russey Organization (MRO), an organization that walks alongside youth living in orphanages. When they become too old to live there, when they "age out" of care, MRO continues to be involved in their lives.

Sarah had already worked for years researching standards of care and implementing those policies. Now she began researching how to support kids with a particular focus on children transitioning from institutional care into communities.

"Do people, including those who fund and run orphanages, consider what happens to children when they age out?" Sarah asked.

Across the globe, children around the age of eighteen become adults. They begin to have more freedom and responsibilities. Usually, this comes in slow stages as families and educational programs prepare the children over their lives to step out into the world on their own.

Most children do not wake up one day functioning as an adult. The transition takes time. They spend their teen years testing boundaries and developing ideas, beliefs, and identities separate from their parents or guardians. They help around their home, learn a trade from a parent, and care for siblings. Then they leave home. These young adult years involve learning to deal with work, schooling, and a budget without someone standing over their shoulder, but adult children know they can still make the trip home for advice and support.

Children in institutions do not get this privilege. Cut off from their communities, families, and even cultures, their transition from orphanage life to adult life can be abrupt, lonely, and often brutal. The term "care leavers" refers to youth who leave or age out of institutional care. The term itself implies that they are stepping out from protection.

Two decades ago, Sarah gathered 514 teenagers from thirty-five orphanages and children's homes with the purpose of collecting unbiased information. She and her team organized the teenagers into fifteen different groups and led a workshop with each group. The groups were arranged so that multiple orphanages would be represented in each group. These groups then answered a series of questions while engaging in creative activities.

"Where do you come from?" "Do you have siblings?" "Are they in the orphanage with you?" "What's your level of education?" "When do you have to leave the orphanage?"

Answers: "I don't know." "When I get a job."

Many of the children had not considered their futures beyond the walls of their institution.

The questions continued. "What life skills do you need?" "What vocational training do you think you'll need?"

The young people wrote their answers and connected them to form a bridge going over the water to show them there was a way to get over their concerns.

"What do you think it will be like on the day you leave the orphanage?" "Where do you want to live?" "Whom do you want to live with?" "And what do you want to do as an adult?"

The facilitators recorded the teenagers' emotions along with their answers. When Sarah and her team collated the information, it became clear the children feared for their futures. Their fears included: gangs, homelessness, violence, and being alone for the rest of their lives. Regardless of their care facility's type, style, or even size, every teen expressed great trepidation and unpreparedness for their lives outside the orphanages.

Two main conclusions came from these workshops. First, people take children to orphanages because they see them as vulnerable. However, the care centers (orphanages) are not taking away this vulnerability. They are merely delaying or even increasing it.

Second, the results indicate that orphanages create orphans in Cambodia. Sarah elaborated, "All the things the kids said pointed to them being scared to leave. They do not have the support to be safe. As a result, they are hypervulnerable to exploitation, abuse, and suicide."

One young man told her, "I feel like a duck let out of a cage, afraid someone might cook me."

They did the same research five years later, adding a control group with village kids who lived with family and community. Again, they gave all participants the same activities and questions.

The young people in the communities had similar ideas and feelings of fear of leaving home. The stark difference was that the kids in the orphanage felt a much higher sense of utter doom. The youth who had grown up in a community were much more upbeat. They may have had concerns, but they knew they always had a home.

On the other hand, for children leaving orphanages, the questions triggered deep fear about the future. They began to question why they ended up in the orphanage in the first place. The institutional upbringing taught them to think that education and a decent job were their most crucial needs, instead of belonging and love.

Many children thought they could fall back on the orphanage, only to realize once they left those doors that the director no longer took any responsibility for them. Moreover, it became clear that their institutionalization alienated them from society. Many did not speak fluent Khmer, so Sarah and her staff had to translate their questionnaires into English.

After collating the research, her team threw a massive meal for the participating kids. Then, they presented the results of their study.

"The orphanage kids felt so empowered and heard," Sarah said, referring to the presentation. "All the kids agreed it was spot-on to their experience."

When they presented the research to orphanage directors at a Chab Dai meeting, however, it was not so well received. In an indignant uproar, the directors all began shouting that the children were lying. "They were all furious," Sarah remembered. "It was every single child in our research agreeing with one another. There was no way these kids were all lying. It was a collective, shared experience regardless of the model of orphanage or institution."

An interview with a former Cambodian orphanage director and his wife yielded similar information. Taevy told me how her husband worked hard in his tiny orphanage to teach the children skills and give them responsibility. However, after they left, the kids kept showing up at their door, needing money, needing help. They struggled to hold a job. Many quit their education programs after a while. Aimless, they got into trouble. After giving one young man a motorbike for work, he crashed it within a month and returned to ask for more.

The kids had received handouts their entire lives. Once they were adults, they had no idea how to care for themselves.

One of the most significant issues with residential care is that children are rarely given a voice or shown options for their care, lives, future, and well-being. CIF and hundreds of international family-based care organizations agree with the policy that children should be actively involved and consulted in the decisions made for their transition or reintegration into society.

Anny has spoken with hundreds of children in orphanages and adults who have aged out. Only a handful said they preferred the orphanage. When she further inquired, she found that those children all came from highly abusive households where they did not feel safe. The rest of them would have preferred to live with their parents or other family members.

Finally, regardless of the size or quality of institutional care, studies show that children will leave with attachment disorders, mental health illnesses, developmental delays, a lack of social skills, a lack of networks outside of the orphanage, and institutional behavior. As a result, they are more vulnerable to being trafficked and abused.

ACCIR's Kinnected program worded it well when it said, "In most cultures, family and extended networks play a vital role in major life events such as marriage, childbirth, and child-rearing. They are also instrumental in finding jobs, providing living arrangements and social safety nets. In many cultures, identity is often tied to your family line . . . When a young person leaves residential care . . . they lack these lifelong relationships and support networks."

According to Dr. Krish Kandiah with the Homecoming Project, studies estimate that one in three care leavers will become homeless, one in five will gain a criminal record, and one in ten will commit suicide. Similarly, a study by Lumos shows children who age out of orphanages are ten times more likely to be involved in prostitution, forty times more likely to get a criminal record, and 500 times more likely to commit suicide than their peers.

Healthy attachment matters. Family and community matters. Whether children are two or eighteen, they deserve to belong and to have a safe place to turn.

Adopting a Boy in a Sea of Girls

The lush rice fields, skirted by palms and flanked by water buffalo, made this a scene of perfection. Recent rain had left the landscape in full bloom with bright blue skies and brilliant cumulus clouds.

We were on our way to CIF's very first village. The area currently has more than forty children in the care of foster families, not including all of the young adults who grew up in this community but who are now in university, getting married, or pursuing a trade in another city.

Initially, Children in Families received criticism for placing most of its children in the countryside. Organizations and other people from Phnom Penh preferred to place children in the city, where they would have opportunities to excel. They saw village life as too provincial and lacking in progress. Yet the vast sky and slow pace of life promised the possibility of a healthy and healing childhood.

At the first home, we turned into an expansive yard, swept clean. Random food carts, motorbikes, and cows wandered past. A middle-aged woman with a sweet face greeted me. The social worker leaned in. "That is Sokea."

Just then, a twelve-year-old boy, Rotana, pulled into the yard on a motorbike with several plastic chairs tethered to the back. He jumped down, shyly glancing my way before blushing and averting his gaze. He was stocky with thick hair that poked out in every direction. Dimples added to his rosy, cheerful appearance. Dara, his father, emerged from their door and gave me a kind greeting. Soon we all sat in the plastic chairs under their stilted wooden house while the family's oldest daughter and their first grandchild rocked peacefully in the hammock.

Dara and Sokea are local snack sellers, making breakfast soups to serve outside the school each morning. Both husband and wife informed me they had had little education and struggled to help their children with their schooling. They were not wealthy, even by village standards, yet they provided a clean home and raised animals to supplement their income.

I struggled to get the couple to speak one at a time. Dara and Sokea usually answered in unison, eager to share about their family. I glanced at my translator to make sure he was following. He smiled and shrugged a little.

Nonplussed by our reaction, the couple pressed on with their story. Neighbors had been fostering children through CIF. Observing the people around them, they realized they had more than enough love to give and wanted a boy.

More than twenty years ago, in the same village, teenage Sokea cared for her disabled mother. Malnutrition, hard labor under the Khmer Rouge, and abandonment by her husband had left Sokea's mother sick in body and spirit.

Sokea met the young Dara from a nearby village at the market. They both worked hard at farm labor to survive. He loved her and wanted to marry her. Her sick mother was of no consequence. It was not part of the Khmer mindset to reject family members; they took care of their own, even if it was a huge and costly burden. Sokea needed him, and he loved her. He hardly had the money for the bride price, yet they found a way.

Then, tragedy struck. Sokea's brother and sister-in-law died in an accident, leaving three nieces orphaned.

The young couple became parents overnight. Dara would inherit three grieving children in marriage and a disabled old woman. But he held no resentment; it was duty and life. It was family, nothing more, nothing less.

What they were more reflective about, however, was their form of parenting.

"We did not know any better," Sokea shared.

The young Sokea and Dara used physical violence against the girls. Verbal abuse, slapping, and inconsistency with consequences ruled the family home. While life was not always turmoil, the girls did not attend school regularly. There were no boundaries. Chaos reigned as they each handled hardship in their broken ways.

Sokea and Dara's parents had beaten them as children. Crude words had rained down upon their young ears. Then parents disappeared, only to reappear weeks or months later. Post-war Cambodia was a grueling place, the countryside even more so. People worked hard and were exhausted. They were always fighting starvation. Death and loss were as common as the seasonal rains.

Culturally, domestic abuse was common and accepted. Neither Sokea nor Dara was ever particularly violent, and the couple loved their family. However, they considered slapping and shouting to be the proper way to handle a child's misbehavior.

As the nieces grew and moved out, Dara and Sokea had three daughters of their own. Dara was completely surrounded by girls.

One day, the youngest toddled over to him in her second-hand dress that had been through five girls before. Taking her tiny hands in his to steady her from tipping over, he daydreamed of a boy to skin his knees and climb trees and help with their motorbike. She was petite with soft baby hairs pinned down, and he loved her dearly, yet he longed for a son.

Dara and Sokea knew the neighbors fostered young children. They had attended some of CIF's community family training and learned about nutrition. Perhaps they could take in a boy.

Soon, they were going to meetings for potential foster parents. Despite their lack of education and meager earnings, the community leaders and CIF staff found the couple incredibly teachable and eager to learn. At every training, the staff saw Dara and Sokea working to implement what they learned in their household.

They became more thoughtful in their responses to their daughter's outbursts. The family also decluttered their home and implemented hygienic practices. More vegetables were incorporated into their diets, with fewer sugary drinks.

All the steps taken were small, but they became habits that formed a healthier lifestyle.

When it came time for the village chief, local police, community leaders, and social workers to decide on families to add to the growing foster care list, it was unanimous that Sokea and Dara would make incredible foster parents.

A few years after their names went on that list, Kunthea, the social worker, called them. A baby boy needed a family. He'd been rescued by an NGO from a potential trafficking situation, and it was unsafe to return him to his biological mother. The following day the three-month-old Rotana was placed in their arms.

"He felt like one blood, one family," his mother said as she recalled holding him for the first time. Never once in the twelve years since has Dara or Sokea thought of him as anything less than biological.

Not only did the couple take him immediately into their hearts, but his sisters also adore him. He has several older male cousins who love him dearly and act like brothers to him.

The sweet baby from a traumatic background turned into a chubby toddler spoiled with love. Soon, he was taking apart toys and putting them back together. His glossy dark eyes lit up in fascination with all things mechanical.

Once when Rotana went missing, they found him attempting to drive the neighbor's small tractor. His feet dangled high above the pedals. His father would slowly pry his fingers from the steering wheel, and little Rotana cried in consternation.

Nothing changed as he grew. The boy is fascinated by all things mechanical. Toy tractors and bulldozers line his walls even as he saves his pocket money for more. Broken fans and loose wiring on a motorbike distract him from school.

If he shows up to school late, it's because he passed a broken-down vehicle, tractor, or road equipment and stopped for a closer look. His parents' only anxiety revolves around his obsession with large vehicles.

"We went to the city [Phnom Penh] to visit our other daughters who work there. We pointed out all the fancy cars and told Rotana that if he studied hard, one day he would be able to buy one, but he didn't care. He would much rather have a digger or bulldozer," his mother laughed. "He's a good kid. We worry about our boys more than our girls. Boys seem to get into much more trouble here with drugs and violence. Rotana behaves well, however. He is peaceful and does not cause fights. He stays out of trouble."

I looked at his bright, gentle face and struggled to imagine him in a fight.

His father cut in, "We want to lead him in a direction to contribute to society. Of course, boys can be more of a challenge than our girls, but we like the challenge."

Not only did they change Rotana's life, but he also changed them. Through the support of the CIF social workers, Dara and Sokea are different parents. Sokea reached out and placed a hand on Kunthea's knee. Kunthea isn't just their social worker; she's also a foster parent and neighbor to the couple. After more than a decade of Kunthea's and CIF's support Dara and Sokea have grown immensely.

"We observe her [Kunthea] and how she raises her children. She does a good job; we strive to be parents like her," Dara said. "These aren't just words for us. She practices what she teaches."

Before CIF put down roots in the community, the village was a reasonably safe place to live. However, because of CIF, many improvements have taken place, not only for foster families but for all the community. The contributions included uniforms and school supplies, support for struggling families, and encouragement in sanitation. Wells were dug, toilets installed, and water filters now make it safer to drink.

"People are much cleaner. CIF taught me a lot about sanitation and the standard of living. As long as CIF organizes an event, anyone in the village can attend, even if they are not one of our [CIF's] families."

Later, Kunthea told me how incredible the couple is. They are the standard of growth she wishes for all families in the community.

While Rotana found his way into their hearts, they made the decision to be better parents. Sanitation, diet, and consistency with boundaries were not the only changes. Before, they found themselves using unkind language with their children. Horrified to learn how words affect development and can crush the spirit of children, Dara and Sokea committed to guarding their tongues.

"My parents love the boy more than us," Rotana's older sister put in, playfully looking at him with a grin. However, it was not necessarily more love, she explained, but better parenting techniques to help them show affection differently. As a result, their daughter now has a better example of how to care for her child.

For most of the interview, Rotana sat in the back, rocking his baby niece in the hammock. He adores her as much as his sisters spoiled and doted on him.

I asked if he was going to teach her to work on tractors. He responded, "I'm going to teach her how to drive tractors!"

Everyone laughed.

While their anxiety over his lack of interest in school remains, consulting with CIF's social workers and knowing they have support relieves many concerns.

Gazing at him with pride, Dara and Sokea shared their joy at finally legally adopting him. No longer is he their son in their hearts alone. As of this year, Rotana is officially their son, forever theirs and able to inherit.

Dara and Sokea are two simple people with little education, living in a tiny village where rice fields and chickens make up most of life. The world would hardly look at their meager snack vending and think they left a mark, yet their desire to love and grow as parents is already reaching multiple generations. From Sokea's disabled mother to orphaned nieces, a traumatized baby they took into their hearts, raising him as their son, and now even a grandchild. In their humble state, they approached parenting with an eagerness to learn. Not only have they changed their family life, but they've also impacted their community. Even the village leaders sing their praises.

As a result, CIF invited the couple to teach other foster families and parents in the area. It's incredible what a little support and heaps of love can do.

A Childless Couple

Stopping outside a local church, we picked up Lim, one of our social workers. Then Leak, another staff member, navigated a series of rural back roads. After a while, we turned onto a narrow pathway only about a tire's width above now-dry rice paddies. In a few places, fence posts and tree branches nearly hedged us in. I sucked in my breath, subconsciously hoping we would fit.

After a while, we turned into one of these farmhouses that dotted the landscape, scaring away chickens and dogs. A woman squatted, stoking the fire under a blackened kettle. One of the tallest Cambodian men I have ever seen stepped around the corner of the house. He looked like a movie star on the set of a rural farm rather than the typical weathered farmer. Flashing a perfect row of white teeth, he smiled and greeted the staff like old friends as his wife stood up from her cooking and joined us.

She was gorgeous too, elegant and graceful even in her daily workwear. I assumed they were in their late twenties. Lim introduced them as Srey Mao and Sengly.

Although materially poor, like the other families we had visited, their home and yard were immaculate. Their possessions were all neatly stowed away on shelves or in cupboards. Srey Mao's mother greeted us as a toddler came careening headfirst from their barn area. Seeing strangers, he changed the course of his mad dash and threw himself on his mother with incredible force. He buried his face in her shoulder, then nervously peeked out at me.

The young couple had been married awhile when it became clear they could not have biological children. However, a few neighbors had fostered children through CIF, and they slowly began the conversation about the possibility of taking in a baby. As they spent years watching the neighbor children develop into good kids, their fears of adoption abated.

"We wanted a girl," Srey Mao shared. "Girls are easier; they are more faithful to their families."

I have heard countless times from Cambodians that girls will stick around and care for their parents even after marriage, whereas male children will leave.

"We began to meet with the social workers and attend meetings by CIF to learn more," she continued. "And we applied for a baby girl."

The couple waited three years for a daughter, but as so many other families also wanted baby girls, none became available. Then, in early 2020, they received a call from Lim about a baby boy rescued from a tragic situation.

Sengly shared that initially they were going to say, "No," but they both sensed they should take time to consider it. Their hearts longed for a child, and their home had felt empty for so long. So, after pondering and discussing it with each other and Srey Mao's mother, who lived on their property, they decided maybe a boy would be a good fit.

Srey Mao said, "We were so hesitant, then we got this nine-month-old baby. We had so many fears. But as we cared for him, our whole hearts bonded."

Sengly nodded in agreement as the toddler, Davin, wiggled from his mother's arms and climbed over to his father. I watched as Sengly looked into the eyes of little Davin, pulling him closer. They both grinned at each other.

As they shared their story, they took me back to the early days with Davin.

Srey Mao awoke nearly every hour in the night, rising from the sleeping mat she shared with her husband and their new baby. Davin looked peaceful, nestled between the two of them. She brushed his wispy hair back from his face. He was filling in, getting chubbier with each day.

The social workers had not given unnecessary details, but they knew that during his three months in emergency care, the child had been underweight and desperately ill. His tiny fingers wrapped around hers in his sleep, and she could not believe that a mother out there would neglect his care like that. She wondered about her foolishness for ever wanting a girl when this baby boy was perfect.

The days were long. Davin cried a lot and demanded constant attention. Srey Mao's mother was a gift to have near. She lived on the property with them and cared for their disabled auntie.

Lim came around several times a week in the early days. She taught them hygienic bottle feeding and brought formula and diapers.

While it remains cultural for parents to believe that too much physical contact will make a child spoiled and needy, CIF's staff taught the family the opposite. Regular physical contact helps children form solid attachments. Holding, feeding, and comforting children when they cry supports healthy emotional growth.

Srey Mao and her mother grew up believing they should prop up a baby with a bottle and leave them on their own, like so many Khmer women before them. However, Lim taught them to hold and feed him, make eye contact, and speak kindly to him. Srey Mao cherished these moments, loving her time watching Davin grow as he showed signs of recognition and intelligence flash in his tiny eyes. He soaked in the world around him.

Davin adored his father, Sengly. One day, as Srey Mao led their cattle in from the fields, she saw Sengly holding Davin in his arms, speaking to the baby. The boy reached his chubby arms, grabbing Sengly's beard in his tiny fists. Suddenly, gurgling joyfully, the baby began to babble back to his father. She stopped in her tracks; her heart swelled as she realized, "Davin knows us. He knows Sengly is his dad."

CIF warned them early on that due to Davin's abuse and neglect in his first months of life, he was likely to experience developmental delays and potentially be disabled for life. Lim, who fostered several children with developmental delays and chronic illness, helped prepare them. Yet as the months marched on, Davin hit each growth and developmental milestone with incredible success. Finally, the couple dared hope perhaps their boy would be healthy.

//

Most of their relatives live several hours away. The little family was at risk of being isolated, yet Lim appeared rain or shine to check in. She was only a phone call away in a crisis or when a concern arose.

One day, while Sengly was in the fields and Srey Mao's mother was visiting a neighbor, Davin grew weak and lethargic. Srey Mao felt his forehead, and it was like fire. Panicking, she fumbled for her phone to call Lim. Lim's calm voice walked her through everything they needed to check, and it became clear Davin was seriously ill. Fifteen minutes later, Lim drove down their narrow lane, whisking both mother and son to the hospital. The medical and emotional support that CIF gave was crucial to the family.

As with the previous families I interviewed, the teaching that impacted Sengly, Srey Mao, and her mother the most was how they spoke to each other and their son. After becoming aware of how negative and unkind their language could be, they all implemented more honoring ways to communicate.

Davin's grandmother said, "I raised children in a very different way. There is so much in the new way of parenting, but it seems much better, much healthier."

Srey Mao said, "Parenting is different than I thought it

would be. Before, it was quiet on our farm. Now that we have Davin, we are much busier and more active, and there is much more noise, but we love him more than we ever expected."

Recently, they were able to adopt Davin officially. Adoption means CIF will slowly remove visits and financial aid to the family. This is a cost they must consider carefully, especially since they are poor, but Sengly said they had no doubts about adopting Davin.

During our interview, Davin managed to climb into each parent's lap, chase the dogs, and get into several things he was not allowed to touch. Finally, his dad picked up the constantly moving toddler and held him. Together, they seemed like best friends.

Getting over his shyness, Davin showed me his toy car. He had taken it apart and attempted to put it back together. He sat in it, indicating I should pull him around the yard. He grew convinced I was not a threat, but a friend. His parents watched, laughing, as we pretended to crash into several things.

A sign of healthy attachment to primary caregivers is a child's ability to discern strangers from familiar people. To take time to assess if a person is safe or not. Only after Davin took shelter in his parents' arms for a while and listened to them talk to me did he decide that I was safe, and this, of course, was in the presence of his family.

People who visit orphanages marvel at the children's instant desire to entertain strangers or throw themselves into their arms. Countless times I have heard how friendly and affectionate these children were to visitors. Unfortunately, this behavior is dangerous and a sign that children never learned to regulate emotionally or to form healthy bonds. Davin, a gregarious child, took shelter with his family when people unfamiliar to him came to his home. He gauged his response to me based on his parents' actions around me. As they grew more comfortable, so did he.

While he knows Lim well and greets her with a smile and a shout, he still does not run to her when he gets tired, hungry, or needs to be held. Instead, he followed his mother every time she left our view, whether to climb the stairs into their stilted home and grab a pillow or to pop into their auntie's small house to bring her lunch.

Lim finally shared her input, "I did not think he would thrive as well as he has. There was so much trauma in the beginning. But he keeps showing us all how smart he is."

As though on cue, the freshly bathed Davin came scampering out from where his father had just dressed him. He grabbed a piece of paper and pen. With his tongue sticking sideways out of his mouth in concentration, the boy scribbled pretend letters and figures all over the paper. He then squatted, head tilted in a thinking pose, finger tapping his dimpled chin. He appeared to be soaking in all that Lim was saying.

Srey Mao looked at him, laughing, and said, "He listens to all of our conversations and asks for clarification when he is not sure what we are talking about."

Lim added, "Davin shows his family daily just how smart he is. He has significantly improved and grown a lot. I see that love is an amazing healer."

The couple would eventually like to take in more children, but find Davin is enough for the present. When they bring up getting him a sibling, he firmly states, "No, no, no!"

Sengly said he recommends adoption to his friends but understands that not everyone can take a child or has the capacity to do so. It certainly filled their world with love.

The Capacity to Love Another Child

Soknan returned from teaching to find his wife, Lyna, working away on her sewing machine. The house was quiet, too quiet. They were so proud of their four children, who attended university in Phnom Penh. Their kids were bright, pursuing great things in their studies; some were married and planning to start families.

However, something felt amiss at home. He loved his wife and enjoyed time with her, but it felt empty with all their children gone. Soknan stepped outside to smoke and ponder an idea he had wanted to discuss with Lyna. As local teachers who were actively involved in community life, Soknan and Lyna had attended the CIF community programs in their village. They were also among the minority Christians and knew several families in their church caring for children.

Stepping back inside, he thought, "Yes, she'll agree to my idea." As though to indicate her willingness, his wife looked up from her work and smiled.

Lyna sighed in relief when he brought it up. She spent her days sewing for people and missed being busy as a mother. Her sense of purpose lay in nurturing children. Not only had their four children filled their tiny home, but all their friends and neighbor kids had constantly dropped in and out.

Like most couples in the province, Soknan and Lyna had married young and started a family almost immediately. Their firstborn came less than a year after the wedding, and the others closely followed.

Within the week of their discussion, they met with social workers and village leaders to begin fostering. Praying constantly, they anticipated their new child, imagining all the features and personality traits just as though they were dreaming of a child they carried.

A few times, the social worker asked about an available older child. Each time they did not have the peace to take the child. Finally, after four years of waiting, they got a call. A baby boy from a complex background needed a home.

He would not necessarily be theirs to keep. That was the most challenging part; the birth mother still had several months to decide if she would relinquish her rights. They would be part of his emergency care with the potential to foster.

They drove to Phnom Penh to meet him. They were excited to squeeze in a visit with their adult children in the city, but their nerves were frayed by the time they arrived. Would this child be a good fit for their family? How would they know if it was right to take him or not?

They had waited so long, yet fear and doubt met them. Soknan prayed and remembered how earnestly they had been asking for this child. He knew they could trust God to tell them if it was right. Still, as they climbed the stairs with the social worker, Soknan and Lyna felt their knees weaken.

A woman holding a whimpering infant met them at the entrance. As soon as Soknan approached, the baby grew silent. Then, as if he knew it was his father, the tiny hand reached up to Soknan. The eyes widened in curiosity as they met, and the tiny fingers wrapped around Soknan's large, worn ring finger. Everything inside Soknan stilled; peace filled him. Here was his son.

Lyna fell in love just as quickly. "I promise I will love you well," she whispered to him.

They named him Elijah after the mighty prophet of God.

Their whole family rejoiced at the news. Their extended family sent baby clothes in such mass that Elijah had an outfit for every day of his first year.

A few months later, his birth mother signed over her rights. They did not ask about the difficulty he came from, for they feared his story would rob their joy. All they knew was that they loved this baby and would do everything in their power to allow him to thrive.

Laughter filled their home again. Over the next twelve years, they added three grandchildren to the mix due to their older kids being busy in the city with education and work. So, Elijah grew up with his nieces and a nephew who were like little brothers and sisters.

Elijah grew into a sensitive, kind, and brilliant child. His parents' love for reading gave him an advanced educational start in comparison to many of his peers.

The four children share a mat on the floor at night, huddled together under their mosquito net with fans to cool them off. Elijah fights to keep his eyes open to read one more page of history. His five-year-old niece snuggles close in her sleep; her stuffed bear clutched tightly in her arms. He swats away a swarm of gnats around his book light before finally giving in to sleep.

//

If school is in the afternoon, Elijah rises early to pick up the cow dung and pile it in the garden before helping his mother wash up their dishes. Then he walks the youngest to school.

In his downtime, he writes stories and loves reading his textbooks, including his favorite subject, Khmer grammar, which his father teaches.

Soknan and Lyna say that the support of CIF staff has made them better parents. The social workers guided them to positive parenting that did not involve crude speech, physical punishments, or inconsistent threats. The teaching has also spilled into how they raise their three grandchildren. As a result, they are finding the approach CIF taught them is more effective.

"I am a teacher. I have education and knowledge; however, we got a lot of good advice and training from CIF," Soknan shared. "We've been applying what we learned and saw positive results.

"I would share with other parents that people must respect their children and treat them like humans. Do not bully, and reason instead of belittling or abusing. It felt countercultural to respect a child's rights, but we've seen much positive fruit for us as a couple and for the kids."

Both he and Lyna also shared, "We learned that it's important to be consistent. Set firm boundaries and enforce them."

Their interactions with the children influence the neighbors. Children are again coming and going from their home constantly, and those kids experience positive parenting through them. Neighbors see how well-behaved their children are and have learned from their family culture.

//

From the moment Soknan held Elijah, the boy was his son. But there was no legal way to do domestic adoption in their early years with CIF, so they fostered, knowing it was forever. They would always be there for their son as long as they lived. When it became a possibility to adopt, they started the paperwork.

Their only fear was how Elijah would feel. He knew he was their son, and they never treated him differently from their other children, but adoption papers would confirm the different way he came into their family.

Yet on the day they completed the papers, all the older siblings came to celebrate and brought gifts. Now nothing in the world but death could separate them from Elijah.

Perhaps the baby of a prostitute or a young rape case, he is the son of their hearts. That is the only thing that matters. They did not want the stigma around his conception to affect how their family or anyone else treated him, so they never asked. As a result, CIF has the information about his birth mother for his adulthood if he ever has questions and wants to know more about his origins, but his parents do not want to know. All they know is how wonderful he is and how much they love him.

Throughout the interview, Soknan said, "I do not feel worthy of being his dad."

I understood this when I met Elijah. Midinterview, Soknan had disappeared to get the kids from school. Elijah was a beautiful child, and his presence was also peaceful. His dark eyes surveyed me with wonder and curiosity as he inched toward his mother, leaning into her. Then he bowed respectfully toward me, our interpreter, and the social worker.

I asked him questions about his life. Then, looking at his hands in shyness, he told me about his love of swimming and his favorite subject in school, Khmer grammar.

"I like to write stories," he said, glancing up at me.

"You know what, I like to write stories too. It's what I do for my work," I told him.

He smiled.

Soknan and Lyna shared that their experience has made other families want to adopt and foster children in the community.

"They see the results in our family and want a child for themselves. Of course, there is some comparison between families, but mostly we help and support each other," Soknan told me.

He continued, "It is hard to compare, however, because each child's condition is different; each has a different personality. But they [the kids] all seem to do well in the right family and improve over time. But some kids just need more help, like when they have a disability."

Almost all of CIF's social workers and physiotherapists in the provinces have foster children of their own, some with special needs. Likely, Soknan and Lyna would have been good parents with or without the support of CIF. However, they shared with me how much they have learned in the monthly trainings about children's rights, parenting skills, hygiene, and more. Their relationship with CIF's staff has just given them encouragement and extra confidence, knowing that someone is walking alongside them and that others care about their family as much as they do.

After I left the family, the social worker shared more.

"We [local CIF staff] are so at peace with how this family is raising Elijah. They give him excellent care. Both parents are very teachable and apply what they learn daily."

At the end of each interview, as I observe interactions, the home, and the community around us, I run an imaginary reel in my head. I picture what it would look like for this same child to grow up in a children's home because children like Elijah still have this experience across the globe.

I strip the child of their adoptive parents. I put them in a sea of other children from poverty or culturally shameful backgrounds. I remove Elijah's nieces and nephew, with whom he walks to school each day and near whom he sleeps each night. Instead, I place him on a bed in a large room with children not related. I change out their caregivers every year or so. I label him with words like "abandoned" or "orphaned," and I wonder what it does to his identity, rather than "son," "brother," "wanted," and "loved."

I put him with all those other children behind a metal gate and a high wall, shielded from their community rather than running free down their neighborhood road or walking home from school.

Worst of all, I see his gentle, quiet nature rendering him invisible in a world of children vying for affection and love. I see him being made a target for bullies instead of being celebrated by two parents and four older siblings who adore him exactly for who he is.

Then, I try to imagine his family without him in it. The longing in Lyna's heart for another child to love goes unquenched. The pride in Soknan's eyes as he gazes at his boy and shares how much he has learned being Elijah's father. Those lessons that baby would have never taught him about faith and prayer.

I think of the community and neighbors who have learned how to parent their children better from Soknan and Lyna's example.

By placing children into orphanages, we rob them of being wanted and loved and deny families and communities a chance to grow, learn, and live sacrificially for children. We take away the God-given right of cultures and nations to develop and nurture children holistically and healthily.

NOW WHAT?

An Introduction to Global Solutions

"Do the best you can until you know better.
Then when you know better, do better."
—Maya Angelou

While this book focuses mainly on the orphanage problem and solutions in Cambodia, this is not just a Cambodian issue. It's a global issue.

When I met an orphanage director from Central Asia on holiday in Thailand, she was excited to learn about family-based care in Cambodia. She assumed, however, that the former communist nation she worked in would not receive children in the same way.

"That works in Cambodia because the culture is already family focused," she responded.

I challenged her beliefs. Family is natural in all cultures, and people love children across cultures. Of course, brokenness and vulnerable people also exist in all cultures, and not all families are safe. That is precisely why CIF and other similar organizations exist.

To counter the argument that family-based care only works in certain cultures, I contacted people working in orphanages and family-based care globally. For the sake of length, I had to leave out most of their stories, but they were essentially the same as those in Cambodia. They gave the same reasons for family separation and vulnerability. They described the same results when children grow up institutionalized and the same reactions when people learn that orphaned children have a place in their communities.

//

Experts globally agree on an alternative care continuum. This means that if children absolutely cannot stay with their biological parents, there are options for them, starting with the least invasive and disruptive. Kinship and foster care would be looked at as permanent options. While emergency care, a small group home (less than ten children), small residential care, or large institution would all be temporary options that would need reevaluation. While international adoption is a permanent solution, it massively disrupted children's lives and should only be considered when all local options have been exhausted.

//

The final part of this book will help empower you, the reader, and those you know who serve among vulnerable communities, keep children from entering institutions in the first place and, for those already in orphanages, ways of transitioning them out of institutional care and into family care in any culture.

What does it look like to deinstitutionalize children and put them back into their communities? How do donors and people who serve vulnerable children help shift the narrative and the funds?

There is a right way and a wrong way to go about this. After all, millions of children's lives are impacted by how we handle these questions. While slapping up buildings and filling beds with children is quick and easy, transitioning orphanages into community centers and placing children in healthy families takes much more time and care.

In Their Own Words— Thailand Orphans

Kimberly Quinley, founder and executive director of Step Ahead Foundation Thailand, shared two stories written by young adults who grew up in Thai orphanages. I decided only to edit these for grammar and leave the words as accurate to the writer as possible because I wanted you, the reader, to hear directly from them.

//

Story 1:
After my father left our family, my mother, who was not educated, took me to live with my uncle, who runs a small orphanage. My mother and my sister went to live with my other auntie, so I have very little memory from my childhood of my mother. Soon, she took both of us to another orphanage. She stayed the night, but we found she was already gone when we woke up.

From what I understand, the intention of starting this foundation/orphanage is to give children a family and a home to live. However, after a while, the family grew bigger, and there were more supporters as well as the construction of a new, more prominent building. Finally, we became an orphanage.

We got an education, bed, clothing, food, and all four requisites but lacked warmth and love. Certainly, not everybody feels that, because my sister and I still have a mother who comes and visits twice a year. I am close to one of the found-ers, who I love like my own father, but in an orphanage, there are many children who are real orphans and aren't close to any of the staff.

Also, thirty children with eight adults can't answer every child's need for love and warmth.

In looking after a considerable number of children, each child has their own differences. Each has different abilities and passions but is put into the same box. By doing everything the same, having a definite life schedule, and having a border to walk, the true potential cannot be fully developed, and it is a pity.

We meet many volunteers who come and go. I feel thank-ful that each of them came to teach us languages, do activities, and donate things because when no volunteers come, we don't have any activities to do. But I also feel like I was abandoned all the time.

Soon enough, we began to understand that there won't be anybody who stays with us forever, and in reality, every-body can't always live with us anyway. But for a child who has experienced abandonment and is continuously abandoned, perhaps by a thousand people, it hurts until it becomes numb. From a cheerful child playing with the volunteers, which is not normal for a child who has just met a stranger to play that much, but it was to receive attention and love. When we grow up and start to understand that they won't be with us for long, it becomes useless in building relationships. We then begin to hold on to our group and interact less with the vol-unteers.

I lived in an orphanage for twelve years, yet we met a houseparent who changed every two years. Some couples are nice, some couples are really religious, some couples use vio-lence by kicking children out of their chairs or sexually abus-ing some of us, some couples are just doing their job. We called every single one of them "Mom" and "Dad." They hurt us, sexually abused us, and left us. We can't tell anybody because we fear getting hurt or nobody believing us.

It then became hard for us to understand the love of God. What is true love? What is the love of a father and mother?

Many of us try to look for love from another place. Some didn't choose the right path and some didn't see hope for their future, choosing to use their life to hurt themselves.

After graduating high school, I left the orphanage and faced the world on my own. It was really hard because we don't have life skills or know how to take care of ourselves, even though it became something that pushed me to survive and seek opportunities. Not everyone does that.

For me, I learned about God since I was a kid. Some volunteers came to see us very often. We like to listen to the story of God, which encouraged us.

One of the founders, who I respect like my own father, passed away last year, but when he was sick and lying on the bed waiting for death, he would still pray for me and talk about the love of God.

This made me decide around mid-last year to truly seek this God and build a personal relationship with Him. Right now, I'm trying to understand the situation and heal myself to move on and walk forward. I don't want other children to experience what I had to experience.

Children need love, care, and protection as much as food and shelter.

//

Story 2: Where is Love?

The moment I was put into the orphanage was the day my life became hell.

It was like my heart was on fire, and the fire was burning all the time.

I wanted to cry out, "Someone help me, please! Help me, please!"

But no one was there for me.

No one ever held me and told me that they loved me.

No one ever spent time talking to me.

No one ever asked me, "Do you feel cold? Do you feel sick? Do you need something?"

When we sang songs about how God is good and God is love—

Even as a child, I questioned this all the time.

I questioned, "What does love mean?"

All I recall is the harsh punishment for all my wrongs and mistakes.

Where is love?

If you can imagine, you walk into an orphanage.

There are twenty, sixty, and eighty children living all together.

There are not enough staff hired to care for all the children.

I don't blame anyone now as I know they had limits.

They couldn't possibly provide what I needed.

But I can tell you this: no child will ever find human love in an orphanage.

What children need more than food and education is real love in a family.

//

Where is love?

I was raised in a Christian family. As a young child, I remember my mother always praying before we ate meals together. She taught me how to talk to God. I loved when she visited me at the orphanage.

At the orphanage, I talked to God too. I sang Christian songs; I prayed the Christian prayers.

But my brain was questioning all the time.

I love God, by the way. He is my best friend.

He was my only friend as a child growing up in the orphanage.

I also begged. I pleaded. I told God I would give up all my clothes

and toys if someone would take me out of the orphanage and love me.

It never happened.

After twelve years, I was finally out. I was finally free.

But if I am honest, I am still searching for the meaning of human love.

Where is love?

Protecting Families
in Thailand

In the late 1980s, Kimberly Quinley was an American teacher and used her summer breaks to serve in an orphanage in North Thailand. Initially, her knowledge of the children's lives was limited without her understanding of the Thai language. However, over time, she realized the orphanage would empty each school holiday. After inquiring, she realized they had families in the surrounding area and villages.

Viewing the minority groups through wealthy, Western eyes, she quickly assumed that material needs equated to a standard of care and lifestyle. Crucial factors were not considered when making these decisions for families. While children are physical beings, they also are spiritual, mental, and emotional. Where did love, community, and belonging fit into the residential care model?

Kimberly moved to Thailand long-term in 1989 after marrying. She and John were primarily working in church planting and had moved away from serving in orphanages, and she had begun to rethink the orphanage model due to her own experiences.

//

Kimberly's introduction to family-based care began in the wake of the December 26, 2004 tsunami. She helped three families remain together as orphanages were being slapped up all around them.

She watched the crisis unfolding and spent time gathering more and more knowledge on family-based care. Craig Greenfield, the founder of Alongsiders International, came to Thailand to meet her in those early years. She read his book, *Urban Halo*, in which he shares his early years in Cambodia, living in Phnom Penh's most notorious slum. Craig and his wife, Nay, were the first to start a family-based care program in Cambodia.

Soon after meeting with Craig, Kimberly began to meet with the Thai government, wanting them to understand what children needed. Her organization took Thai government officials to London for training with Lumos, a family-based care organization started by author J. K. Rowling that operates mostly in Eastern Europe. Another year, the government officials traveled to India for an alternative care conference. She currently helps the Thai government develop strategies for family-based care (also known as alternative care).

She was part of the creation of an alliance of Christian organizations that believe children belong in families, the Strong Families Alliance Thailand (SFAT), which was started in 2016. The Thai government also works closely with them. They conduct workshops that teach the skills for building strong, healthy families and currently work with fifteen organizations and four orphanages.

Like many other family-based care organizations, they will work with orphanages only if they have an exit strategy for their children and are committed not to take in new kids but rather to transition their centers into supporting families and communities.

Kimberly said, "Thailand is growing in this. But very slowly."

While alternative care is better for children, better for families, more sustainable, and takes significantly fewer resources, an onlooker would wonder why orphanages still exist anywhere. The answer: money.

What keeps governments and communities from closing orphanages is money. Orphanages are lucrative for those running them. It is a business model. But while orphanages bring in money, it is the children who pay the highest cost.

//

Dr. Deliah Pop, Director of Programmes and Global Advocacy at Hope and Homes for Children said of improving orphanages, "We don't renovate Hell."

People come to Kimberly Quinley asking how to run their orphanages better. She clarifies to them that her goal is not to improve orphanages but to eradicate them and promote family-based care.

She starts with basic questions for anyone seeking either to create an orphanage or upscale one. "Tell me about your call to orphans. What is your background? Did you do research and get training in this?"

The questions sound simple, but they dig into a deeper issue. People with big hearts and good intentions can cause harm when their intentions exceed their training and knowledge. If you enter a nation knowing nothing of the culture, the needs, what is separating children from families, or even the need for care, how can you create a ministry that meets the needs of the community? Especially if you need to gain skills or experience in working with children.

She quotes Proverbs 19:2 to anyone who comes to Thailand to "rescue" all the kids and babies. "Desire without knowledge is not good, and whoever makes haste with his feet misses his way." (ESV).

"The orphanages in Thailand spoon-feed everyone information that kids are going to live on the streets and be trafficked, but the reality is, Thailand doesn't have that happening."

Thailand is a tourist paradise with pristine beaches, intense nightclubs, and a well-preserved history. The north and west are full of mountain ranges and stunning minority people groups. Unmarred by civil wars and colonial rule, Thailand is significantly wealthier than its Cambodian neighbor, though there still lies a vast disparity between rich and poor. Despite Thailand's GDP being substantially higher than Cambodia's, it has more orphanages per capita than Cambodia. This means that poverty is not the sole reason for family separation.

The reality is, the existence of orphanages in Thailand creates orphans. Foreigners, primarily tourists or short-term Christian visitors, get convinced there is a need for institutions and pour money into them, creating an industry.

Then there's the additional layer of refugees and illegal immigration. Decades of fighting between the minority people of Myanmar and their military caused hundreds of thousands of Karen, Shan, and other groups to seek a haven in Thailand. They became refugees in rugged jungle mountains along the borders. Or they migrate illegally into the cities to find work. Half a century ago, when China became communist, Mao Tse Tung and his followers slaughtered minority groups and religious peoples. Many made their way into Thailand, settling in the north. Persecuted Christians escape from Vietnam and Laos and seek to blend in and find rest in Thailand. Refugees from the Middle East also flock to Bangkok. Among all these groups are unaccompanied minors.

Without proper documentation, these people cannot make a legitimate living, and their children are born without citizenship. Their lack of national status renders schooling an impossibility. These families are among the most vulnerable to family separation. Parents will often be arrested for their illegal status, leaving the children alone. Some go into foster care, others into government shelters.

Kimberly and her team work to get mothers out of detention, so they can be reunited with their children. Her program, Freedom for Families, has a contract with the government allowing women and children to be in her care, together.

A few years ago, she finished writing the policies for the government foster care program and standard of care in Thailand, which involves unaccompanied minors. The solution is not institutions.

Refugee children are at high risk for institutionalization. The lack of access to education leaves the youth alone (and consequently, aimless) for much of the day. Drug use amongst the refugee communities is significant, partially due to organized crime exploiting them as couriers or distributors, partially due to them being close to porous borders, and partially because many do not have much to do with their time. They seek to escape through drugs.

Rather than well-intentioned people investigating the key fundamental causes of these issues, such as lack of documentation, good jobs, and education, people come in and begin to institutionalize the children because they appear abandoned and lacking purpose. Their parents might be labeled as negligent or abusive.

Yet removing the kids does not remove the drugs, trafficking, or documentation issues. If anything, it creates deeper rifts in communities because children grow up separated from the identity of their unique culture and communities. They grow up raised by foreigners who come and go while stuck in a world where they lack options to transition or leave.

The money spent institutionalizing children could be poured into strengthening their communities. This includes programs that create stable jobs for refugee parents, alleviating the need for dangerous or underpaid work or for leaving their children behind to find employment in the city. Access to decent education would give children a safe place to go during the day, opportunities, and a future. And help with getting legal status in Thailand would decriminalize them and open the doors for legal work, university, and freedom of movement.

Another factor creating orphanages, and therefore orphans, in Thailand is the lack of access to education in rural regions.

Tribal villages in the mountains may not have schools, as teachers are less willing to work in remote areas. The few schools that exist have little monitoring, which leads to low attendance and teachers not showing up to work.

Children from these minority people groups may also speak a language other than Thai. Learning is more difficult in a second or third language. Additionally, when the Thai government closes village schools, these children don't have access to education at all, further disadvantaging their people group. Their only option for a decent education is to live in an orphanage in the city.

These children never lacked family. They lacked education. Sadly, they are forced to choose between the two.

Much to her sorrow, Kimberly recruited these children for an orphanage when she was new to the country. "They lived in grass huts and were dirty. Therefore, we assumed they did not have the proper care."

Now she leads people in an activity to analyze the situation. Showing a picture of a shanty house or a gleaming orphanage, she asks participants to evaluate the situation by looking at a holistic view of "Body, soul, spirit, and mind." She said it takes hours, but the activity helps people shift their perspective by seeing the importance of love in addition to meeting physical needs.

Leaders in family-based care around the globe kept telling me the same things. Children do not leave orphanages less vulnerable or more prepared for the world. Their vulnerability is either delayed or increased. They exit with a deep loss of identity. They no longer fit in the world they left behind as a child or the world they are entering as a young adult.

Another repeated theme from interviews with Kimberly and others was the question, "Why are we caring for only the kids and not their parents too?"

Aaron Blue, the founder of the Charis Project in Mae Sot, Thailand, stated, "The business model of the orphanage depends on the family structure falling apart."

On its website Charis Project proclaims, "Families protect children. We protect families."

The Tsunami

On December 26, 2004, the world watched in horror as a massive white water rapid of ocean waves crashed across islands and shorelines in South and Southeast Asia. People, structures, and vehicles washed away in seconds, unable to stand against the unrivaled force of nature. The worst recorded tsunami in history hit the south of Thailand. The epicenter in Sumatra sent shock waves that affected all the surrounding nations and killed around 230,000 people within minutes of hitting the coastlines. In Thailand, nearly 5,400 people lost their lives.

Before the mud cleared and the total death count could be assessed, at least twenty organizations swooped in, opening orphanages. Despite the incredible damage, only 1,100 children lost one or both parents. No child was completely without a family to care for them. Yet before homes could even be repaired and businesses reopened, orphanages were set up.

//

Residents dwelled in tent villages and displaced-person camps. Dau felt dazed since the incident. In her dream-like state, she fed her toddler and looked for day labor, yet her heart was far away. She thought back to that beautiful winter day when the rains had ceased and the air held a fresh excitement. Working in the tourist industry, she had the day off after serving foreign visitors for many hours on Christmas Day.

She decided to take Lawan, her toddler, to visit a friend's house more inland. Rising early, she kissed her husband,

Chatri, on the cheek and handed him his tin of rice and fish. He smiled his gap-toothed grin back at her, face deeply lined from his labor on the fishing boats. They were neither poor nor rich. But their thin walls were saturated with love.

When she kissed him "goodbye," she had little inkling that the day would end without him as would every day after. The emptiness tightened in her chest. During those horrible days and weeks, she pleaded with aid workers to help her find him. Their small dwelling, sea treasures, wedding photos on display, baby pictures of sweet Lawan held tenderly in Chatri's arms—it all was swept away, buried with her heart.

Sometimes the smell of raw fish and sea salt aroused her senses, and she would return to that happy time. Yet months passed, and she stood on the hardened, barren grounds of the tent village, destitute and desperate. Lawan pleaded for food and comfort, traumatized by the sudden changes and losses around her.

Her mind flashed back to drinking tea with her friends, Lawan chasing a kitten; they heard the screams, the roar of the sea as it never sounded before. Sudden terror gripped them as her eyes met her friends. Instinctively, they ran for their children, grabbing them in time to see the water crashing over buildings a few streets down. Catching Lawan in her arms, feet scrambling for higher ground, lungs burning from exertion, her mind cleared of all things but one: "survive." The force took her legs out from under her, and she felt her body being dragged under. She nearly squeezed her daughter to death in her panic to keep her.

As quickly as it hit, the waters receded. She found herself retching and gasping for air, cuts bleeding and bruises forming. Lawan coughed but mainly appeared fine, minus her piercing cries. Unsure of where she was or what had happened, she wandered in a daze. Her best friend called to her; both battered from the trauma. Tears streamed down their faces as the shock set in. Unable to think or move, her friend buckled, pulling them both into the mud. Lawan had calmed, nestled in her mother's breast. But many were never found.

Kimberly and her husband, John, felt drawn to return to the place where they served doing church planting for eight years: ground zero for Thailand's tsunami. They left the very next day after the tsunami to see what they could do to help. As the months passed, they saw how so many came to open orphanages. The issue was displaced families, not orphans. So, Step Ahead Foundation (the organization Kimberly and John founded) opened four child development centers in the area to provide a safe place for children during the day while struggling parents tried to make sense of their new life post-tsunami. While the children were in a safe environment, the families had time to find work, set up businesses, or rebuild. They would return to the displaced-persons camps or temporary homes with siblings and family members.

Dau and Kimberly's lives intersected at the center. Dau dropped Lawan off daily as she searched for employment. One morning as Kimberly pulled up to a center, she noticed a familiar face on the steps of the child development center. It was an orphanage director. As she approached the steps, she heard the sobs of someone clearly in distress. She saw Dau holding Lawan and crying. The orphanage director was speaking with her. Curious and deeply concerned, Kimberly stopped to greet them, "Sawadee kah, Dau and Lawan," as she placed a hand tenderly on Dau's back. She turned to the woman. "May I help you?"

After formal greetings were exchanged, she learned that the orphanage director was recruiting a toddler, Lawan, for her orphanage. Her goal was to find children to fill the beds.

Determination coursed through Kimberly's veins. Parents losing their children to institutions could not be the only option for help. She was unsure how, but she knew she had to start somewhere. Looking Dau directly in her bloodshot eyes, Kimberly found words flowing from herself, "Do you really want to give your daughter away?"

"No. But I have no food and no job. Life has been so hard since Chatri died."

Kimberly suggested, "What if we help you keep your daughter? We'll make sure you have food, and we will help you find a job."

A spark of hope leaped into Dau's heart. Maintaining eye contact, clutching at Lawan, Dau nodded in agreement as she wiped her nose with the back of her hand.

"You would do that for me? For us?"

"Yes," confirmed Kimberly.

Kimberly turned to the orphanage recruiter. "We are finished here. Have a nice day." She put her arm around Dau, and they walked back into the center.

That day, family-based care was born in Southern Thailand. Partnering with Orphan's Promise, Step Ahead began small. Initially, it served three families at risk of separation. However, the program called "Keeping Families Together" has blossomed across Thailand and internationally.

Dau was unsure how life could improve, but she had her baby in her arms, and that was enough.

She was the catalyst for Kimberly to dream and fight for all children in Thailand to grow up in safe and nurturing families.

The African Way

If the emotion "joy" had a face, it would look like my friend Modula. She is a tiny package with a presence that fills a room. There is no such thing as a stranger to Modula. Everyone is a friend.

Modula is from Lesotho, a landlocked country surrounded by South Africa. She describes herself as a farmer who hates to eat her vegetables, a statement always followed by a laugh.

//

One day, Modula, from Lesotho, and I, from America, were eating at a Greek restaurant in Cambodia. We were enjoying a conversation heavily seasoned with laughter when the talk suddenly grew more somber.

I had already learned that in Lesotho, cousins were not called cousins; they were just "brothers" and "sisters."

She further explained that her father passed away when she was very young; if something were to happen to her mother, her aunties would be her mother. So, they were called "mothers."

All of this was entirely natural for her. Her cousins were her brothers and sisters. Her aunties were her mothers. Simple.

It got a bit more complex on her father's side, but one thing stayed with me. There was such a cultural understanding of the importance of family that no one questioned its fact or nature.

If something happened to her mother, she rested in complete and absolute assurance that she and her brother would still have a family. Close family.

Mouth agape, I stared at her.

"Can I put this in my book?"

She did not hesitate. "Of course!"

"Can you explain it again?"

We went through it all slower this time. She must've thought Americans were insane for not understanding basic principles such as caring for family members.

A year later, I was eating dinner with a beautiful Congolese couple and heard similar examples of family and communal structure. Whether biological relatives or merely close family friends within the surrounding community, Congolese take care of children. The husband and wife told me they always knew that if their parents could not care for their children or if they passed away, an auntie or uncle would step in. As an adult, the husband discovered that one of his brothers was not biologically related. The brother's parents had died when he was a young child, and my friend's parents took him in and treated him so much as one of their own that everyone forgot he was not their biological child.

I had to sit with this information for a while. How many other nations in the world had similar principles? How many places were now filling orphanages with children when their original social structure naturally kept the children in families—before we Westerners came in and told them we had a better way?

How many cultures had surrendered their children to our institutions when they were already practicing family-based care? Our interventions were harming, not helping, and somewhere along the way, what was natural was lost.

At a missions conference, Cathleen once sat at a table with a gigantic Ugandan pastor. He was as gentle as he was huge. As they discussed family-based care, he passionately pounded their table, nearly breaking it in half as he declared in a booming voice, "You're right! Orphanages are not the African way!"

Walking Alongside
the Vulnerable

Craig Greenfield is an influential and sometimes controversial voice in orphan care, social justice, and development work. He's written several books that offer a deeper glimpse into his mind, work, and life: *Subversive Mission*, *Subversive Jesus*, and *Urban Halo*.

When he was growing up in New Zealand, his parents had many foster children and refugees living in their home. Through their example and his exposure to the poor, displaced, and abandoned, Craig found God leading him to Phnom Penh's urban poor, living among them for many years. His experiences gave him unique insight, causing him to shift many standard missional paradigms.

He told me, "The orphanage model in Cambodia is particularly damaging because it hits on brokenness within the culture. Many Cambodian parents face immense economic pressures, and the local orphanage offers them a way to address those needs.

"There is a mismatch of the Western view of orphanages versus non-Western. For instance, most Westerners would view orphanages as a place to care for actual orphans or abandoned children. In contrast, a Khmer family views it more as a place to meet their needs like food and education. But now that it has been modeled to them, Khmer families feel they need to send their children away rather than care for them within their nucleus and communal setting."

He shared that institutional life robs children of much more than it gives them. No skills of the parents or extended family can be passed on. There is no opportunity to face and overcome the everyday challenges of living in a community. In essence, the orphans are trained to lack the ability to cope.

He continued, "Orphanages don't take children away from vulnerability; they delay their vulnerability. Orphanages create an antiresilience. The children are not raised to face the world and culture they will live amongst as adults."

During most of his seventeen years in Cambodia, Craig and his wife, Nay, lived in an urban, poor region of Phnom Penh and saw many abandoned and uncared-for children, including several true orphans. However, in their quest to start an orphanage, they quickly rejected the model, realizing it would take responsibility for the children away from the community and alienate them from their own culture. Instead, they found many older widows or aunties who were very much alone. These women had lost their children or never had children. The Khmer family structure, which includes caring for their old, had been broken.

So instead, Craig placed true orphans with these widows, aunties, and uncles. As a result, the community continued to influence the children's lives, and they received stability, love, and family. They belonged in both the broader sense and in the more nucleus sense.

Later, Craig and Nay went on to form the organization Alongsiders International.

Alongsiders' vision states: "We equip young people to walk alongside those who walk alone. To love, welcome, and encourage the most vulnerable and orphaned children within their communities. In this way, more than fifteen thousand children's lives have been transformed."

The local church is also involved in the movement to oversee the training of the young adults and disciple them. It is a movement of one generation transforming the lives of the next.

Craig explains that in almost all developing nations, the youth are a disproportionate majority of the population, with significantly fewer people in the older generations to care for them. He established Alongsiders so that communities and local churches could care for and influence the next generation. Rather than put those vulnerable, marginalized, lonely children in a group home far away, they continue to live in their communities. But now they are not alone; they have someone to share their pain and victories and they have skills to help them overcome their challenges. They are championed and encouraged, all while facing the realities of their community struggles. Only this time, they do it with someone.

Throughout Cambodia and twenty-five other nations spanning the globe, children can have many of their needs met through others in Alongsiders while being empowered to grow and flourish right where they are.

While neither CIF nor Craig wants to leave children in unhealthy families, there is a recognition that brokenness exists everywhere. Abuse and neglect are a concern, and they cannot be overlooked. However, several studies from the US to former Soviet countries have shown that the trauma of removing children from their families can be more devastating than leaving them in poverty or minor abuse.

Rather than isolating children and youth from the negatives of their culture, Craig and Alongsiders work to model a better way of living within the culture. Young people walk alongside children to help show them a way to shift the culture to healthier ways of living and treating one another. The young adults walking alongside children are given regular training and curriculum to work through with the younger kids. Their teaching materials include topics like "Good touch, bad touch," the value of honesty and integrity in relationships, destructive family patterns and how to overcome them, and how God loves them unconditionally.

Often, these children do not need removal from their

homes but someone to see them, hear them, and teach them, a transformation from the inside out rather than outside in. The older mentors grew up in those neighborhoods. They are young adults who overcame and may still be facing adversity. The children are not learning from outsiders with little understanding of their lives. They have someone who truly understands.

The financial costs of a program like Alongsiders are minimal, while raising children in institutions costs millions annually. Estimates by Lumos show that in Haiti alone, orphanages cost one hundred million dollars *minimum* each year, so imagine the cost of orphanages across the globe. As of 2019, Cambodia still had over 400 orphanages operating. A 2018 Reuters article by Emma Batha, titled "Factbox: Most children in orphanages are not orphans," stated that the rate of children in orphanages was increasing in Cambodia despite the decline in actual true orphans.

These statistics paint a discouraging picture. Billions of dollars fuel the orphan industry in Cambodia and globally. At the same time, programs like Alongsiders require only a fraction of the cost to see those same vulnerable children cared for in their communities.

The mentors with Alongsiders are encouraged to use their own funds to treat their little brothers and sisters. Rather than the organization handing out money for expensive activities or spoiling the children with material gifts, the program focuses on one-on-one relationships. It allows the mentor to invest seriously in the child they walk alongside. It also cuts back on the savior or rescuer mentality, which can make the person serving feel superior to the receiver.

The excuse I hear from fans of the orphanage model is, "Well, maybe that just works in Cambodia (or Europe and Latin America) because it is already cultural."

But the concept of Alongsiders has already spread internationally. The program now exists in several nations, spanning Southeast Asia, South Asia, and Africa. Alongsiders is intentional, adapting its training and material to be culturally relevant while keeping the heart of the Gospel and maintaining its core values.

At the end of the day, family and community are the best places for children, and we need to work to improve these spheres of society rather than remove and isolate the vulnerable.

Vulnerable Children Deserve the Highest Care

I wrote about Mick Pease in CIF's early years as he was instrumental in helping train foster families and social workers, but there's so much more to Mick and SFAC, the organizations he founded.

He was a blue-collar laborer in coal mines, but a calling to care for vulnerable children found him and drew him in. He claims, "God just captured my heart with family care."

Growing up in England post-World War II, he and his family were desperately poor. His older sister had severe asthma, putting her at risk of death without continuous medical treatment and evaluation, so she was placed in an institution far away. His parents could rarely visit. After nearly four years, his mother could no longer handle the separation and brought her home, but the damage had been done. Mick later learned she was physically and emotionally abused by staff and other children.

Medical issues separated their family, causing lifelong trauma to the girl. All of this was due to poverty. Neither his parents nor his sister wanted this, yet circumstances tied their hands.

After working in coal mines and studying at Bible college, Mick became a residential social worker. Teens from age fifteen to eighteen lived with him and his wife, Brenda. It was during this time that he realized how little he knew about trauma and supporting kids to live independently. The learning curve was massive, but after a while, he became a social work trainer, working in child protection and involved in adoption and foster care.

Mick said in an interview, "Many kids go into orphanages for non-orphan reasons. In most instances, they enter the orphanage without a degree of assessment and gatekeeping. Orphanages have become an attraction for poor families to place their children in the hope of getting a better life, education, health, or other opportunities,"

Families living in poverty are incentivized to give away their children. If they keep them, the same opportunities are not usually available. Those decisions are often made without consideration of the long-term detrimental effects on the child. Yet long-term thinking is a privilege. Those who survive from day to day can rarely look forward. To tell a parent with hungry children who lack access to medicine and education that the long-term effects on their child will be damaging when the parent is not sure if their child will eat that day is not effective. It is easy to see why an orphanage appears attractive to them.

Often, the child gets no say in the decisions made and is likely unaware of the implications. Meanwhile, many institutions are making decisions on behalf of donors, not residents. Other agendas crowd out the needs of the actual children in their care.

The shift to caring for children internationally came with a trip to Brazil in 1997. While doing short-term work with a children's mission, it struck Mick that all the children were healthy and well-behaved; no extenuating circumstances made it difficult for them to be in families. Their family separation was not due to criminal or behavioral issues.

Not long after being there, he spoke with local pastors about caring for vulnerable children. They kept circling back to international adoption, and Mick continued to re-explain local foster care, receiving blank stares. Domestic adoption and foster care appeared alien to most.

It struck him that the assumption in Brazil was that foreigners from wealthy nations were the only option for orphans and children abandoned by their parents. Mick could not believe what he consistently heard on the subject.

Mick takes issue with the term "orphan," as most children with the label have living parents. They were removed from their homes or abandoned. He also explained, "The term orphan does not accurately describe what we are dealing with [globally]."

A few years later, the reality of the global situation for children in orphanages hit home for Mick. He went to Tajikistan for a short-term trip and saw the same patterns as in Brazil.

Taking care of children outside of a family spanned multiple cultures. While working on the possibility of family care in Central Asia, Mick and his team traveled all over the region, allowing him to talk with a wide array of staff and children in institutional care. The issues he was hearing were the same as in Brazil: poverty was a key driving factor, not abuse, trafficking, or death.

Interviewing children at the orphanages, he asked, "What's life like here? Are you happy? How often do you see your family?"

They all answered that they were happy and doing fine. But then he would ask, "If you had a magic wand and one wish, what would it be?"

Every single child answered, "I want my mom and dad."

No one had ever asked them what they wanted. Everyone assumed they had a better life in the institution. They had activities, education, food, and clothes, yet they all wanted to live with their family like "normal" children.

Mick firmly believes that children must have a voice in their care and in what happens to them. He said, "We have to ask children, 'What is important to you?'"

He also wants to address the people caring for children in institutions. "Many carers from around the world are working from the heart. They are not trained in social work and counseling. But they need more than just a big heart. They must be trained to deal with the children's issues and the long-term implications of residential care. Most of them lack technical expertise.

"The most vulnerable children in this world are outside their immediate family. But who do we give them to look after them? They are being cared for by people who are working from the heart. People who are lowly paid, lowly motivated, lowly trained, and lowly equipped. Is there any wonder these children are just not getting what they deserve? They need more, not less, than others."

Dan Hope, the current CEO of Strengthening Families and Children (SFAC), added, "For Mick, this resonates with his own experience. We ask the untrained and unqualified to care for children with complex needs. It is an issue not only in children's homes but in foster care, kinship care, and reintegration. We need skilled, knowledgeable carers and social workers. Otherwise, we repeat the issues of children living in unsafe or inappropriate places."

//

"Children's homes should not exist for the vast majority; they have other options. It should exist for the children who need it. And let's apply the principles of a family into the children's home."

He defined what a child would look like who needed to be in children's homes. Many are too old to be placed into a new family or have lost trust in the family structure due to severe abuse. Their survival skills have kicked in, and they've rejected the family structure. These are usually children with extreme emotional and behavioral issues who live on the streets. Others have severe disabilities or are part of a sibling group, so it would be harder to find a family to care for their specific needs. Although it is not impossible, it may take longer, and even those children can be part of a family or community eventually.

Mick stated, "We cannot call them unadoptable. Let's change the narrative to every child is adoptable, but sometimes we just do not have the right family for them at that time. Let's ensure the temporary and family homes we give them are well invested in."

His experience also led him to realize that most people running orphanages do not even have legal rights to the kids in their care. Many are not registered with the government. The children in their care are there through their family's voluntary choice. The parents are still the legal guardians. This creates incredible issues regarding major medical decisions, schooling, or moving the child around. No one, not even the well-meaning carers, has any idea who has legal control.

This practice creates greater vulnerability for children. A lot of these organizations lack good quality practices. They do not have a strong foundation or policies.

He shared about an organization in Uganda called Retrak that works specifically with street children, enabling them to shift from distrust of the system to belonging in family and community. Their description states they "work with children and family to ensure children are healthy, emotionally well, safe, educated" and that "families are economically independent." Retrak is now incorporated into the bigger charity, Hope of Justice Global, an anti-trafficking organization.

Their work spread from Uganda into Ethiopia, Kenya, Malawi, and Zimbabwe. The kids deemed unplaceable in a family are finding a place in their communities because the roots of the breakdown in the family are addressed. Rather than looking at children with extreme behavior and trust issues as being beyond help, we need to learn what matters to these children and why they've rejected a family structure. Often their fight-or-flight instincts have been active for too long, and they do not know how to live or process a safe environment. It takes time to earn trust and allow them to rest in love. In Lesotho, there is a similar organization called Sepheo.

//

Mick's organization SFAC starts at the bedrock of family care. Substitute families can be many things, but their work begins with the biological family. Mick quoted Psalm 139, "You created my innermost being, knitted in my mother's womb."

He continued, "We will only ever have one birth mother and one birth father. It is significant and creates identity despite how our family has treated us. That information must be preserved for children and their identity despite circumstances. When they cannot live with their biological family, we have to look for other forms of care, extended family or community. We have friends of our families who become like family despite not being biological. A child may be close to a community member."

He explains that if none of those sources are found, the search can go further to "stranger foster care." There are still people, in all strata of society, who believe in the rights and safety of the child and offer good care. Our efforts should include domestic and international adoption only as a last resort.

Another part of SFAC's work is helping people globally make decisions about who is appropriate to raise a child. Orphanages across the globe are generally poor at vetting and establishing their boundaries about the children they take in. Mick says, "How do we judge that the biological parents are not appropriate to raise their kids? In the UK, there are systems in place to protect at-risk children. The systems aren't perfect, but they exist and are hopefully improving. In those cases, we use the courts to make decisions. In other countries, these systems are not in place."

SFAC trains and equips people who work with vulnerable children to help understand their needs and make the appropriate decision for the child. Wise decisions need to start early in the process for the children. Otherwise, the system is at risk of failing or exploiting them.

At the end of the day, the orphanage model is the wrong starting point since eighty to ninety percent of those in their care have parents. Additionally, orphanages are most often exploitative. They may not start that way, but they are donor driven. They are dependent on donor dollars for continued funding. But their attitude toward children must change. Children are not objects to be used as we tell them. Children need more than food, nice walls, and healthcare. Those things do not bestow identity and belonging on a child.

The church's mindset also needs to change. With the best of intentions, we think we need to rescue children from poverty to give them opportunities. Yet we fail to see that their biological family is the only one they will ever have. Often our "opportunity" comes at the cost of their family.

Mick's expertise and training globally, along with the broader work of SFAC, is making a huge impact on seeing the orphanage narrative shift. He deeply cares about everyone from the orphanage directors to the families and all the key stakeholders involved. He recognizes how nuanced the shift from institutionalization to family care can be and seeks to honor the process and produce the best possible outcomes for everyone involved.

Reintegration

Mick and Hannah Won, Kinnected program manager with ACCI, both gave great insight into reintegration.

Hannah explained that most orphanages across the globe are resistant to reintegration. Her organization only works with the roughly ten percent of orphanages that are open to it. She also mentioned that the orphanages that are most interested in reintegration are already providing the highest level of care for their residents.

If an institution has yet to begin reintegrating children or to stop taking in new ones, they likely have other motivations for running an orphanage. Many have mixed interests in caring for children; they may care about the kids, but other interests like pandering to donors or the emotional pull of rescuing so many vulnerable children creep in. Money without accountability degrades motives.

If orphanages get so much financial support from donors, what might motivate them to transition children out and support family care? What happens to the staff when orphanages reintegrate? An important consideration here is the staff's livelihood. Wouldn't most staff lose their jobs if an orphanage closes, moving ninety percent of the children out of the institution? Not necessarily, Mick said.

"Some staff are exceptional and love the kids," he explained. "I've been in children's homes where the kids have the best relationships with the guard, the driver, the cook, etc. Oftentimes, they have better relationships with these staff than the actual care workers. On the other hand, some staff should not be allowed within a mile of a child. These are people that need to lose their jobs.

"Every person in an orphanage should be assessed by outside experts who know what they are looking at. There will be staff happy to do more, upskill, and put kids in a family. During the transition, these staff need to remain. Children will trickle out. Some family placements will break down, and those kids may need to return. You can't just shut down a children's home overnight. Where would we put all the kids?

"As the children transition out, the orphanage will need significant time to reduce intake. Someone needs to track down families; sometimes, the cooks and drivers can help. They are needed to work with the social workers, taking them around. And while the staff are there, you train all of them about childcare. This will help develop their skills to go elsewhere. Even the laypeople can be set up as key workers since they have a specific responsibility for the children. During the transition, those people will have one-on-one time with each child in their care, getting to know them well. They can follow up when the child is reintegrated, both pre-contact and post-contact. Laypeople can learn what to look for and ask questions to help the children."

Mick explained that when the whole staff are trained, it eases the load of the social workers. Every good person in a children's home can have a role and can upskill. In the long run, their training can also generate a better income. He views it as a broad spectrum.

Mick shared about an organization in Uganda, Child's I Foundation. They had a children's home in the past, but after SFAC helped transition most children out, they had only a baby home. The baby home focused on interactive childcare. He saw the staff doing a great job with desperately sick babies. The carers were trained well and provided a lot of one-on-one care with each baby.

Mick then said to the founder, "You can do better. All the

women working here could take the babies into their homes and care for them there if they had suitable circumstances."

Sure, the babies had medical conditions, but the women were already trained to deal with these issues. He pointed out it could be done at home as long as their homes were safe and sanitary.

This step allowed the organization to continue providing income for its staff and also gave the babies the opportunity to make healthy attachments in a family environment. Basically, Mick said, you "sell" family care as an opportunity for everyone to thrive.

Dan Hope shared that during the COVID pandemic, a children's home they worked with had to divide the children up to be cared for in the homes of their staff members. He said, "Post-COVID, the carers all said they wanted the children to remain in their individual homes and that the children's behavior and development had improved."

The good or even marginally good children's homes will see an opportunity for growth and take it. The rest, the bad, exploitative orphanages, are selling kids. They use children as bait on the hook to catch donors. They will probably never shift or transition to family care on their own and are the ones that need to be closed permanently.

Decades ago, the UN published its Declaration of the Rights of the Child. In it, the UN explained that part of human rights for children was to exhaust all forms of alternative care before placing children in institutions. Yet orphanages are thriving across the globe, and new ones are even opening.

Institutions that do not start out exploitative and terrible often still have no interest in decreasing their numbers by only taking in children with no other viable options.

Then there are the orphanages who are truly exploitative from the beginning. They exist to make a profit off of children. They can involve sexual abuse, trafficking, and organized crime. Cambodia has fewer of these, while in nations like Nepal and others in Eastern Europe, these are rife.

One of the issues to tackle in Southeast Asia relates to religious schools that also act as orphanages. It gets tricky when deinstitutionalizing impedes local religion and traditions. Across the Buddhist world, children without families or those living in poverty are placed in monastic schools and trained as Buddhist monks.

People are less inclined to question the practice of training orphans as monks and are unlikely to monitor these Buddhist "orphanages." Calling into question the local religious leaders has serious cultural repercussions. Also, attempting to deinstitutionalize these orphanages comes up against the religious practices. This leads to severe abuse and exploitation. In March 2023, Radio Free Asia reported that an orphanage run by Buddhist nuns outside of Yangon, Myanmar found children so severely abused, they had been permanently disabled from neglect and beatings.

The same goes for local Christian pastors. In Myanmar especially, but also in Cambodia, pastors will take in a few abandoned or orphaned children. This is fine; it would be considered fostering. But then more people begin to leave their children with the pastors, expecting better care. Or foreign donors come along and hear about the pastor and give money to support the family. This incentivizes the church leaders to take in more children; too many children arrive, and an orphanage must unofficially begin. Slowly, the caretaking becomes about donations rather than providing a home for a couple of children.

Regardless of the faith the orphanage is founded on, many crop up unofficially and are unregistered. This leaves the leaders with unlimited power over vulnerable children with no accountability and oversight.

//

Officially, Hannah joined ACCI's staff in 2017 to continue in the field of reintegration. Its Kinnected program exists across nations. Its pastor workshops train local church leaders in family-based care, but they work to tackle donor bases as well. Orphanages are money driven, plain and simple.

The Kinnected program provides a way for donors to do their due diligence. Before giving to or continuing to support an institution, several questions should be asked. People usually give because of a personal connection and not because of facts or numbers. Facts can't convince donors to give elsewhere if they have an emotional tie to an orphanage or the director. People need viable alternatives to support institutions through a transition. It does not work to merely sever contact or paint the leader as bad, even if they are. The information needs to create space to point donors and leaders to a healthy transition.

While Hannah's beginning to reintegration was incredibly difficult, she told me that when she reached out to Cathleen in her first year of this, she received incredible encouragement and support. All the times she wanted to quit, she had CIF championing and giving input to the process. Grateful, she pushed through and came out the other side with a more profound experience that now reaches far into several nations and strengthens families and communities.

Deinstitutionalization

Several of my interviewees addressed the topic of deinstitutionalization, and many stated similar things, all while working in different cultural contexts.

Sarah Chhin addressed this with me when I heard about her history of caring for vulnerable and institutionalized children in Cambodia. She also did a *Think Orphan* podcast interview in September 2016, titled "Why Family Matters."

I combined her conversation with me and more details I gleaned from listening to her on the podcast.

What is deinstitutionalization?

ACCI defines it as a process of changing the way care is provided for children. It's a bigger process than simple reintegration. It encompasses family-based care and family-supportive programs within communities. It shifts funding and endeavors to keep children from entering residential care in the first place.

In 2012, seventy-two percent of the young people living in orphanages in Cambodia had parents. Nearly all the others have extended family.

Because they either did not have schools in their villages or did not have money for their children to go to school, parents were sending their children to orphanages for educational purposes. It sparked the Cambodian government to take an interest. They asked, "What does it mean to get children out of orphanages and back home?"

Rebecca Nhep, of the Kinnected program with ACCI, said, "The process is not going to happen overnight. There is a lot of overlap and increased cost in the short run for better gain in the long run. To deinstitutionalize safely, you must invest in the transition phase. It must be child-centered, child-focused, and in the children's best interest. What usually happens is that the social work components will increase. Standards of care need to increase. This needs to be safe and effective. And then, there will be supporting families and communities to bring their kids back home. They may even need support once the children are transitioned. But once kids are transitioned out, there is a massive cost drop. It's much cheaper for family-based care." Much better for the families and children too.

In 2012, the government inspection team Rebecca helped create went to an orphanage. It was so bad it had to be immediately closed down. There was no other option. The children and their carers were taken to the local government orphanage for the short term. Mlup Russey was brought in as a technical advisor to reintegrate these kids.

Soon, they were flanked with issues like kidnappings, court cases, and even rape. As they worked, they created step-by-step guidelines to reunify families.

"Reunification and reintegration are different," Sarah explained.

ACCI states, "Reintegration preparation should begin as soon as a child enters residential care. It is a process of identifying the obstacles that need to be overcome for the child to leave residential care and then actively working towards these goals, ensuring that the child has the necessary skills to function in society and community and achieve full social integration."

Sometimes reintegration involves placing children with non-biological families.

While they define reunification as "the process of reuniting children with their original families, it is not simply the act of returning a child home. It is a broader process that includes child and family consultation, assessments, developing care plans and rebuilding bonds through home visits, etc."

The government has gone on to close more abusive, neglectful orphanages. Mlup Russey has emergency foster care, and eighty percent of those placements come from abusive orphanages. Mlup Russey then works to reintegrate and reunify them.

"The goal became to reduce the number of children living in orphanages by thirty percent. The focus is a do-no-harm, best practice. We don't want orphanages closed without monitoring and due process. Otherwise, that can be dangerous."

In her *Think Orphan* podcast interview, Sarah was asked, "Are orphanages ever OK?"

"I do not advocate the automatic closure of all residential centers," she responded. "Some cases, as a last resort, will need long-term residential care. However, from the eyes of the child, it needs to look, feel, and be like a family. There are always emergency cases that need temporary help."

Rebecca Nhep also elaborated on this topic. "There will be a few children in those settings who cannot get into a permanent family. But that determination should be based on real evidence."

"Ask, 'What care can the child access?'" She continued, "[The decisions] need to be in the child's best interest. A child may not be best in a family environment, but it's rare. Or all efforts to find a family for the child may be exhausted. So, with very high standards and processes in place, we need to put the child in residential care, but this decision needs to be reviewed regularly. Always treat it as temporary with the attempt to continue to assess the child's situation. You need a good social work process in play."

But she indicated she believes the days of massive institutions should be over.

Mick's advice was similar for people who want to start an orphanage. Some older children will need to be in a care home, although usually that should be temporary, not long-term. However, if an orphanage is already established, he says to ensure the only children in it are the ones without any option for a safe family. And, for them, we need to ensure that their caregivers are the absolute best quality possible, prepared and supported to look after vulnerable children.

//

All kids need care as close to a family setting as possible. Rebecca defines family as including biological parents, blood relatives, legal guardians (foster families), and permanent parent-child relationships in adoptions.

Foster care and kinship care must have minimum standards, age limits, potential for non-traditional families like child-headed households, and guardians who have the means to care for and do training. Social workers need to go into the community to do family assessments.

If family is not an option for children, she addresses the question, "How do facilitators best make a residential care facility look like a family?"

"If they are Cambodian, then they know what a Khmer family looks like and how they work with lots of people in the same rooms. They know the different setups families would have across the country."

If it were a foreigner overseeing the residential care, she would have them use their eyes and find out what Cambodian families look like. "You don't want them [the children] to live a lifestyle that is not sustainable and not natural for their culture. The children must be brought up in the culture they are a part of and need to be part of." She emphasized this last point strongly.

//

Mick went on to point out that with the term "deinstitutionalization," there is a huge disengagement that happens. "It's better to engage orphanages with the idea that 'Children need families.' You are not slamming the orphanage door shut but helping them see that kids do better in a family."

However, deinstitutionalization needs to happen globally. It is not merely about closing down orphanages. It begins with limiting the flow of children into orphanages.

"We need to support the communities from where these children are coming. A colossal amount of money has gone into orphanages for decades. If we use that to develop community services that support family care, we help families keep their children and raise their living standards in the community. This includes investing in technical services."

He continued, "We have to get our heads and donor money around supporting organizations who train and value people to care for children properly."

He explained the church has a fabulous opportunity to play this role. "Our money needs to go into paying people on the ground to deliver the proper service for family care. Children belong in safe families. How do we equip those families to do their jobs well?"

Merely telling people about family care and adjusting their perspective is not enough. Large-scale awareness is a good start, but much more foundation-building comes into the process.

"People can't just be captured by family care. You need to give them something to do with it. In the early stages at SFAC, we address the 'why.' Why is family care better? Why do kids do better in homes?"

Then the training must shift to the "what." "What does family care mean? What does it look like, and what could it look like? This can depend on culture, legislation, and resources available. There are varying factors in the 'what.'"

The next move is into the "how." "How do you implement family care? That's when policies get set up, transitioning kids back into families, implementing laws to get things in order."

Mick ensures the staff transitioning children into families

understand local laws and are clear on them. They need to understand the "how of implementing good practices." This involves oversight, supervision, and check-ins from the outside. In the transition phase, there needs to be a strict gauge for children's needs being met and how to look for evidence and proof of proper care. There needs to be risk analysis. Every decision made for a child has a risk factor. There needs to be evidence the decisions made are caring and appropriate.

Mick was encouraged because his initial years were mostly advocacy, and now he does a lot more of teaching the "how."

"The thing lacking in many organizations are good quality practices with people who've actually done the work. Those with experience need to take it and help others lay foundations. We are dealing with people's lives here."

Volunteering with Vulnerable Children

One of the questions the hosts of the *Think Orphan* podcast ask their experts is, "Do short-term missions have a role in orphan care?"

When Sarah Chhin was interviewed, she answered, "Short-term used to mean many months and years. Now that seems like a long-term contract. [The volunteers] were chosen to work in fields they were trained in. Then, they were given three additional months of training to do the volunteer work."

She continued, "A two-week mission, unskilled, is misguided."

ACCI states, volunteering at orphanages "encourages the proliferation of residential care, compounds the myth regarding the number of children who are orphaned and in need of adoption and feeds the unscrupulous orphanage business, which separates children from their families to generate funds from donors and tourists. Children are often expected to perform for guests, beg in the streets or hold 'orphan events' to raise funds for their own care. This is highly unethical and exploitative, and tourists and volunteers unwittingly create a market for such practices through their visiting and volunteering."

The research is clear: the children's response to volunteers is a symptom of reactive trauma disorder. Kids should have a certain level of fear of strangers. Yet they flock to strangers in orphanages, bidding for their attention.

"Their abnormal behavior is being reinforced by volunteers all coming in," Sarah explained. "They do not know why they were abandoned in the first place. They never understand it. So, teams coming and leaving them constantly and caregivers leaving create emotional and psychological difficulties. They end up with delays and developmental issues because of this constant changeover. It's a huge problem. That's not even going into the exposure to abuse."

Rebecca explained, "Short-term workers should not be taking caretaker roles. They must learn what it means to advocate for vulnerable children and their families. They need to understand the issues."

So, what are things short-term teams can do?

There are things people can offer with professional backgrounds with skills; examples include youth work and social work.

Sarah said, "There are tasks that they can do to support the local workers and upskill. For people without skills, stock-taking teams have put together a welcome pack for kids. The packs have things care-leavers can take to survive on their own."

"Short-terms cannot get enough language to do most work on the ground. Leave that to the local experts and give help and support to them in ways they feel are needed."

Sarah told me the story of one short-term volunteer who saw an old lady tediously laboring in her field. So, the volunteer spent a whole day picking the stones from an old lady's rice field to help her. She met a real need and built a relationship.

The best advice: "Come in and build a relationship first. Then find out what is needed."

Ask, "What would you do with your neighbors?"

"You wouldn't just show up at their house and tell them you would help them with specific things. No, you'd build trust and relationship and find out what they need first."

Rebecca wrapped up the advice, "It's a complex and nuanced issue. There is a role for short-term missions in the orphan-care sector. However, it's best not to have people interacting directly with children. Thankfully, there are ways to serve that are not at the expense of a child or a birth family and their well-being."

Our Responsibility

Afterword

The topic of caring for vulnerable children globally may be too big to tackle in one book. But I can confidently say that decades of research show that family is best for children. Orphanages, institutions, and children's homes have consistently proven to be harmful to children when used for long-term care. In short, the world does not have an orphan issue, but rather an orphanage issue.

With nearly ten years spent in Cambodia, the majority of my time has been serving with CIF, while I also worked throughout Southeast and South Asia on smaller projects. Once this book is released, I plan to move to a neighboring country to continue to work in family-based care where tens of thousands of refugees are fleeing across the border from decades-long conflict. Family separation, trafficking, and drug abuse is a huge risk in these incredibly vulnerable communities. They have faced decades of violence, trauma, poverty, and lack basic resources.

The last thing we should be doing is separating these families needlessly. In the midst of so much loss, they should be empowered to keep their children, their language, and their ethnic identity.

If you have the desire and passion for serving vulnerable children, research local laws, find out what the actual needs of communities are, and learn what already exists regarding care for orphaned, abused, or abandoned children.

You might find that the abandoned or orphaned children problem is linked to something bigger that needs addressing. A friend told me about fellow missionaries with her organization. The southern African nation where they served had countless children living on the streets and involved in violent gangs.

Their knee-jerk reaction was to start fixing the problem. Instead, they moved into that community and spent two years building relationships, not building any programs. Their initial response to the problem would only have helped a few kids by removing and isolating them from their culture; however, once they noted root issues in the breakdown in family, community, and options for these kids, they set to work addressing the real problems, working alongside locals who also had a heart for the youth.

Within a few years, gang violence, drug problems, and homeless youth were nearly eradicated from this community. So, we need to check our agenda before we serve or give.

If you feel "called" to help vulnerable and orphaned families, then do your research. What does family look like where you serve? What options already exist for children? Look at the root of family separation and vulnerability. Use your gifting and skills to keep families together.

When we discover the problems with institutional care, it can be easy to grow critical of the people on the ground doing something. Instead, we can help them to adopt better practices rather than alienating them with our attitude.

We still have a responsibility to make those around us aware. We also have a massive obligation with our money. If you support organizations globally that work with vulnerable populations, do your due diligence. The resources have lists of questions you can ask.

If you support orphanages, children's homes, or institutions, do not take what you are told at face value. You may not be seeing the whole picture yet. Is there really an orphan problem where they are? How are they reintegrating and connecting the children to family and community? Does the organization really need to exist in its current form?

Billions of dollars fuel orphanages. They exist primarily because they are lucrative. If you currently support children's homes, orphanages, or institutions, use your donations to create change by encouraging orphanage directors and staff to shift to family-based care. They need to establish stringent gatekeeping for taking in any new children. In addition, they must have regular reevaluations for every child in their care to be placed in a safe family or returned to their family of origin. If there is no contingency plan in place for each child, then request they begin and monitor the follow-through.

If directors of orphanages get angry when questioned, that's a huge red flag. If they do not want accountability, they should not get funding.

Most people who support orphanages have a personal and emotional investment in the directors or the children. I have heard countless times, "Oh, but Sister So-And-So who runs that children's home is wonderful. A hero who cares about children."

Yet I often find out the person saying this met their "hero" on a short-term trip, where they sat and heard their moving stories of rescue and care. I know many kind people running orphanages. But I still disagree with their model of care. And I would still want them to learn, grow, change, and do what is best for the children in their care. I love those people, but it's because I love and respect them that I want them to be accountable and do what is best for children.

If you or your faith community personally know orphanage and children's home directors, use your relationship to promote better practices and change. If you are not already funding one, then don't start. But rather support organizations and programs that work holistically with families.

Family preservation and family-based care are only small-scale in nations like Cambodia and Thailand partially because we need more funding to pay staff and create enough resources to reach the entire country. If CIF, SFAC, Mlup Russey, or countless other organizations that support family care received the same funding as orphanages, there would be no need for orphanages. There would be enough funding to help every vulnerable child. With only fifteen percent of what it takes to care for a child in an orphanage in Cambodia, CIF can keep that same child in a loving family. The financial impact on strengthening families and keeping them together is so significant and can be stretched much further.

Now that we know better, let's do better. Let's work to place all children in loving families. It's where they belong.

Author's Note

Since I have been researching, writing, and speaking on this topic since 2016, a lot of my resources have been compiled over the years and are extensive beyond listing. Many of the statistics and information quoted in this book are agreed upon by countless entities and organizations working in family-based care.

If you want to learn more on this topic, check out:

Children In Families
ACCI's Kinnected Program
Better Care Network
Think Orphan Podcast
1 Million Home
Hope and Homes for Children
Lumos (wearelumos.org)
Mick Pease's book *Children Belong in Families*
Conor Grennan's book *Little Princes*
Books by Craig Greenfield

Resources

1. Think Orphan Podcast. Episode 52, host Phil Darke on May 9, 2017, guest Dr. Delia Pop

2. ACCI's Kinnected FAQ https://www.kinnected.org.au/faq-1

3. World Report on Violence Against Children published by the UN in 2006

4. Children In Adversity infograph CIF research. childreninfamilies.org

5. www.developmentaccord.com

6. Better Care Network interview with CIF staff, September 12, 2019

Acknowledgments

I want to begin by thanking Cathleen and Dale Jones. This book would not exist without their insight and vulnerability. I am grateful for all of the staff at CIF I served alongside for nearly seven years. It was their passion and hard work that kept me going through all of the ups-and-downs of international living. I am also grateful for the editing prowess of Elizabeth Trotter. Not only is she a significantly better writer than I am, her knowledge of Cambodia and love for the nation helped shape the framework for this book. There are so many others who've poured into me over these past three years, but more than anything, I want to thank the families of Cambodia who sacrificially cared for hundreds of abandoned, sick, and children in need of love through CIF's programs. They deserve the highest praise.

About Atmosphere Press

Founded in 2015, Atmosphere Press was built on the principles of Honesty, Transparency, Professionalism, Kindness, and Making Your Book Awesome. As an ethical and author-friendly hybrid press, we stay true to that founding mission today.

If you're a reader, enter our giveaway for a free book here:

SCAN TO ENTER
BOOK GIVEAWAY

If you're a writer, submit your manuscript for consideration here:

SCAN TO SUBMIT
MANUSCRIPT

And always feel free to visit Atmosphere Press and our authors online at atmospherepress.com. See you there soon!

About the Author

ERIN FOLEY is an American with an international heart. After spending a portion of her childhood in Latin America, she served in Papua New Guinea and Australia with YWAM Medical Ships for two years. She currently lives in Southeast Asia, where she's been teaching and working with NGOs for nearly a decade.

Erin is the author of *Kapuna: How Love Transformed a Culture*, which received the North American Book Award 2015 for Best Travel Non-Fiction and the 2015 Idaho Author Awards First Place in Biographies, Autobiographies, and Memoirs.

She studied Art, Photography, and Journalism at Hillsdale College in Michigan, USA. Her passions include teaching inductive Bible studies, urban gardening, good coffee, wombats, family-based care, and, of course, books.